DWELLINGS
The House across the World

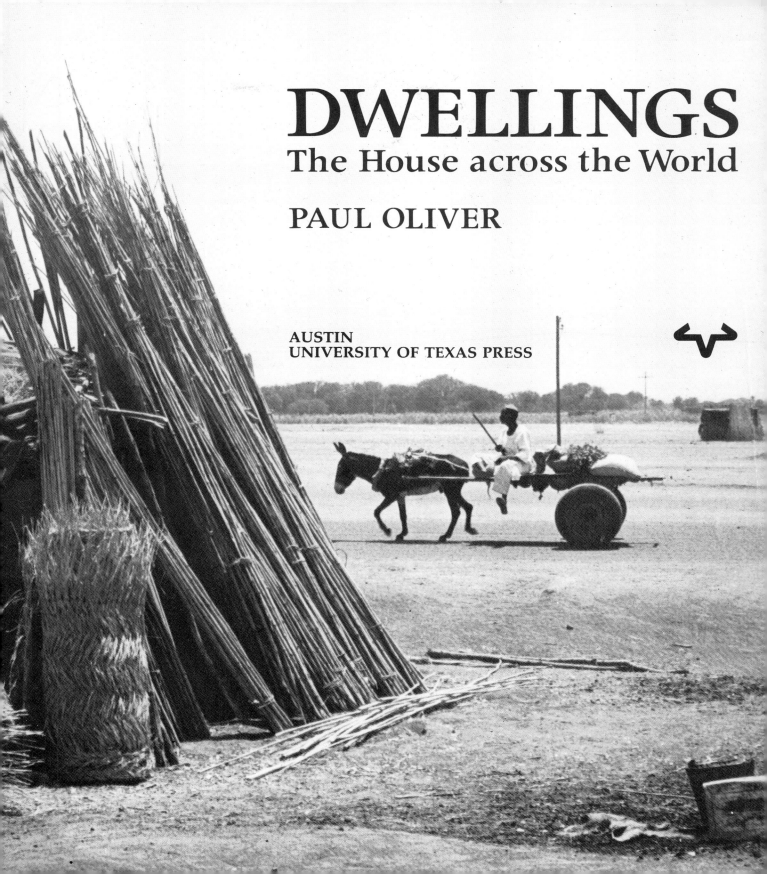

DWELLINGS
The House across the World

PAUL OLIVER

AUSTIN
UNIVERSITY OF TEXAS PRESS

To those students of many countries who have worked with me

International Standard Book Number 0–292–71554–4 (cloth);
0–292–71555–2 (paper)
Library of Congress Catalog Card Number 87–50177
Printed in Great Britain

First University of Texas Press Edition, 1987

Title-page: part of a materials depot serving the needs of migrants
from Chad who intend to settle outside Khartoum. Awode, Sudan.

CONTENTS

ACKNOWLEDGEMENTS

In writing a study which is based on many years of field work and research I am indebted to scores of colleagues, friends, and past students in many parts of the world, not to mention innumerable people with local knowledge, who have helped me in countless ways. Unfortunately it is not possible to name them all here, though my appreciation for their invitations to lecture, opportunities to conduct research, and patience while I pursued details which at times may have seemed of marginal relevance, is deeply felt.

Throughout these years, and in many difficult circumstances, my wife Val has accompanied me and shared in the work; in the writing of this book she has been continual critic and adviser, and has undertaken the task of assembling the Bibliography and Index. To Val I owe an incalculable debt of gratitude.

With other commitments in education, writing this book would not have been possible without a release for six months from teaching in the Department of Architecture at Oxford Polytechnic. Some of the expenses incurred were met with research allowances from Oxford Polytechnic. Not only am I most grateful for this assistance, I also wish to convey to my colleagues my thanks for their help, knowing how time spent on research places additional burdens on others in education. I feel I must express my special thanks to two of my colleagues: Ian Davis for his continued interest and support throughout this study, and Geoffrey Bennett for his technical advice.

In a work of this kind illustrations are of particular importance, and much of the architectural detail has been made explicit through Stuart Parker's invaluable drawings; they have been augmented by some of my own. Though half of the photographs were taken by myself in the field, I have been greatly helped by many friends who have made their files available to me, none more than David Hicks, a number of whose photographs are included here. Among those I particularly wish to thank are Yasemin Aysan, Tim Bruce-Dick, Pat Crooke, Miles Danby, Robert M. W. Dixon, Irene Leake, Jolyon Leslie, Diedre McDermott, Philip Opher, Geoffrey Payne, Ramoń Pelinski, Joseph Reser, Graham Paul Smith, David Sneath, Robin Spence, Graham Stewart, Kate Stirling, John Turner and Hanspeter Wagner.

In addition, I had much kind help with illustrations from individuals within larger bodies, among them Nic Eastwood, Audio-Visual Dept., and the Centre for American and Commonwealth Arts and Studies (AMCAS) at the University of Exeter; Liz Edwards, Librarian of the Pitt Rivers Museum, Oxford; Sandy Laumark, Directrice, CARE (Mali); John Norton of the Development Workshop; Suha Ozkan, Deputy Secretary General of the Aga Khan Award for Architecture (AKAA); and the Photography Services of the Public Archives, Ottawa, Canada. I am most grateful to them all for their help. In this connection I must offer a special word of thanks to Eric Boone of the Educational Methods Unit, Oxford Polytechnic for his careful processing of much of this material.

Additional photographs for the book were obtained through the efforts of Caroline Lucas. Eileen Cook and Jean Smith patiently, and with much good humour, transferred my notorious typing to the word processor. Finally, Katherine Carr and Marie Leahy have been careful editors whose advice has been most welcome; my sincere thanks to all of them.

Paul Oliver
Oxford, 1986

INTRODUCTION

All houses are dwellings; but all dwellings are not houses. To dwell is to make one's abode: to live in, or at, or on, or about a place. For some this implies a permanent structure, for others a temporary accommodation, for still others it is where they live, even if there is little evidence of building.

Dwelling is both process and artefact. It is the process of living at a location and it is the physical expression of doing so. There are peoples whose dwellings are little more than depressions in the long grass or rough shelters of branches and leaves. And there are peoples whose dwellings are massive structures, finely wrought in durable materials and sometimes centuries old. But the dwelling place is more than the structure, as the soul is more than the body that contains it; for untold millions of people the bond between themselves and their dwelling-place transcends the physical limitations of their habitation.

It is this double significance of dwelling—dwelling as the activity of living or residing, and dwelling as the place or structure which is the focus of residence—which encompasses the manifold cultural and material aspects of domestic habitation. 'Shelter' indeed summarizes much of its meaning, implying the basic desire for protective enclosure which is common to most, if not all, peoples of the earth, and the structures which they build to meet that end. 'Habitation' likewise has this dual connotation, though both terms have stronger associative ties with the building than with the nature of its occupancy which, in English at any rate, 'dwelling' signifies.

No one can say how many dwellings there are. Not to the nearest million, or even to the nearest hundred million. With a world population in excess of five thousand million people, eight or nine hundred million dwellings are possible. Of these only a miniscule proportion were designed by architects; one per cent might well be an over-estimate. Speculative and professional builders of suburban houses might be added in, but still the total of dwellings that were built with professional or official involvement is likely to be less than five per cent. By far the majority

House with walls of woven palm leaves and palm leaf thatched roof. Tamil Nadu, India.

Above Old, finely-carved upper-storey window of a house in Kirtipur, Nepal. Its present occupiers cannot afford to repair the walls or the broken lattices. The windows are of generous size to admit benign spirits.

Right Fourteenth-century cottage at Didbrook, Gloucestershire. Its cruck frame of ground-to-apex coupled timbers is of a type widely distributed in England which has been laboriously documented.

of dwellings in the world, whatever estimated statistics one may settle for, were built by the people themselves without professional intervention. These dwellings, the homes of the people, are the subject of this book.

Aspects of dwelling—the Swiss alpine house, the English cottage, the American log cabin, for instance—have been the focus of detailed study over several decades. Their aesthetic appeal, their echoes of long, if romanticized, history have attracted both scholarly investigations and the clicking camera shutters of countless tourists. Conservation lobbies and tourist boards alike have recognized their value as objects symbolic of a heritage. But though there are parallel enthusiasms in other countries, principally European, and though approved and singular examples have been herded together in open-air museums since the 1930s, the emphasis on the artefact has often been at the expense of any understanding of the reasons for their form, how they met the requirements of the users at the time of building, and how they may have been adapted to suit changing needs. In many countries elsewhere in the world, dwelling types have received far less attention, even if numerous studies have been made of aspects of specific local traditions. Much of the information that we have on the dwellings of the world depends on the dedicated researches of amateurs, many self-taught, who have become interested in the habitat of peoples in regions where they live.

There is, as yet, no discipline, no specialized field, that exists for the study of dwellings or the larger compass of all types of vernacular architecture. If such a discipline were to emerge it would probably be one that combines some of the elements of both architecture and anthropology. This dual character has possibly accounted for the limited number of comparative research studies in the field, for anthropological enquiry is not a customary part of architectural education, and an understanding of architectural principles has never been considered a significant aspect of the training of an anthropologist. Consequently, notes and records of indigenous building, though made by architects in a number of countries, are frequently short on the use or meaning of the buildings, while anthropological writings will frequently give considerable details of social customs or kinship structures with the barest recognition of the architectural contexts in which they may occur. The lack of a common graphic language, or even a common technical one (all professional areas being prone to develop their own jargon) means that there are very few instances where interdisciplinary teams have studied specific dwellings and settlements to bring their various skills and perceptions to bear upon the subject, leading to a unified collective study. Potentially, it is from interdisciplinary work that the most rewarding results could be obtained.

A great deal of effort has been expended on the terminology of buildings that have not been designed by architects or master builders. In 1969 I discussed some of the usages then current: today they are much the same.[1] 'Primitive architecture' is the most invidious, and also imprecise, implying either a primitive origin to 'architecture' which the buildings represent, or 'primitive' peoples who build them; 'traditional' architecture is better, for it acknowledges the inheritance of the past. For this reason though, it is applicable to much formal, designed architecture. The term which has gained widest acceptance is 'vernacular' architecture, with its linguistic comparison to the language of the common people: the folk equivalent of formal architecture, as vernacular speech is to the language of the court or college. 'Indigenous' architecture is perhaps a more accurate term, certainly less metaphoric, though it cannot be applied effectively to imported forms and to the buildings of peoples that are not native to a region.[2] Wishing to place the emphasis upon the primary nature of such building, I proposed 'shelter' as an alternative term. Though this has had relatively widespread use it does carry connotations of the rudimentary and the temporary.[3]

Rather than create artificial, and generally insupportable, distinctions (e.g. primitive, vernacular, popular) in some notional progression, I am choosing here to discuss the 'dwelling' and, in context, to

Annular windmills used for pumping water by the houses, barns and stores of farmholdings on the central plain, Mallorca.

identify its source: tribal, nomad, peasant, migrant, folk, or popular, using 'shelter' or 'vernacular' where the context warrants it. These terms embrace many other forms of building which are not professionally designed structures—many barns, watermills and windmills, and market-halls among them. These other buildings are closely related to dwellings, acting as the storehouses, stables, byres, meeting houses, markets, and places of worship which help sustain the physical and spiritual life. As such they are intimately bound within the settlements where the groups of people reside. Dwellings are sometimes separate from other forms of building that serve purposes related to living, and sometimes they encompass them: the shelter protects both animals and family; the shrine is in the corner of the room, and in some cultures is even synonymous with the house itself. Dwellings are the focus for a variety of functions, some contained within them, others provided within specialized buildings nearby.

Few of mankind's artefacts have the longevity of houses. Boats and bowls, ploughs and pitchers, tools and totems may last for a century or more, and some may be in use for much longer. Nevertheless, the continuity of use of the dwelling in many societies exceeds the utilitarian life of virtually every other artefact. Consequently, the occupancy of countless dwellings has been through successive generations of families, whose association with the building, the settlements and the land is intimately bound with their own identity. But dwellings also outlast lineages, change hands, are sold, re-occupied, remodelled, and adapted, their survival to the present being a record of responsiveness to altering life-styles and societies in change. In many other instances, though, the fabric of the dwelling is not, in itself, permanent; the structure is dismantled or demolished, to be reassembled later on a different site, but in similar form. In such cases it is the idea of the dwelling that persists, expressed in the continuity of form, plan, structure and use. A vast number of buildings in use today are the products of the past, or, when they are still being built, perpetuate the forms that satisfied the same societies in earlier times.

When cultures change, old buildings may be adapted to new ways of living, and new buildings are altered in form to accommodate them. This temporal problem—that buildings have a history, sometimes relatively static, sometimes evolved and changing, sometimes of form rather than substance—is only one of the many that make difficult a comparative study of dwelling types that occur throughout the world, bearing in mind the vast range of conditions, states and countries in which they are to be found. There is no effective way of including examples from every country, nor would this be in itself a significant goal. There are some 180 countries in the world, a statistic which is politically significant but which in terms of land area and population (Vatican City and Monaco apart) ranges from Nauru with fewer than 7,000 people living in an area of 21 km^2 to the 260 million Russians residing in over a million times that area, to the 700 million in India or the 1,000 million in the Chinese Republic.[4] Unions of states and federated republics might be better considered in their constituent states, but even so, the dispersed population of many countries and the high concentration of others make any such geographical/political representation impossible within reasonable limitations of space.

There are many other factors that can affect the nature of dwellings across the world, such as the availability of certain materials, like wood or stone, or the varying kinds of climate, altitude and environment in which different peoples live. Taking them into consideration has influenced the way in which they are discussed in this book, and the sequence in which they occur. To have looked at the dwelling types of each continent in turn would have involved some needless repetitions; for instance the techniques of building in clay are comparable in many different parts of the world, certain construction and plan types are employed in both Asia and North Africa, and so on. So instead I have chosen to concentrate on certain principles, both environmental and cultural, which shaped the variety of dwelling types that exist today. They involve for example, economy and settlement types; material resources, both organic and inorganic; forms of dwelling, the technologies and processes by which they are built; climatic and environmental considerations; the way that space is organized and used within the dwelling to meet the demands of daily living; symbolism and meaning, craftsmanship and decoration; the impact of twentieth-century social change and its effect on the expanding cities; rapid urbanization, and the problem of housing which now confronts the world.

What I have tried to show is that the focus of the family and the bonds of community life are powerfully integrated into the dwelling in its cultural and environmental context. Moreover, I have sought to demonstrate that men, women, and their children have both the capacity and the desire to shape their personal environments and to relate them to those of other members of their societies. Traditionally they have had the skills and competence, the sensibility and the know-how to build them effectively with regard to the land, the climate, and the resources they have at hand. Embodying the values and needs that are special to them, they have built homes in ways that have often achieved, in their integrity and authenticity, beauty of form and harmony of design.

I have chosen to illustrate the points I have wished to make by presenting specific cases rather than by dipping freely into hundreds of examples. In the process perhaps we know the people and their cultures, as well as their dwellings, a little better, even if we forfeit the diversity of a broader range of briefly cited instances.

Although some of my examples have been drawn from Europe and the United States, and even one or two from Great Britain, I have not used many such sources. There are two reasons: firstly, there is a considerable literature on the vernacular architecture of Britain and the 'folk architecture' of the United States, and there are national surveys, folk architecture museums, and the like in several European countries; these are easily available, and viewable. Secondly, the traditions of self-built and community-built dwellings which are the focus of much of my discussion, died long ago in much of Europe and virtually all of Britain and only survive vestigially in the United States; I wish to draw attention to the liv-

Two-roomed cabin of massive, untrimmed pine logs, built single-handedly by Pawnee Bill (Major Gordon Lillie). Oklahoma.

ing and recent traditions. Almost inevitably, these have been largely in what are unsatisfactorily termed 'The Third World', the 'Developing World' or the 'Less Developed Countries', labels which are by no means easily defined and which are, in one way or another, divisive. As far as possible I have avoided using them, not wishing to make so arbitrary a distinction between nations, when my main emphasis is on *cultures*. Considering cultures has meant that, within any one chapter, I have had to draw my examples from various parts of the globe. This, I realise, can be somewhat confusing, so I have used 'case examples' examined at some length, rather than innumerable comparisons of similar or differing conditions.

Selecting the appropriate case examples has involved the weighing up of a number of factors: availability and accessibility of the information, the appropriateness of the example to the point that I wish to illustrate and, where possible, my personal knowledge of them. Where the references are based on my own research I have indicated this in the Notes to the relevant chapter where I have also given references to other studies. Fuller details are listed in the Bibliography.

FINLAND

RUSSIA (UNION OF SOVIET SOCIALIST REPUBLICS)

ENGLAND
IR
27
FR DDR PO
88
99
FRANCE 81
82 S
IT YU 17
89
SPAIN 60
PORTUGAL 16
4
48
68 91
TU
MOROCCO 64
CT 80
ALGERIA
3
2
MAURITANIA 101
31 29 101
SENEGAL NIGER 11 CHAD
MALI 101 96
GB BF 76
34 36
92 49
IC GH 9 NIGERIA
41 31 31
43 12
CA
CONGO
ZAÏRE
ANGOLA
ZA MA 109
MO
85 ZI
NAMIBIA BO
100-71
71
75 74
LE
SOUTH
AFRICA

GR 54 6
IS 47
SY IRAQ
13
59
21
32
EGYPT
SAUDI
ARABIA
77
46
86
Y
97
ETHIOPIA
84 SOMALIA
52 19
KENYA
58 69 56
TANZANIA

TURKEY 23
20
AFGHAN-
ISTAN
103 78
44
IRAN
14
PAKISTAN 37
40 83
28 72
105 53
106
22
INDIA
5
18
67
93
SRI LANKA

MONGOLIA
104
50
94
TIBET
NEPAL
66 66
BD
25
BU
TH
CHINA
51 90
JAPA
61
MALAYSIA
95 SA
15 42
SUMATRA BORNEO SU 98
45
INDONESIA JAVA BALI
PHILIPPINES
79
6

MADAGASCAR 87

AUSTRALIA

8
N
GU

73

MORGAGE
LIBYA
SUDAN

ABBREVIATIONS

BD BANGLADESH   PO POLAND
BF BURKINO FASO   PR PUERTO RICO
BO BOTSWANA   S SWITZERLAND
BU BURMA   SA SARAWAK
CA CAMEROON   SU SULAWESI
CR COSTA RICA   SY SYRIA
CT CRETE   TH THAILAND
DDR EAST GERMANY   TU TUNISIA
FR WEST GERMANY   Y YEMEN
GB GUINEA BISSAU   YU YUGOSLAVIA
GH GHANA   ZA ZAMBIA
GR GREECE   ZI ZIMBABWE
GU GUATEMALA
IC IVORY COAST
IR IRELAND
IS ISRAEL
IT ITALY
JA JAMAICA
LE LESOTHO
MA MALAWI
MO MOZAMBIQUE
NI NICARAGUA

Maori village at Rotorua in 1930. By this time the house posts were no longer carved and most Maoris were already rejecting traditional dwelling types. (*AMCAS*)

All this means that the examples are relatively recent, for the emphasis of this book is on our own times or at least from the end of World War II to the present. I have chosen not to use the familiar fiction, sometimes called the 'ethnological present', which implies that societies, and their buildings, exist in a constant, unchanging state, when in fact the cultures concerned have died out and their dwellings disappeared—in some cases before the beginning of the century.[5] In a few instances where it seemed necessary I have referred to older dwelling types that ceased to be in use before then, but the period since has been critical, for so much has been damaged, threatened, or lost within recent memory. Remarkable though they were, many indigenous dwelling types still in use fifty years ago have vanished forever, to linger only in the memories of old men and in photographic archives. With them has also gone much of the accumulated wisdom and experience of living in the world's diverse regions and conditions.

These changes have been marked in recent years as individuals, families, and whole communities leave the rural areas and, often with no homes to go to,

migrate to the cities. In the early post-war period a report from the United Nations on world housing conditions, stated that there was no country without a housing problem; even if Europe doubled its pre-war output of 800,000 houses it would take until 1975 to meet its housing needs. With the advantage of hindsight it is clear that neither housing target nor universal housing problems were met by that date, nor have they been met since.[6]

Thirty-five years later in December 1982 the General Assembly of the United Nations declared 1987 to be the International Year of Shelter for the Homeless. Far from having coped with the problem of ensuring that all people have dwellings of their own, we are in a world where hundreds of millions of people are now, by whatever definition we use, classified as 'homeless'. As the world's population continues to grow, as the cities of the Third World expand in their multi-millions, as resources become exploited and land scarce in degrees which make it progressively more difficult for individuals and families to satisfy their housing needs, there is an increasing pressure on the State and on nations to provide houses. Housing the homeless is seen as a national, even an international, responsibility which can only be solved by intervention in what has been, for much of the world's populations in the past, their own affair. Unfortunately, the solution has usually been in the form of anonymous apartments in the sky, or militaristic ranks of low-cost housing schemes. Rarely does such 'housing provision' take into account the culture of specific communities, and the mass-produced dwelling seldom reflects the values of the family.

We leave it to national and local governments, and the architects or planners employed by them to cope with the inadequate living conditions of the poor and the dispossessed. But in my view this should be as much the concern of all of us as is providing food to the starving, water and sanitation to the thirsty and disease-prone, or bringing relief to refugees and the victims of disasters. Housing, however, is far more complex than the nonetheless difficult problems of transporting grain, shipping bales of blankets and clothing, or drilling wells. Not only is the scale far greater, but the factors that influence the locations, building types, construction, uses and meanings of dwellings are much more numerous.

In a great many cultures the dwelling is the largest artefact that a man, a woman, or their family may ever construct; in many others it is the single most important item that they may ever call their own; in some it is also the most expensive, most costly investment, as purchase or as rent, that they will ever make in their lives. But the dwelling is more than the materials from which it is made, the labour that has gone into its construction, or the time and money that may have been expended on it: the dwelling is the theatre of our lives, where the major dramas of birth and death, of procreation and recreation, of labour and of being in labour are played out and in which a succession of scenes of daily lives is perpetually enacted. Yet the metaphor is inadequate: the play can be performed without the stage; the theatre stands empty for most of the time, awaiting the performers and their audience. Dwellings are more than that; the relationship of man to his home is intimate and essential. There are virtually no peoples in the world that do not build or shape their dwellings, no cultures for whom a form of shelter does not exist. But human societies differ, and the differences are profound; they are expressed at many levels in the dwellings of mankind.

If the International Year of Shelter for the Homeless is to mean more than the mere emergency provision of roofs and walls, we need to know much more about these qualities that shape the dwelling of differing societies. By doing so we may be more effective in assisting them in gaining appropriate living conditions—and in the process, learn more about our own.

Top Between the highway and high-rise middle-class apartment blocks squatters' shanties perch on a narrow Bombay short-line. By the year 2000 Bombay may have a population exceeding 16 million, doubling its present size.

Right The dwelling is the focus of many cultural rituals. The marriage of two nomadic couples of the Ayt Atta tribe takes place to the sound of drums and singing. Central High Atlas.

1.

SHELTER OF THE NOMADS

Arms spread from a stocky figure like a well-swaddled child, slit eyes and smiling face beaming from a halo of fur, the Eskimo standing before his snow-block house has illustrated countless children's books. If there is one exotic term for a house that a Western child knows, it is 'igloo'. An 'igloo' has served with harpoon, husky dogs, and sledge as a symbol of anything cold from ice cream to the acme of the salesman's skills in disposing of refrigerators. With so much pre-conditioning it is difficult to re-examine objectively the habitat of the Inuit, as the Eskimo peoples are sometimes classified. They are dispersed around half of the polar world, from the Bering Straits and Alaska to the shores of Greenland. Nomadic hunters whose main source of food and raw material for clothing and artefacts comes from sea mammals, Eskimos are principally coastal dwellers with a cycle of movements and activities largely determined by the length and severity of the Arctic winter, and the conditions of ice and snow prevailing over both land and sea.

SURVIVING IN THE ARCTIC

Eskimo territory lies mainly north of the 53 °F (12 °C) August isotherm which defines the northernmost limits of the tree-line and the territories of the forest Amer-Indians. While it loops north of the Arctic Circle in the Yukon it embraces much of Hudson Bay and sweeps deeply into Labrador to the east and the Bering Sea coast of Alaska to the west. Eskimos depend largely on catching fish—a family may consume five thousand in a year—and hunting seal and caribou, picking berries and fruits when the warmer, short summer season permits. The many months spent in the confines of the snow or sod *iglu* (house) might seem circumscribed and confined, but Eskimos are sociable and travel hundreds of miles by sledge to visit relatives and friends. In the vast wastes of tundra and snow, coastal fogs and winter blizzards obscure the landmarks of the indented coastline, so such travel away from the minute humps of the dwellings demands extraordinary navigational skills and spatial cognition. But these they indisputably have, as the remarkable maps drawn by Eskimos, collected and published as early as 1942 have shown.[1] Their acute observation and awareness of their inhospitable environment and their mastery of survival

Map of Eskimo territories in North America and Greenland, north of the arboreal edge and the 12 °C August isotherm.

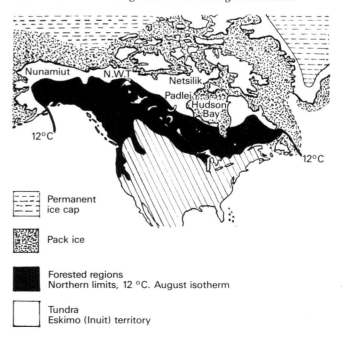

Nunamiut — N.W.T — Netsilik — Padlei — Hudson Bay — 12°C — 12°C

- Permanent ice cap
- Pack ice
- Forested regions Northern limits, 12 °C. August isotherm
- Tundra Eskimo (Inuit) territory

Eskimo hunter in the process of building an iglu, in the Padlei region, North West Territories (NWT). A bone snow knife is used to trim the blocks cut from the snow beyond the sledge.

arts, the invention and making of everything from their harpoons and net gauges to their snow goggles and visors, from their stone vessels and lamps to their clothing and dwellings, ensured their capacity to live in the Arctic.

Eskimos speak a common language, more or less mutually intelligible among hunting bands dispersed over a million square miles, and they share, broadly speaking, a common culture. There are differences between the ways of life of the Alaskan Eskimos and those of the Central territories in the islands of northern Canada or those of Greenland where some live 800 miles north of the Arctic Circle, but all are exposed to a most rigorous climate and a harsh and inhospitable environment. There is evidence to show that Eskimos have evolved a physical resistance to chronic exposure to extreme cold, with hand blood-flow twice that of whites from temperate climates;[2] even so, their main resistance to excessively low temperatures was achieved with great ingenuity. Mummified Eskimo bodies five centuries old were discovered at Qilakit-soq, Greenland wearing clothes of sealskin sewn with sinew, waterproofed with seal oil, and with undergarments made from the feathers of cormorant, duck and goose feathers; garments of a kind that were still serv-

ing their purpose centuries later.[3] Such clothing protected the individual; the dwelling or *iglu* protected the family group.

Snow houses were seldom built by Alaskan Eskimos and infrequently by those in Greenland; they were used as winter dwellings by the Central Eskimo and smaller ones were built as temporary shelters by hunters. Though their use is virtually at an end they were still employed by some groups of the Central (Netsilik) Eskimo in the 1960s.[4] The method of building was much the same irrespective of their size. A level site or, if possible, one that was banked slightly, was chosen for the new iglu and suitable snow located by testing for its consistency with a fine caribou antler probe. Blocks cut from a snow-drift that had been built up from several falls were inclined to shear, so a snow layer from a single fall was sought. It was cleared of top snow, with a hide snow shovel, and the drift swiftly cut or sawn into blocks with a slightly curved ivory snow-knife, *orsulung*. These might be as much as 3 feet (1 m) long, 2 feet (0.5 m) wide and 8 inches (0.2 m) thick (though smaller blocks of similar proportion have often been reported), and each block was cut with a scarcely perceptible curve. After a circle had been scribed some 15 feet (5 m) across, the initial layer was laid in a ring, the first block then being cut back to the site level, and the subsequent blocks each cut at an incline so

Constructing an iglu. A spiral of slightly curved blocks is made, each leaning on its neighbour and inclined inwards.

that the layer formed the first stage of a continuous spiral. The next blocks were laid so that the joints were broken (or did not coincide) and chamfered so that as they inclined inwards they rested against the preceding block. In this way the spiral continued to slope inwards without the dome collapsing during the course of the work. One man would work inside; another outside the dome, cutting and packing the blocks and filling any gaps with loose snow. A key block or two would be placed in position, supported by the man within, who stood, if necessary, on a bench of snow to reach the top.

Once the vaulted dome was complete an opening was cut close to the floor level, and a tunnel, sometimes with storage chambers, made for the approach. This was lower than the internal floor level so that cold air would remain trapped within it, and not enter the iglu. In some iglus the entrance was approached by a subterranean channel, in others by an angled tunnel. In all cases the aperture was small, so that little cold air was admitted when the snow block door or grizzly bear skin was moved aside. Inside, a snow bench, the *iqliq*, the width of the dome, was built up to a height of two or three feet, which served as the living and sleeping platform. In front of it at floor level, the first third of the space was the *natiq*, or general purpose area, which housed the stores of fish, the cooking utensils, and household articles. It was also used to receive visitors. Some

Inuit groups lined the roof of their houses with caribou hides to form an inner skin which acted as additional insulation. With blubber lamps and bodyheat it was possible for the internal temperature to be raised to 60 °F (15.5 °C) or more when the outside temperature was down to −40 °F (−40 °C). To keep the interior ventilated a small hole, the *qangirn*, was made in the dome wall, but others would be pierced when stale air had to be released as the need arose. Inside there was some light to be had from the blubber oil lamp with its moss wick, but daylight was obtained through an arched opening cut through the snow dome above the entrance; a translucent layer of sewn seal intestine linings formed a window, or a block of clear ice was used which was formed from snow melted in a sealskin bag and whose curved shape fitted the surface of the dome. Sometimes a window might be cut in the side of the iglu and the block removed used as a reflector to catch and deflect the last rays of the sun into the dwelling.[5]

Inside the iglu the family sat on the iqliq, backs close to the wall, legs extended but not overhanging the edge so making sure of being out of the cold at floor level. The platform would be covered with moss and sealskins or hides to insulate the occupants from the cold, and a stove used for making tea would help raise the temperature. Fish had to be gutted and cleaned, small animals from the trap lines skinned and quartered, clothes had to be sewn, and hides prepared—though it was taboo to do so when the men were hunting. There were proscriptions on what could be done within the iglu, some based on superstition, some clearly evolved because of the need to live amicably in close contiguity. Honesty and calm were valued, anger and extreme behaviour repressed. In the evenings the family would engage in games, play with the children, smoke, drink tea, tell stories, or receive visitors, eventually to undress and climb swiftly into the fur-lined sleeping bags of sealskin.

A group of Netsilik, the Utku, in the early 1960s numbered just thirty-five people in eight households, the sole inhabitants of some 35,000 miles of territory.[6] But in spite of their isolation the Eskimos, given the opportunity, are gregarious. Communal club houses,

Interior of a large iglu near Chesterfield Inlet, NWT. Eskimos (left) are seated on the *iqliq;* food is being cooked at the far end.

karigi (or *gaggi*), were built by the men and were a focus for ceremonial life. Song-dances, in which both men and women participated, gave opportunities for repressed feelings to be relieved through derisive song duels, and major feasts and ceremonies were held in the karigi in which hung protective amulets in which spirits resided. In some instances the karigi might be made from the joining of three or more snow houses; sometimes a special, large snow house of twenty feet or more in diameter might be built, capable of holding as many as sixty people.

Unquestionably an extremely efficient form of dwelling, the snow house was devised from the most economical means; the vault was constructed without formwork through the use of the spiral and chamfered blocks, the dome offering the maximum volume possible with the minimum surface area. Moreover, the dome had no internal corners or areas where stagnant or cold pockets of air could form, the contours permitting the conservation of heat and energy and assisting in the circulation of air. With the internal skin a volume of cold air could be trapped between the hides and the internal surface of the iglu, preventing the snow shell from melting with the build-up of heat within.

It was an adaptable dwelling, which could permit the addition of domical cells for storage or extensions when two or more families wished to link up during the long winter. Elsewhere in the four thousand mile span of Eskimo dwellings, other types of *iglu* were built. On the Arctic coast of Alaska the *anegiuchak* was favoured, also made of snow blocks but square in plan and with a gabled roof over which loose snow was piled.[7] Or the *killegun* was built, a temporary structure made of block walls cut from the ground snow. The hole left was some 3 feet (1 m) deep, the four walls rose a similar amount above the snow surface, and a ridge pole was used to support a canvas roof. Inside, a tent was pitched to produce a double-skinned dwelling so efficiently insulated as to permit a temperature of over 100 °F (38 °C) to be reached, with the aid of a camp stove (1964), when there were 50 °F of frost (− 18 °F, − 28 °C) outside.

It is possible that the snow house derives from the temporary shelter of the Alaskan Nunamiut Eskimos.[8] This consisted of a domical framework of willow wands over which a layer of snow was shovelled, heated stones inside being used to anneal the snow into a shell. But there is also a possibility that houses of whalebone rib frames may have preceded the snow house; at any rate the remains of ancient whalebone-framed houses, or *quarmang*, have been found in all regions and some were still in use early in the century. Most others were replaced, even in Greenland, by the early seventeenth century, with dwellings of stone and turf or sod. Many of these were cut into a hillside; others were partly subterranean. Heavy stones were corbelled out on the cantilever principle to support a roof slab, over which turf and stones were packed. These Greenland houses were not dissimilar to the snow house in form, but a rectangular stone and turf house largely replaced it, sometimes providing accommodation for several families.[9]

A *tupiq,* or Eskimo tent made of caribou skins, under a light layer of snow. The entrance is at a lower level than the stove at the rear. A can of powdered milk is being unloaded from a large sledge in the foreground.

To the West, in Alaska, where driftwood could be obtained in considerable quantity, log houses were constructed which were packed over with sod; the internal form was approximately rectilinear, but the snow platform iqliq, a narrow and low entrance passage, and gut-skin windows were common to nearly all types. Where possible, the karigi were also constructed from log, plank or stone and sod as in Alaska, where the club houses were associated with specific whaling crews. As the winter ended the snow house became uncomfortable, with snow blocks melting, roofs falling in, and the smell of faeces outside becoming evident. In the transitional period between seasons a *qaqmaq* might be built, consisting of circular walls of snow blocks with a tent roof or with a tent pitched within the enclosure, its guy-ropes fixed with pegs to the wall.

After the biting cold of the winter the brief summers brought the possibility of hunting game—and clouds of mosquitoes and biting flies. Nearly all Eskimo 'bands' turned to making tent dwellings or *tupiq*, constructed from slender poles made of pieces of antler or willow wands lashed together. Two pairs of crossed poles, the smaller at the entrance, the larger at the front edge of the iqliq, formed the basic elements, with an arc of poles defining the back of the tent and resting on the fork of the rear crossed supports. Between the two pairs of crossed poles ran a ridge-piece and the whole frame was covered with a tight fitting membrane of seal-skin or hide. In form, therefore, it was related to that of the iglu in both its snow and sod types, higher and more spacious at the iqliq, narrower at the entrance.

What can be learned from the example of Eskimo shelter types? It is evident that in a region where natural organic materials in the form of timber and grasses are virtually non-existent, and where suitable structural members may only be obtained from sea creatures such as whale or seal, great inventiveness was required to devise and to adapt existing resources to become building material. Permafrost inhibits deep digging in some regions, and six or eight foot thick layers of ice may cover rock, though in some parts turf and stone may be obtainable. Thus, even if access

Typical construction of a *tupiq* or summer tent of the Central Eskimo. A number of variants have been recorded.

to specific materials is not a determinant of shelter it is a significant factor in the devising and construction of built form. Peoples in isolation from other cultures have evolved construction techniques and discovered for themselves fundamental structural principles— like the snow house unsupported vault.

Survival in the polar regions would not be possible for extended periods without effective means of shelter that would insulate a family against the rigours of extreme cold, and exposure to winds, fogs and precipitation. Climate, therefore, is a major factor in the development of building types. Without clothes or shelter a human being will soon die when exposed to a temperature of $-5\,°C$ ($23\,°F$). Eskimos have been able to live in the severe conditions of the Arctic because they have developed clothing and dwelling that will give them the protection that is vital, and the technologies that have made them possible. Even so, relative to the landmass, there are very few Eskimos; in some areas as few as one to a thousand square miles. They are widely dispersed along the frozen rivers and harsh, serrated coasts of the northern Polar regions; in terms of human population as a whole their existence is marginal.

Expediency, and the maximizing of the potential of available resources, shapes the response to materials and their structural possibilities; adaptability and the perception of benefits against custom influence change; the need to create adequate conditions for the pursuit of living and social activities moulds the response to climate. Whether the Eskimos live permanently in sod houses or other iglus, whether they make use of temporary shelters of snow block or hide, and when they make the change, are all conditioned by their economy and the means of obtaining food, raw materials, and articles for daily living; whether they construct large, communal snow houses for community gatherings, ceremonials, and religious occasions is ultimately dependent on their values and belief systems.

In the ensuing chapters the aspects of dwelling that are epitomized by the iglu will be examined through other examples and case studies (though regrettably, not at the same length). They may show how these various aspects of dwelling are integrated in the total context of a way of life within a given environment: how dwelling as artefact relates to dwelling as process.

LIVING IN THE DESERT

Though we are accustomed to thinking of mankind in relation to nations and territories, only thirty per cent of the world's surface is land. Of this, immense areas are very thinly inhabited or have no inhabitants at all: most of Canada, Alaska and Greenland; much of Russia and Siberia; large tracts of Mongolia, the Middle East, Arabia, and North Africa; the Amazon basin and most of Australia. These regions are largely barren lands, from the short grass steppes of Russia, the gravel plains of the Gobi, or the rocky highlands of the Sahara, to the moss and lichen-covered wilderness of the tundra and ice shelves of the Poles. Some are arid, with high temperatures and low rainfall, others cold, and subject to searing winds. Combining poor soils and thin vegetation these territories are generally unsuitable for cultivation, though they may still be host to many species of animals, birds, and hardy plants.

Inhospitable they might seem, but many of the world's barren regions sustain dispersed nomadic populations whose ability in adapting to their environment is often remarkable. Take the San for example, popularly known as the 'Bushmen', of the Kalahari of Namibia and Botswana. The Kalahari is a desert, but one which has scrub plains, thin grasslands, and in the Dobe region of the north, forests of mongongo. The small, honey-coloured !Kung San, who speak a 'click' language (! indicates one of the five vocal 'clicks') are believed to be among the survivors of the oldest African peoples. Until recently they were classified as 'hunter-gatherers' though food obtained by hunting represented less than a third of their diet: hunting provided excitement and variety. Over many millennia they developed the capacity to extract from the desert life-sustaining bulbs, tubers, stalks, truffles, and the nuts of the mongongo tree. Water was obtained from waterholes, water-conserving plants gathered in the rainy season in ostrich-egg containers, or even filtered through stalks from holes in the ground.[10]

A !Kung San hunting group would comprise thirty or so individuals from three or four extended families, though their numbers and composition were flexible. Edible resources were soon exhausted in the area around a camp, and after longer forays were made to obtain food, the group would move away. Because they had to move camp frequently their material culture—their artefacts and possessions—were necessarily limited and light, though they included cooking vessels, bows and arrows, snares, rudimentary clothing, and sandals. In the dry season some groups might stay in one camp site for several months, in the wet season they might move often; factors which affected the form and durability of their dwellings.[11]

At a distance of a few metres their *scherms*, or *kuas*, were virtually indistinguishable from their surroundings; ranged around the periphery of a clearing they would be backed into the grass bordering the site, or might even incorporate the cover of leaves and branches of a living bush. Short-stay huts could be built within an hour from branches, wands, and grasses but a long-stay scherm was more carefully constructed. Thin peeled sticks would be inserted in the ground, in a circle of less than two metres diameter, and the ends tied with the bark of saplings to

provide a light, pointed dome. Horizontal wands were woven into the frame at intervals and bundles of grass tied to them to give a thatch covering. Though the men cleared the site and assisted in inserting the poles, most of the construction and covering was done by the women, who might spend some fifteen hours on a structure that would last, with only a minimum of maintenance, for three months.[12]

Though their kuas were more important as storehouses and site markers than as places in which to sleep, the !Kung San were emotionally attached to them. While the scherm was private, the dwelling-space included the hearth area before it, and this was where cooking, eating and tool-making took place. Beyond the central clearing was a communal space for the trance-inducing and healing dances that were important in Bushmen social life. Such light frame houses seldom lasted long after the group had moved on; if the group returned to the site and it was still habitable, the huts might be reoccupied but it was customary to seek a new site, fresh branches and grass being gathered for the next structure.

In areas where the frame hut took a more developed form, or where suitable lengths of sticks were not readily available, frame poles were carried between settlement sites by many nomadic peoples. But whereas the Bushmen travelled light and did not need pack animals, the transporting of building elements necessitates the use of donkeys or camels to carry them. This is the case with the Rendille, who live in the desert between Lake Turkana and the Ndoto mountains of Kenya.[13] They are nomadic pastoralists whose movements are dictated by the need to find forage and water for their camels, in a dry region which has an average annual rainfall of less than 250 mm—and in some years, none at all.

Looking rather like a large whelk, the Rendille *min* or dwelling is not a symmetrical dome, but rather two-thirds of a hemisphere, with an inclined front. Two pairs of long curved poles, pre-formed to a flattened arc by heating and considerable use, are lashed together; one pair provides the leading edge of the part-hemispherical frame, the other a second curved brace to the rear. Other lengths of thin stick are bent

!Kung Bushman *kua* in the course of construction. Kalahari Desert, Namibia.

over and lashed to these stronger elements to form the domical part of the hut, while straight poles are inclined inwards to form the frame for the front. Women make the light structure and cover it with sisal. At the rear a few animal hides are hung, which can be removed for ventilation if the interior gets too hot. A long rope is bound round the whole structure, and though it is light and quivers in the fierce winds that blow from Lake Turkana it makes a resistant shelter.

On plan, the min departs from a circle, being wider at the front than at the rear; the two forms that make up the whole structure differentiate the areas within the hut. Inside the forward space of the min is used to store the milking vessels, firewood and sandals; the

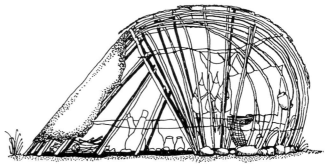

The Rendille shelter, or *min*, cover removed. The internal space is differentiated in use. North-west Kenya. (*After Grum*)

rear, domical section provides a sleeping area for the woman and her husband with palm stem mats unrolled over the floor and skin sleeping mats on the ground. Personal possessions such as stoppered cala- bashes, hide containers and household equipment are

suspended from the ribs or hang round the back of
the hut.

While the women build the huts the men define the
nabo, or council enclosure, and light the fire that will
provide the firebrands for all the huts. An enclosure
of acacia branches is built round the settlement with
its entrance facing west; all the huts have their
entrances facing the main access to the compound,
ranged in an order of seniority that reflects the sub-
clan and status of the occupants. Enclosures for the
animals are also built of acacia and each member of
the camp has a well defined role in the animals' care.

When the grazing is thin the elders of the Rendille
camp debate their next move. Dismantling the huts
takes two or three hours, the poles and mats of each
min carefully loaded on two or three pack camels.
With the long spars rising high from its back like the
mast of a dhow, the camel justifies its name of 'ship of
the desert' as the train moves off to find another
campsite by nightfall. Anders Grum, a Danish archi-
tect-anthropologist, with the help of a venerable Rendille man traced the movements of one nomadic
group. Over more than seventy years it covered some
twelve thousand miles, in long, zig-zagging routes,
making use of the whole Rendille territory and sometimes penetrating well beyond.[14]

Many other East African tribes like the Boran of
Somalia, have similar houses, transporting the long,
curved poles and sometimes woven wattle doors on
their pack animals as they migrate to new grazing
lands. Because the structures are covered with mats,
they are frequently termed and classified as tents.[15]
But they are more accurately (though not more
simply) described as frame-and-mat dwellings. There
are important structural differences between this type
of hut and the majority of tents for it is built by restraining the bent poles that form the structural frame
in tension, the mat covering being laid over the surface, and only lightly tensioned, if at all, by tying it to
the frame. True tents, however, tension the covering
itself, without placing it on a frame but by stretching
it over poles to keep it clear of the ground.

Probably the best-known tent is the A-section form
with a rectangular plan and low brailing walls, used

Nomadic peoples of Kenya, Ethiopia, and Somalia of the 'Horn of
Africa' use pack camels or donkeys to transport the frames, mats,
and wickerwork door of their dwellings.

by armies the world over. But apart from those who
have acquired them in refugee camps or relief programmes, few tent nomads use this type. Quite the
most common is one or other variant of the so-called
'black tent'. Spread across the map like a black tent
itself, the culture of pastoral nomads stretches from
Mauretania and southern Morocco to the west, to the
aBrog of Tibet in the east. In some respects, the
conditions in which Tibetan nomads live differ
considerably from those of the arid-zone nomads of
the Middle East—the altitude, the extremes of cold

and heat, the high pastures, the herding of yaks rather than camels or goats. But they share with their lowland desert neighbours the use of the black tent, though the Tibetan tent is much heavier being made from the belly-fringe hair of yak steers, and the pins and toggles made of yak-horn.[16] While there are many variations of form and detail in the tents of differing peoples of Iraq, Turkey, Arabia, or Algeria, they have much in common, suggesting perhaps, a single source far back in time, before the Song of Solomon was composed: 'I am black, but comely, O ye daughters of Jerusalem, as the tents of Kedar . . .'

All black tents are made from strips of cloth sewn edge to edge to form a large surface. The strips, woven on ground looms, are narrow enough for the women to sit astride them in the process of weaving the goat-hair yarn. In essence, the tent cloth is a membrane held in tension with guy ropes and stretched over, or between, a number of poles. East of the Arabian Gulf the tents are mainly stretched along their *length*, for tension across the cover would separate the strips at the seams. Tents in Arabia and North Africa are strengthened by transverse reinforcing tension bands of webbing which take the strain *across* the membrane. Many tents are strained over a curved ridge-piece supported by one or two poles, or even over a number of such ridge-pieces, to give a typically humped effect; the ridge prevents the supporting internal poles from piercing the membrane. If the black colour of the goat hair might be expected to absorb the sun's rays and make the tent interior uncomfortably hot, the dark hue means that the cover casts a dense shade and insulates against radiation heat. Natural oils in the goat hair are not washed out by dying and consequently the open weave, which permits the circulation of air, contracts tightly to produce an impervious shield in the rare, sudden rains, retaining heat as the temperature drops. In Morocco, where rain, and even snow, fall quite often, the ridge is high and the pitch of the tent steep, but in the more arid regions the pitch of the tent is flatter.[17] Tents east of the Gulf tend to be more box-like, with low-pitch covers and high side walls. Of these, the *khune* of the Basseri is representative of how the tents

A row of Bedouin 'black' tents, near Gafsa, Tunisia. The humped profile is produced by a curved wooden T-frame over which the tent cloth is strained.

Breakfast in the black tent of Moroccan transhumants. The tent culture stretches from Mauritania in West Africa to Tibet.

are used in practice.

One of a confederacy of tribes, the Basseri of the Fars region of Southern Iran are herders of goats and sheep. Their tribe is divided into a dozen descent groups which are subdivided into *oulads*, or family clusters, numbering about a hundred tents. Every oulad has specific rights to summer pasture which have been assigned by the chiefs, to which they

Tent in the Fars region, Iran, showing supporting poles. In many examples wooden fasteners take some of the strain of the tent cloth.

migrate following an *il-rah* or 'tribal road'. This is a traditional route on which they can claim rights to grazing, water and camp sites at specific times of the year. Other tribes may share parts of the same il-rah at different times so that the limited resources of the pasture are utilized to the full. Fredrik Barth, who lived with the Basseri, noted that it is necessary for the health of their animals that they are moved frequently and the migratory routes make the best use, at appropriate times of the year, of the different ecological areas of the Fars region.[18]

A tent accommodates a Basseri household of five or six persons, each household owning up to a dozen donkeys as pack animals, and around a hundred sheep and goats in their flocks. Often they travel in large groups of as many as forty tents but when the winter forage is thin the tents are spread out, with only four or five camping near one another and other clusters camping several kilometres apart. Because the nature of the camp sites varies there is no strict ordering of the tents, but they are often ranged in a rough semi-circle. When the tent cloths are raised wooden 'stay fasteners' or loops along the edges of the cloth take the guy ropes, which are strained over the notched ends of the supporting poles so that the poles do not bear directly on the material. Five poles on the long dimension and three on the short sides of the membrane, which is some six metres by four in size, take the strain. In a large tent the length of the cloth is supported by a discontinuous ridge of T-shaped elements, each made from a pole inserted into a ridge length. Towards the rear the tent is further divided by a high screen of personal belongings in woven sacks, which creates a private space beyond. Skin vessels for milk and water line one side, and a depression near the front of the khune acts as a firepit.

When it is considered time to move on, camp is struck before sunrise and a mounted advance guard rides swiftly to reconnoitre a new camp site. By noon the straggling line of animals will have arrived and the tents will be pitched again; the women will have settled down to their domestic tasks, cooking, spinning or weaving while the men obtain wood and water, do the repairs, twist new ropes, and tend the animals, as their predecessors have done for generations.

FROM TENT TO HOUSE

Although individual nomadic groups may use a single type of tent or frame-and-mat dwelling, larger complexes of peoples spread over a considerable area may use a variety of structures. These may be simple deviations from a norm or they may have fundamental differences which are specific to a group or clan. Obviously, differentiation contributes to a sense of belonging to a distinct group, and helps identification over a distance. Supported by single poles or crossed poles the many lengths of ridge-pieces used by Bedouin and Berber groups have this secondary function, the size of a ridge giving a specific contour to a tent which is perceivable at a distance by eyes used to the sharp discernment of details in the desert or steppe. Differences may also arise from traditional custom, access to usable materials, and the influence of contiguous peoples: the Tuareg are a case in point.

Inhabiting a large area of the Central Sahara the tribes known as the Tuareg number around half a million people. In Arabic, 'Tuareg' is said to mean 'the abandoned people'—those who have departed from the strict tenets of Islam. Tall, lean, haughty and, in the past, warlike, the men wear indigo blue veils, a

fact which has had a peculiarly romantic appeal for European travellers. Strong class and caste distinctions between the nobility and the black *harratin*, the vassals, are observed through complex rules and protocols. Centuries ago these people of Berber origin moved south to breed the camels which are their pride, but also to raise goats in the Algerian desert and even a few zebu, or humped cattle, further south in Niger. They survive in the mountains and gravel plains of the Hoggar and the Ayr massif because of the presence of occasional oases, waterholes and wells, and through the tenacity of desert acacias and fodder plants like tullult grass and aramas.

Formerly the Tuareg were raiders; today, many are traders in camels while others transport salt from Bilma across the fearful sands of the Teneré desert, south of the Ayr mountains. They barter for cereals, tea and cotton cloth, exchanging them for goods made of dyed goatskin—camel hide does not take tanning. In leather they are skilled workers, but neither the men nor the women weave. Consequently, the tents of the Kel Hoggar are covered in membranes of sewn skins, and not of woven goat hair. When a young Tuareg of the Hoggar mountains marries he and his family are expected to give a bride-wealth of camels; his bride's family provides the tent cover and poles,

A tent, made from approximately forty goat skins, of the Ahaggar Tuareg living in Tamesna, west of the Ayr Mountains, Niger, Southern Sahara.

bed frame, soft furnishings, cooking utensils, donkeys, and as many as forty goats. Significantly, the wedding is termed *éhen* - also the word for tent. Women make the cover, sewing the skins in rows to make long strips, or *tarda*, of which there may be five or more. Forty skins might be used to make a membrane of twenty square metres but Tuareg tents of the nobility have been noted that are five times that size. The trailing ends of the leather are made into tassels for decorative effect, and the skins of legs and neck are used to attach the guy ropes.

Skin tents among the Tuareg may take many forms: one typology lists some thirty support systems over which the membranes are stretched.[19] Of these a number consist of two or more arches, made from tamarisk roots, placed at right angles to the long dimension of the tent, the ends of the membrane being supported by cross-pieces resting on forked poles. Other types are supported by three or perhaps five cross-pieces, those in the centre being higher than the ends. Alternatively, a central pole is inserted into a notched ridge-piece to form a 'T'-member, clearly demonstrating the source of the system in the Arabic tent. In these and all other systems the curved poles, ridge-piece, or transverse cross-pieces spread the load of the skin membrane, which is under tension. As the membrane is not attached to them there is no risk of uneven strain, lateral shifting of the tent in high winds doing no damage as they slide over the arches and other members. Poles at the edges take the guy ropes and keep the cover taut.

Daytime temperatures can be high in the desert with 122 °F (50 °C) by no means uncommon and underfoot temperatures of 70 °C. Yet at night, frost is frequent, and snow falls in the mountains. With the sides open for through ventilation the tent can be an effective shade cover, but it is uncomfortable when the sides have to be closed in desert winds and storms. Mats woven from azefu grass are used as screens around the tents and rough stone walls are built as windbreaks. Exposed to the harsh extremes of the climate the skins eventually deteriorate: they are renewed a strip or two at a time, from the centre outwards, the worn outer edge strips being removed.

It is a cyclic process, exactly the same as that used by the Bedouin and Berber when they renew the strips in their goat-hair tents, further confirming that the Tuareg originally obtained their tent forms from the Arabs and adapted them to the use of hides, rather than hair.

Among the Kel Geres, and other Tuareg peoples of the Ayr massif in the southern Sahara, another form of portable structure is used—the frame-and-mat type employed by many peoples of the Sudan and East Africa. Nicolaisen identified seven types of frame, though the most common is made of three or four hoops, the central arches being higher than the sides. Each hoop is made of two lengths of acacia root pre-formed by heating them when green and tying with cords until they dry out to the desired shape. One length is greater than the other in each hoop, that at the front being longer than the rear, so that when they are tied together the joins are not at the crest. Transverse cross-pieces at the ends are lashed to corner supports, while long poles are run across the hoops from end to end of the structure and held in tension by tying them to the frame and the central arch; the whole structure resembles the inverted hull framework of a boat supported on slender poles. Over the framework, mats made of plant stems are secured with cord to the horizontal cross-pieces and the bottom of the framework. Further mats of dum palm are placed in both directions so that all parts of the roof have a double thickness. Finally, when sandstorms make it necessary, a long dum palm mat is brought round the whole tent, leaving a small opening for access; otherwise the mat may be partially rolled, or omitted altogether, to allow ventilation beneath the cover. Portable frame-and-mat dwellings of this type are carried by donkeys, who also transport the heavy carved wooden bed-frames that are the standard furniture of the Tuareg household.

It seems that the Tuareg have been willing to borrow shelter types and structural techniques from other nomads, and to adapt them to their own needs. In the south of the Sahara the types meet and, literally, overlap: both forms of dwelling may be found in one camp, and sometimes the frame-and-mat struc-

Above Skin tent of the Taramanset, one of the Tuareg tribes. The tent cover has been raised to allow through-ventilation, and shows the use of the interior space.

Right Frame of a Tuareg mat hut as used by the Ayr Tuareg. Long poles are held in tension by curving them over three hoops and fixing them to horizontal members at each end.

ture may be covered with a skin tent to keep out summer rains. Rain showers, however, have not been a problem for several years; on the contrary, shortage of water and hence of forage, has had a profound effect on Tuareg culture. Thousands have been forced to migrate to the cities and refugee camps.

Not all Tuareg are nomads; increasingly, the tribes of the southern region have taken up forms of agriculture and lead a more sedentary life. Their dwelling

types include the sturdy but elementary square frame used by the farmers of Hoggar, the *ekeber*, which consists of three poles a side, and a higher, central forked post. This takes the burden of radiating rafters which are lashed to the 'wall plates', the horizontal members of the wall frames, over which bundles of bullrushes or hay may be placed to form both the walls and the roof covering. There are other huts that are cylindrical in form, with low pitched roofs covered in

Left Mat covered frame hut of the northern Tamashek tribe of the Tuareg, adapted from those of the Bella, former black slaves. Timbuktu, Mali.

Below Interior of a frame hut covered with mats of woven palm stems. The heavy wooden bed frame is traditional among the Tuareg. It would be borne by a donkey, when moving camp.

Migrants from Tibesti in northern Chad use the frame structures of their traditional dwellings on settling in the Sudan, covering them with sacking. Eventually they will build more permanent homes.

thatch, while many Tuareg have adopted the dome structure, common among many of the savannah and Sahel peoples, of a ring of poles tied together at the centre and covered with thatch. Some Tuareg have built permanent dwellings of stone or, under the influence of the French, of mud brick, while others used conical mud balls to build the rectangular, flat-roofed house whose form is characteristic of the Hausa of northern Nigeria.[20] Such mud and stone houses of Tuareg agriculturalists began to appear in

settlements in this century, and have started to assume village forms which reflect the adjustment of caste and class systems based on old nomadic traditions to the more recent farming practices.

In the future many nomadic peoples will be abandoning their pastoral, hunting or food-gathering ways of life on the margins of the habitable world. Under the pressures of environmental deterioration and political change they may be obliged to adopt a sedentary life. If so, their exceptional survival skills, and their traditional building techniques using immediate resources for their portable dwellings, will soon be forgotten in the processes of adaptation to alien patterns of living and unfamiliar house types.

2.

RURAL SETTLEMENTS

'They have so used the premises from time when memory is not' stated a report to King Richard II on the condition of farming on Dartmoor. Six hundred years later the 'commoners' who farm the 'ancient tenements' of the moors still jealously defend their rights. Dartmoor is a dramatic wilderness plateau in the south-west peninsula of England, wholly within the county of Devon. Almost denuded of trees its broad furze and bracken-clad moors, scattered with the 'clitter' of boulders rise to heavily weathered 'tors', granite outcrops like nipples on the round-breasted hills. It can be dry and parched in the summer but in winter it is often fog-bound and wet and subject to storms; there are signs of many Bronze Age settlements and hut circles sited to take advantage of the protection that the moors could give.[1]

MOORLAND FARMSTEADS

In a saddle between two hills at Houndtor the remains of a cluster of granite-walled dwellings can be seen, dating from the ninth century. They are an early form of the 'longhouse' in which the farmer and his family shared a cross-passage with the livestock, gaining warmth from the heat of the animals.[2] At the uphill end of the longhouse was the 'livier' or dwelling while the cattle were wintered in the 'shippen' at the lower end, with its stone-lined channel for the slurry to drain. Hay was stored in the 'tallet' or loft overhead, to be pitch-forked to the animals below.[3]

One-storeyed buildings with roofs of hard-won timber frames and thick thatch, longhouses were constructed of granite boulders which cleave into large but manageable blocks. Though the Houndtor longhouses are now no more than an archeological site, an early form of the longhouse still stands in a fold between two tors at Sherrill (Sherwell), where it is used as a cattle byre. Smoke blackening of the roof timbers confirms that it once had a livier with a central hearth but no chimney. Immense blocks of moorstone, probably taken from a Bronze Age kistaven or burial chamber, flank the cross-passage entrance. Another longhouse, now much altered runs at an angle to the lower end and between them are granite pig troughs and a monolithic circular cider-apple press. Close by is a third farmhouse, whose occupiers in the 1970s still cooked over open hearths and maintained the farm with the traditional systems of their childhood.[4]

Half a mile further down the valley is Babeny. Now all one farm, it was once three, facing on to a plot still known as the green. One of the ancient longhouses, though largely ruinous, is used as a bull pen, but its livier, with an immense granite lintel over the fireplace, is open to the sky. The farmhouse is a nineteenth-century one, standing on the hard pan of a former farm building. Unlike Sherrill, Babeny is a 'tenement' in the royal forest of the Duchy of Cornwall which was defined in the 'Perambulation' of AD 1240. In spite of its altitude and heavy rainfall, oats and even barley were grown, and in 1303 the tenants built a grinding mill on the meeting of two rivers; its leat can still be traced. Above the farm is an ash-house in which were placed the ashes from the gorse burnt in the furze-oven. The ash was used to harden floors, to make lye soap and to help fertilize the soil. But perhaps the most permanent reminders of Babeny and Sherrill's long history are the low stone walls which outline the strip fields and the 'newtakes' claimed from the 'outfield' of the moor. Though Babeny today is one farm with a new (1960) open-sided tractor store, its present use is deeply rooted in its past.[5]

Small though they are, these hamlets illustrate many of the factors that influence settlement, of which access to water is vital. The capacity of the land to support a populace is reflected in its density while the nature of the farming system is an indication of the type and quality of its soils. They were largely self-sufficient—the owner of Sherrill in the 1970s still took pride in making her own butter, baking her own bread, spinning and weaving the wool from her own sheep and raising a mixed stock of cattle, sheep, horses, pigs, and fowl. The moors are not readily cultivated on a large scale and are more suitable to cattle and sheep farming, but there was an evident need to diversify farming activities as in the winter months the hamlets could be isolated. Stone was abundant for the building of 'linhays' and barns, but roof timbers had to be brought in by waggon. Examination of the terrain shows the importance of communication routes that gave access to rural fairs

Remains of an early longhouse at Houndtor Vale, Dartmoor, Devon, showing the entrance to the cross-passage. Above and left, would have been the 'livier' or living quarters; animals would be stabled to the right on the hill-slope.

Single-storey longhouse at Sherrill with its entrance built from massive moorstones from a Bronze Age *kistaven*. The present farmhouse may be seen beyond.

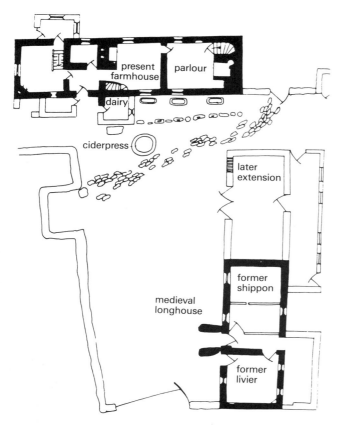

Plan of Sherrill farm, Dartmoor, Devon, with former medieval longhouse and existing farmhouse.

and cattle markets, and the grass keep from the South Hams of west Devon.[6] Today, horseboxes, tractors, and lorries have shortened the time spent in travelling, but the narrow lanes still regulate the flow, and a time-distance ratio between house and field or open pasture still applies.

CONTINUITY AND CHANGE

We know something of the background to the settlements of Dartmoor because of the long history of official records in Britain, though more is known of Babeny than of its neighbour, because it is leased from the Duchy of Cornwall. An efficient bureaucracy which has a tradition of keeping administrative records, parish registers, and official archives can make the unravelling of the skeins of settlement history possible. Genealogies, accounts of tithes and taxes, court records of legal disputes, the entry of births, marriages and deaths or the sale of plots and 'parcels' of land, all contribute to an understanding of the establishment, growth, stability, or decay of a community. Augmented with details on methods of cultivation, production, processing, storing and marketing, on demographic trends and the impact of wars, migration, intermarriage, or economic pressures a reconstruction of the past of a community is possible.

This was the attraction of a Swiss settlement to the anthropologist Robert Netting, who used such records to examine the life of the mountain village of Törbel in the Valais. Perched on an Alpine slope within sight of the Matterhorn, it was protected from the threat of avalanches by forests above. Törbel had a long tradition of common use of some lands and private ownership of others; a tightly-knit, if vigilant and even suspicious, community with family commitment to the production of its limited but healthy diet, and communal participation in the seasonal transhumance of its cattle. Alternating the fallowing of rye fields, rotating crops of rye and potatoes, composting animal dung and gathering forest humus for its nutrients the farmers over the centuries had developed a form of land husbandry that was sensitive to the specific soil structure and climate of their Alpine settlement. An irrigation system had been established as early as the twelfth century, and this had to be maintained in good repair, the farm families using it on a sixteen-day cycle to water the vines on the steep mountain terraces. Törbel seems to have been a community which has maintained its equilibrium over the centuries through judicious farming and effective internal social controls. But Netting noted that the parish records revealed an expansion of the population in the late eighteenth century and a decline in the mortality rate, which he believed to have been due to the beneficial effect on health and fertility of the introduction of potatoes to the mountain economy.[7]

More people meant a demand for more accommoda-

The village of Törbel, showing the relationship of the closely packed houses and *speicher* (stores) to the field plots. Valais, Switzerland.

tion. Houses and land had been the subject of investment since the thirteenth century and analysis of notarized transactions and later, bills of sale, meant that from the 1600s the exchange and ownership of property was well documented. Young married couples had difficulty in acquiring property unless parental land was made available to them or they gained it through the partition of the inheritance on the death of a farmer father. Törbel's houses were built of horizontally-laid notched timbers, under local slate roofs. The earliest, the *Heidenhauser*—literally 'heathen' houses—were of split logs; later the baulks were sawn. *Speicher* or storehouses, and field granaries mounted on mushroom-shaped staddle stones

were similarly built. Because of their sturdy construction and the steady state of the settlement many of them remained in use for centuries and are still in use. Each house had a *Wohnstube*, which combined the functions of living room and bedroom, and a kitchen with an open hearth. Beneath the house a cellar kept cheese edible for years and was used for the summer store of meat. Clustered closely together with narrow paths between them the houses allowed little room for expansion, and in large families trundle beds were used for children who did not share the parental bed. Recently though, changes have come to Törbel. Chalets have been built on the outskirts of the village and new houses have appeared on inherited lands. Many people commute to the towns but others, with evident satisfaction in their way of life and pride in the new amenities that they have received, still farm

Farm complex at Törbel with house to the right and barns, granary (on 'staddle stones' to deter rodents) on the slope below. All buildings are of 'notched' horizontal baulks of timber with stone slab roofs.

in the village.[8]

Emphasizing the ecology of the mountain settlement, Netting's account depicts the life of a community in historical depth, charting its institutions and delineating the problems and choices before the farming families over the passing of generations. But villages have a spatial as well as a temporal dimension; his study did not include the plans of settlement, land holdings, dwellings, church, and workshops that would have given a rounded picture of the settlement in its location, and the processes of change that may have occurred within its form. As an Africanist, however, he was drawn to Törbel precisely because the social record of its past could be assembled, an undertaking far more certain in the reliability of its sources and infinitely fuller in its documentation than that of the Kofyar hill-farmers of the Jos plateau in Northern Nigeria whom he had previously studied.

Sometimes passing through the Jos region, sometimes settling, the Fulani are a people with a complex history whose migrations from Senegal and the western Sudan began in the thirteenth century.

Slender and aquiline, they intermarried with those with whom they came into contact or whom they conquered in battle, while retaining their language. Fulani nomads, the *Bororo'en* were and are an independent cattle-herding group but the *Fulbe na'i* are semi-sedentary, the young men seasonally migrating with the herds. A ruling and professional class, the *Toroobe* have considerable power, becoming able administrators in Muslim society and exacting taxes from their less fortunate brethren, the *Fulbe siire*. Both groups established themselves 2,000 miles from Senegal in the Adamawa and Benue river region of what is now Cameroon, by the eighteenth century.[9]

Bé is a Fulani village between Garoua and Rei-Baba on the Mayo-Kebbi, a tributary of the Benue. The Fulbe siire have adapted the economy and often the dwelling types of the indigenous peoples. At the beginning of the century the Fulani of the region were divided between the wealthy slave owners, their slaves, and free men, but with the abolition of slavery the power of the *Laamido*, or Fulani emir, was reduced and partly replaced by that of the administrators at Garoua.

In 1949-50 Bé was visited by a team of Parisian architects from l'Ecole Nationale Supérieure des Beaux-Arts. They surveyed some of the *sarés*, or compounds, but found them rather formless, with labyrinthine routes between their mud walls. Dwellings in the sarés included pole-framed, circular-plan huts with wall cladding of woven straw, and domed, thatched roofs; cylindrical earth houses with conical pole-and-thatch roofs; and earthen houses of square plan and flat roofs in the Islamic style of northern Nigeria. A saré comprised a number of such dwellings. At the entrance was a reception hut, sometimes with another hut nearby built by a young unmarried son. Beyond a screen wall, an enclosure contained the huts of the wives arranged in a loose arc around the compound headman's hut, the *fattuude*, which was often of the square type. Granaries, a kitchen hut, a grinding shelter, a stable, a well, and at the rear of each saré, latrines and a dunghill, were recorded by the team.[10]

At much the same time Bé was visited by the

Typical larger house in Törbel with stone cellar. The small size of some of the rooms is indicated by the timbers of the cross-wall. A vertical pole helps to clench the gable end of the storehouse.

Fulani *saré* or compound showing houses with circular plan. Some have mud-plastered pole walls; others have been repaired with reed and bamboo bound with straw; a number combine both systems.

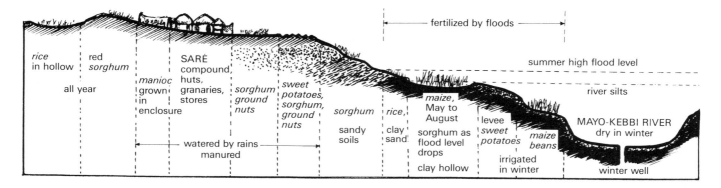

rice
in hollow | red *sorghum* | | SARÉ compound, huts, granaries, stores | | | | | | | | | | fertilized by floods

all year | | *manioc* grown in enclosure | | *sorghum ground nuts* | *sweet potatoes, sorghum, ground nuts* | | sorghum | rice, | *maize,* May to August | levee *sweet potatoes* | | summer high flood level / river silts

watered by rains manured | sandy soils | clay sand | sorghum as flood level drops / clay hollow | maize beans / irrigated in winter | MAYO-KEBBI RIVER dry in winter / winter well

Section through a *saré* at Bé on the Mayo-Kebbi River, Cameroon. Principal crops and methods of winter and summer irrigation are shown. (*After Dumont*)

French agricultural economist René Dumont, who noted the fields around the saré which produced alternate crops of sorghum and groundnuts. A plot of manioc was situated close to the saré, fenced against goats, and a short distance away sweet potatoes were growing in ridged fields, the crop alternated with groundnuts, sorghum or beans. Further afield on the hill-slopes rice was growing in hollows among the sorghum fields, and below the saré nearer to the river red millet was planted. Rice was grown at the flood limit and quick-growing maize corn, or sorghum seedlings transplanted from the upper nursery beds were sown as the waters of the Mayo-Kebbi fell. Flooded in the summer and manually irrigated in the winter the alluvial banks of the river were used for growing a variety of vegetables—aubergines, calabashes, marrows and pumpkins. Apart from satisfying his family's needs, a farmer could produce some 600 kilos of millet, sweet potatoes, and groundnuts for sale. With the proceeds he could buy cotton which could be dyed and woven in the compound, and such goats and cattle as he could afford. Forty goats were needed for a bride-price, but the number of cattle that he owned, not to say the size of the dunghill they produced, were an indication to the world of his prosperity.[11]

A score of years later Bé was visited again, this time by Nicholas David, an anthropological archeologist who studied the social structure and living patterns of the inhabitants, making detailed records of 36 of the 56 Fulani compounds in the village. In 1966 cotton had been introduced as a cash crop but the growing of groundnuts and sorghum continued, the diet augmented by fishing in the Kebbi river—unmentioned by Dumont. A compound, David noted, would have a minimum of two huts, one for a man, his wife and pre-pubertal children, and another for a kitchen. But if he took a second wife she would also require a minimum of two huts, and a grinding hut would also be found where there were two wives. Hearthstones were located inside the kitchen huts and in the open for dry season cooking. Water vessels were sunk in the ground, baskets for storing groundnuts were suspended, and plastered grass granary bins were set on rocks to keep away rodents. Some larger compounds were agglomerates of the sarés of two or more friendly or related families, while guest huts and bachelor huts were also sited in the sarés.

When a member of the family died the body would be interred near the guest hut but the deceased's own hut would be abandoned. Soon the puddled earth would be used for the building of another hut nearby. The roofs were frequently infested by white ants which could consume one in six months, the average life of a hut being around ten years. Every other year a hut within a compound became uninhabitable, and the whole saré would be replaced within a span of fifteen years. In the process, functions often changed. As new huts were built for new wives old ones were recycled or used for other purposes: deteriorating sleeping huts might become a kitchen, a kitchen

Above Members of a Fulani family, having brought their goats from pasture. Recycled materials or structures from dwelling huts may be used for animal pens and disused houses may become stores.

Right Plan of a *saré* at Bé, showing the compounds of two wives surrounded by woven straw mat fences. (*After David*)

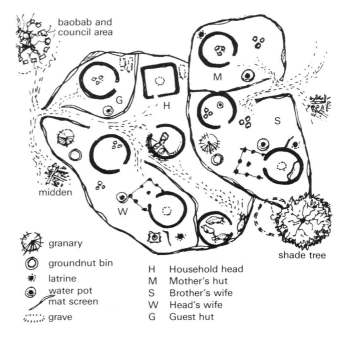

baobab and council area

midden

M

S

H

G

W

shade tree

⊛ granary
◎ groundnut bin
⊛ latrine
⊛ water pot
〜 mat screen
░ grave

H Household head
M Mother's hut
S Brother's wife
W Head's wife
G Guest hut

might be used as a storage hut or animal pen. Though the overall generalized appearance of the compounds may not seem to have altered since the visit of the Beaux-Arts architects or René Dumont, in fact the village of Bé as seen by Nicholas David was a different one in every detail. Change in this society was physically expressed in the buildings but the presence of bicycles and transistor radios was evidence of other changes taking place.[12]

Apart from what we may learn from these reports about the Fulani compounds of Bé, we may note that each observer, objective according to his own discipline, sees the settlement in a different way. The architects, seeking formal beauty and consistency found the variety of forms disconcerting and haphazard; they were only marginally concerned with the reflection of the social structure within them. To the agricultural economist the village demonstrated a type of horticultural land utilization which was efficient, though mainly fertilized by river silt: he deplored the wasted potential of ashes and manure in the prestige dunghill and the middens. For the anthropologist the plans of the compounds reflected social custom and family structure, and the cycle of labour. Each observer had his own purpose in conducting the study and points to make: most original perhaps was Nicholas David. He sought to demonstrate to archeologists with the use of the compound plan as research material, that their interpretations could well be wrong: such a plan would reveal neither the complexity of the social forces at work nor its organization, neither the ambiguous use of the buildings nor the changes that had taken place over a short passage of time.

From these studies we get an incomplete picture of Bé as a settlement—like the Törbel example there is no overall plan, and neither is there a plan of the land holdings of each saré. Moreover, each report was selective; while acknowledging the presence of the palace of the Laamido, the relationship of the sarés to it and of the inhabitants to the Toroobe was not made explicit. There were immigrant Gesira already settled in Bé when Nicholas David was there and in the interim many hundreds of Fulani have settled in the Adamawa region. Change continues.[13]

If there is much that remains untold we learn something of the importance of subsistence economy and land utilization in the patterning of these settlements and we have an understanding of some of the factors that might affect their physical organization.

Bé however, is a specific case. Other Fulani sarés may share characteristics with its compounds but the village has no mirror image: though many of the general features of climate, land use, economy, social structure, and history may have their echoes in other societies, this particular blend of interaction and evolution is uniquely its own. It is this singular nature of

settlements within society that has so often been overlooked when generalized characteristics have been used to justify 'mass housing' for diverse peoples—a subject to which I shall return. And it must be borne in mind now, as we consider some of the constituents and commonalities between various settlement types.

HAMLET AND VILLAGE

These examples I have discussed could all be considered as 'upland' settlements, though their altitudes are different. They are also inland settlements, far from the sea in the Swiss and Cameroon examples, far enough (in view of the problems of communications and the marked difference in the topography), for the Devon instance to be considered as 'inland'. It has been shown by the Polish geographer Staszewski, that the bulk of the world's population occupies lowland territories—perhaps 15 per cent live at an altitude above 700 metres and over half live below 200 metres. But the factors that influence whether communities live in high or low altitudes are numerous: in much of South America it is healthier to live in mountain regions. In Colombia and Ecuador, eight out of ten people live in the Andes; in Bolivia, three-quarters of the population live above 10,000 feet (3,000 m).[14] Altitude and latitude interact, and in northern latitudes more people live in the lowlands. Again, it has been noted that the greatest densities of the world's population live close to the sea, with three-quarters of the cities of over four million inhabitants being located on sea or lake shores and most of the rest located by the principal rivers.[15] But the world's population is far from wholly concentrated in these cities, at least not *yet*, more than half still being rural.

In contrast with the agricultural societies who raise crops and livestock on farm lands, many of the peoples who dwell near rivers, lakes, or the sea depend on fish as their principal source of food. If they are fortunate, or careful in the extent of their fishing, they can nurture the fish and produce a surplus which can be traded with peoples inland. Riverain and lacustrine peoples can be endangered by seasonal flooding which may raise the level of the waters above floor levels. Their situation is often less sheltered than that of forest dwellers and the exposure means that unchecked winds may also add to the hazards. Coastal peoples and those on tidal reaches of rivers are also subjected to considerable daily variations in water levels, and there are other problems caused by the instability of silts and river mud, and sometimes the undertow of receding tidal waters. It would seem safer to build on land, and many riverain and lacustrine peoples do; but there is also a strong incentive to live over the fish stocks and so protect them. Whole villages, even entire towns, are to be found built over water, the dwellings being erected on piles or 'stilts' requiring catwalks and jetties to connect them.

Between coasts and uplands may be found, in differing continents and contexts, the marshes and swamps, the rain forests, jungles and woodlands, the savannahs, prairies and veldts, the undulating foothills, and the hot and cold deserts of the world. These are where the bulk of the rural populations dwell in farmsteads, homesteads, villages, and rural townships that may be numbered not in thousands, but in millions: India alone is reckoned to have more than half a million villages. Movements of nomads who settled millennia ago, invading hordes and migrating families who established their claims to land and water, defended their territories and established their lineages, determined much of the patterning of settlements that can be perceived today. Beneath the foundations of untold houses are the floors and foundations of their predecessors; to the archeologist the land is a palimpsest on which can be read the unfolding of man's settlement history. But if generations have built on the lands of their ancestors, new territories are still being opened up, virgin forests are still being felled to make, often with irreparable environmental harm, new claims upon the land.

Arguments have been powerfully made for a physical and environmental determinism that considers that advantageous climates and temperatures, soils and seasons give shape to man's culture;

Piles raise these dwellings above the river flood level, in the coastal province of Choco, Colombia. Open platforms form part of the living space. Split bamboo is used for side walls and the roof is of palm thatch.

they have been rebutted as vigorously by those who argue that culture determines building and settlement form.[16] But there is much evidence to show that both apply, as we have seen in the examples above.

Ecological factors profoundly affect population

Indications of the significance of millennia to a site are to be found at Carnac, Brittany, where village houses follow the lines of megalithic stone rows.

densities; marshy regions which have been exploited for the growing of rice have permitted densities which have reached well over one thousand people per square kilometre in some parts of rural Asia; no other cereal enables so large a number of people to be nourished by so small a cultivated area. What is often termed the 'carrying capacity' of the land to support a population relates to the form of food production and the kind of society which utilizes it. When the maximum population is reached, beyond which the carrying capacity of the land is exceeded, either new lands must be sought or expanded into, or there must be change in the intensiveness of the cultivation system. Nevertheless, the poorest agricultural lands and the simplest of tools can multiply by as much as forty times the number of hunter-gatherers that it can sustain—but hunters can survive where agriculture is not possible.[17] The processes of agricultural and technological change do not necessitate a corresponding change in settlement, but they certainly contribute.

The economics of settlements relate to time-distance factors which affect the ability of a population to work its lands. Those crops that require constant attention or are required most are closest to the settlement, those that can be maintained with less intensive use of labour and time are further away; at the farthest horizons the land may be unexploited.[18] There is a tendency for settlers to disperse themselves regularly in a polka-dot pattern across new and unbroken terrain. As land is cleared for cultivation and land utilization expands concentrically, the areas come into contact with each other, 'close-packed' like hexagons over the field. With the establishment of hamlets and the making of roads trading begins between the centres. Enterprising settlements exploit the trade potential to produce a profit, expanding to become villages which serve a number of hamlets, a hierarchy of trading centres being established.[19]

Territorial boundaries are the result of the meeting of lands under production; when the available land has been occupied, production increases to meet an expanding population with more intensive agriculture. However, the acquisition by force of adjacent lands has often been the less peaceable solution to the problems of land and population pressures, hence defence of the territory has been in the past a significant factor in settlement organization and location. Often the boundaries of an agreed territory are defined by topographical features—mountain ridges, rivers, shorelines. But in thinly-populated forest regions the treeline edge itself may be the boundary, the forest dwellers apprehensive of those whose territory lies in the plains.

There are manifold reasons why villages have formed, and security is undoubtedly one. Isolated homesteads are vulnerable to marauders, and the need for protection and to ensure the family line into future generations was a powerful imperative for joining others. There is safety in numbers, but there is a narrowing too; many villagers are secure in their group but suspicious of, and hostile to, outsiders. A people like the Yanomamö of Brazil have a limited perception of the space beyond their villages, the lands within reach of a raiding party often being the limit of their knowledge of the world.[20]

However, man is a social being and the need to be in the company of others extends beyond safety and self-preservation. Companionship, friendship, argument, the need to share problems and seek or give advice, and to debate issues of mutual concern, all play their part. A broadening of local knowledge and experience, the news of events, the exchange of ideas and information and the expansion of the intellect and the heart are made more possible in the social life of the village and small township. Economically, the advantage of barter, exchange and trade, the opportunity to sell produce and to purchase others, are incentives to use the village and, for many, to be a

Top An isolated Indian farmstead in the comparatively thinly populated Guerrero State, Mexico. The few patches of cultivation reveal the low 'carrying capacity' of the land.

Right Skilful use of terraces has enabled the people of Charikot, Nepal, to exploit the full potential of their lands. In the foreground stream waters power grain-mills.

A hamlet with a well to the right, and the church, the centre of the community life, beyond. The ruins of an old house stand among fruit trees, a new house follows the traditional plan. Murcia, Spain.

to the Scott Committee which reported on land utilization in rural Britain, any 'compact grouping of over 1,500 people constituted a town'. The geographer Dovring noted that while the median size of villages in the Balkans was above a thousand, in Italy and Spain it was in excess of 5,000.[21] And of course, populations are not constant. Villages grow into towns, others decline with the migration of their young people to the cities. It is their rural situation and their dependence on a living from the land, lake, or sea as much as their scale that distinguishes them from the manufacturing and marketing economies of towns and cities today.

PATTERNS OF SETTLEMENT

Spatial and demographic aspects of settlement are properly the province of economic and population geographers who have much to say on these subjects, while the traditional themes of land utilization and settlement location have been enlarged by the study of ecosystems and the place of human ecology within them. In turn, these have considerable bearing upon social organization as a part of the study of social systems, inevitably overlapping and interweaving with some current trends in anthropology and planning theory. Important as these subjects are, they are specialized in themselves, and highly complex in their ramifications upon each other. Obviously space does not permit discussion here, in a book which is essentially concerned with the individual dwelling. In making some brief comments on the form of the hamlet, village, or township—insofar as these can be defined—I am obliged to make broad generalizations which could be extensively modified in many contexts and contradicted in others.

part of it. That the village, like the hamlet or the farmstead, has an economic base is, in one sense its *raison d'être*. But, as in so much related to dwelling, it is the interaction of many elements and the dominance in specific circumstances of some over others—the advantageous site, the market, the feudal manor, the sacred ground—for instance—which may account for the quality, shape and ultimately, the size of the settlement.

A huddle of houses brought together by the need for mutual support, the hamlet is often occupied by people with close kinship ties. Many have no focus beyond a well, a bend in the road, or some other small but, for the resident, distinguishing feature. Some may have a shrine or chapel and the size of the settlement might range from two or three to a dozen habitations in which as many as a hundred people may live. There is no easily definable transition from hamlet to village; the distinction is blurred and evident more in the nature of the scale and complexity of the relationships between members of the community and the world beyond, than in any numerical definition. Numbers of inhabitants are likewise no reliable index to the nature of the village or small township:

Sufficient has been said to indicate the relationship of the economy to the settlement pattern. It is evident in the 'dispersed settlement'[22] where farm workers live close to their crops and is particularly marked in a plantation system. Until the 1960s, when sharecropping in the Deep South of the United States virtually ended, the cotton fields of the southern monoculture were dotted with the cabins of the 'croppers'. In Mississippi, Arkansas, or Alabama two-roomed frame shacks with verandahs had only a yard and a few garden plots before the cotton fields stretched out to the low horizon.[23] This pattern is to be seen today in the dwellings of the *campesinos*, the tenant farmers and peasants of Central America. On the slopes of the coffee plantations of Costa Rica the poor, but often brightly painted and flower-bedecked houses nestle in the deep green, densely planted coffee bushes. Below in the lush rain forest on the shores of the Caribbean beyond Limón, neat wooden houses, some with thatched roofs, some under corrugated iron sheeting stand in clearings dispersed at intervals of a hundred metres or more.[24]

Where the land is more intensively cultivated but the ecology is more fragile, as it is in the savannah regions of West Africa, a tighter control may be exercised on the siting of dwellings. Compounds of the Tallensi are sited on the least cultivatable land, often among the curious rock piles that are scattered through their region of northern Ghana. Allocations of land for new compounds is determined by the *Tendaana*, or land priest, who intercedes with the ancestors by appropriate rituals and libations to seek their guidance on the appropriate site. Compounds form 'molecular settlements', partially dispersed, but linked by footpaths through the tall stands of maize and elephant grass. Though the compounds are a bow-shot apart, their siting is closely related to the amount of arable land that a mature extended family can be expected to work,[25] to their relationships with kin occupying other compounds, and to the re-use of ground consecrated for building.

Many of the peoples in this region were conquered by Mossi invaders from the north, some of the chiefs still being of Mossi origin. Their compounds were encircled with walls which linked the huts and

Top A settlement of *campesino* (peasant) houses, dispersed among smallholdings within reach of the coffee plantations which provide the main source of employment. Costa Rica, Central Valley.

Right Tendaana or land-priest (left), and the chief of a Tallensi 'molecular' village, in front of a family compound. Northern Ghana.

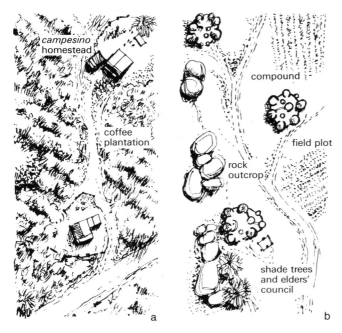

Morphology of typical settlement patterns, including
(a) 'dispersed' settlement of *campesino* dwellings, Costa Rica; (b) a
'molecular' Tallensi compound, Northern Ghana; (c) a 'nucleated'
walled *ksar* in the Draa Valley, Morocco; (d) a 'linear' Ashanti
village, forest regions of Ghana, becoming a 'grid' settlement.

afforded some measure of defence, but their molecular dispersal undoubtedly made them vulnerable to attack. Defence, as has been noted, is an important factor in the siting of many settlements.[26]

Several hundred miles further west on the pre-Saharan southern slopes of the High Atlas the landscape is desolate, rock-strewn, and arid, but it is broken by the Valley of the Draa, which provides a fertile if unreliable strip which waters the palm groves. Along the Draa are the 'nucleated settlements' of both Berbers and Arabs. Formerly under frequent attack from other groups and from nomadic tribes they defended themselves in walled *ksour*. Comprising an agglomeration of densely packed ochre-hued earth and stone houses they were threaded with narrow lanes and culs-de-sac which reached the dwellings by circuitous routes. A representative ksar may have as its key nuclei a mosque, an ancient *souq* or market-place, *kasba*, ceremonial dance space, shops

and wells. Such a walled, nucleated settlement has no room for expansion within its boundaries, and in recent years a large open market, rudimentary post office, cafe and further shops will have been built beyond the walls. These are to be found beside an improved road which now links the *ksour* along the Draa and, in the process, a form of 'ribbon development' is beginning.[27]

'Linear settlements' may follow a topographical feature which inhibits their growth in depth—a hill ridge for instance, or a deep but fertile cleft. Generally they have grown along a communication route, dwellings on either side benefiting by their access to passing trade. Villages of the Ashanti of Ghana were traditionally sited along the main street, the *abonten*, which ran either north-south or east-west. In even the minor villages the abonten would be over 100 feet (30 m) wide and many were far wider, with drainage channels along the sides and a camber to the red surface of the laterite road. The house of the chief, the *ahemfie*, with the Queen Mother's house and court to its left, faced a central clearing with large shade trees, the site for traditional ceremonials and village meet-

Typical *ksar* or walled, nucleated settlement, on the southern
flank of the eastern High Atlas Mountains. Er-Rachidia, Morocco.

ings. Further along the street would be situated the
abosomfie, the priest's shrine, and between were clustered, parallel to the road, the houses of the villagers
grouped according to their clans. Often these were
single rectangular houses but most had additional
paito, or open-sided 'verandah' rooms arranged
around a courtyard. Formerly the houses were of wattle, plastered with clay, and often whitewashed, but
solid walls of packed earth are now customary and
the former thatched roofs are covered with the
ubiquitous corrugated iron. Traditionally all Ashanti
houses were single-storey, but some chiefs' houses
today are two-storeyed. On the edge of the village a
market, a school, and even a church will generally be
found.[28]

In many linear villages problems arise when the
round trip to basic amenities becomes inconvenient,
or the participation of the inhabitants in village social
life is restricted by their relative isolation at the limits
of the settlement. Under these circumstances there is a

The main street which determines the linear form of an Ashanti
forest village. The chief's house (two-storeyed in this instance)
overlooks the principal space used for public meetings and
ceremonials. Ghana, West Africa.

tendency to develop parallel secondary and tertiary
streets, cross-linked to the main communication
route. The resultant 'grid settlement' with its
checkerboard arrangement of dwellings is characteristic of the larger Ashanti settlement. In many societies
it is a traditional form, but it is also frequently generated by the focus of some forms of a communal 'open
space settlement', the main square or plaza of, for
instance, Spanish or Portuguese colonial origin which
is common throughout Central and South America.[29]

When it is compared with many other settlement
patterns such as those summarized above, the grid is
sometimes in violent disagreement with the 'organic'
growth of villages according to the nature of land utilization, topography, the spatial requirements of communities and families, and the available resources.
Such is the diversity of settlement types and locations
that though some morphological similarities may be
identified which make broad classifications possible,
the variety of factors which influence man's settlements are, in indigenous contexts, unique to their
specific circumstances.

Opposite A group of replica Haida houses with heraldic totem
poles. This type of house is no longer built, though there has
been a revival of pole carving. University of British Columbia
Totem Park, Vancouver, BC, Canada.

Tuareg grass shelter, in the Acacus Mountains on the Libya/Algeria border.
Formerly these were used only by the *harratin* vassal caste.

Opposite Black tents of the Qashgai, one of the tribes of the Fars region, Iran.
They have a more box-like form than the low-profile Bedouin tents.

Camp of the !Kung San Bushmen at sunset. Though the *kua* or dwelling is private, most domestic activities take place outside. Namibia.

Opposite Early Dartmoor longhouse with cross-passage entrance built of granite slabs from a Bronze Age burial chamber. A monolithic granite apple mill, centre. Devon, England.

Compound of semi-sedentary Fulani, whose earthen dwelling huts are occupied seasonally. The small child by one of them is grinding corn. Northern Nigeria/Cameroon.

Yanomamö Amer-Indians are hostile to strangers and take pride in feuding and raiding. Their defensive communal jungle houses, of which this is a small section, are circular in plan around a central open space. Venezuela/Brazil.

A compact, nucleated settlement in a fertile valley between mountain ranges. Terracing conserves water and careful cultivation exploits the 'carrying capacity' of the land. Naqil, Yemen.

3.

TYPES AND PROCESSES

Looseness of terminology confusing shape with form, paying scant regard to plan, and with little acknowledgement of structural differences, has resulted in numerous vague descriptions of dwelling types. Generalized statements that summarize a building form as 'in the bee-hive style' or a 'typical round hut with a thatched roof' abound in travellers' and anthropologists' writings; that the buildings of adjacent villages may differ from one another is frequently not perceived, or not thought to be significant when it is. I do not wish to minimize the difficulties in drawing up any typology of buildings, which may vary considerably over quite a small area. Guinea-Bissau for instance, is a small West African state of less than 14,000 square miles and a 1974 population of half a million. A Swedish team identified six major 'form-types' of houses within the state, one of which, the 'planta baixa circular' as they termed it, alone having five sub-types within it. They identified nine major plan types and several section variations in their typology, but their extensive illustrations and individual plans of houses reveal that these categories compromised the many subtle variations of plan, section and form, made more complex by a diversity of materials and details, which were to be found even within a single village.[1]

Often it is the variants from a norm which give indigenous dwellings their interest and meaning; to identify Mediterranean island vernacular as 'cubic' is to do injustice to an immense variety of buildings. Commonly used, it is a term which could be applicable whether the building were built of timber, stone or earth. Such description by form is of only limited use and typologies which derive from the structural and material characteristics can give a better indication of the distinctions that exist between shelter types.

PHYSICAL PRINCIPLES

All buildings, whatever their function, have to meet certain physical constraints. Whether they are the outcome of a long tradition of received techniques, assembled by trial, error, and experimentation, or based on detailed mathematical calculations and the application of formulae, ultimately the basic laws of physics will determine whether they will stand up or collapse. If, for example, a fluted marble column in Athens stands on a carved marble base, and a house post in New Guinea stands on a lump of stone, the base in each case exerts an upward thrust equal to the total load on the post or column. Or again, though a solid beam may be made of oak, steel, or reinforced concrete, if all its dimensions are trebled it will be three times as long—but it will be twenty-seven times greater in volume, weight, and strength. In other words, no matter how simple or sophisticated a building may be it is subject to the same physical laws.

Understanding the general physical principles that affect the 'structure' of a building, and the means and methods of assembly of materials employed in its 'construction' helps us to appreciate the achievements of indigenous builders. It can also help us to recognize why buildings may lurch or collapse through structural weakness or failure, and may assist in the making of recommendations on the improvement of building methods and use of materials in the interests of economy and safety.

All materials have weight, and all buildings are affected by the forces of gravity; structural systems

A corner post stands on interlocking timber cills, resting on stone blocks. The house is 'overbuilt'; a lighter support system could have taken the roof load. Kulu Valley, Himachal Pradesh.

loads has often led to 'overbuilding', with walls of a mass and weight greatly in excess of what is necessary for ordinary domestic purposes. That some buildings survive over many centuries is often attributable to this overbuilding which enables them to cope with unexpected stresses. Conversely though, some buildings are deliberately underbuilt so that they will be less dangerous if destroyed; the collapse of buildings in a Pacific cyclone, for instance, is the result of their *not* having been built to withstand the ferocity of high winds, which create a sudden addition to the live loads.

In addition, therefore, to the stresses imposed by the elements used in the building itself, there are other stresses which may vary considerably according to climatic conditions, the relative stability of the site, and the way of life of the occupants. Stresses on building components can be broadly classified as 'tension', a stress which pulls apart the particles of matter and has a stretching effect, such as the strain on a guy rope; 'compression' where the particles are pushed against each other with a shortening effect as in a column or solid wall; and 'shear' which causes the particles to slide, as for example, where a floor joist meets a wall. A building material that is ideal for coping with one kind of stress is not necessarily good for another: adobe (earth) brick may behave under compression forces very well but be poor in its capacity to resist shear forces. Most materials meet certain kinds of stresses better than others and part of the essential skill in building lies in the selection, preparation and assembly of materials appropriate to meet the strains the chosen form imposes.

If access to a wide range of materials is available, the most suitable can be selected. Many northern European countries are particularly well endowed with a variety of timber species, clays, and rocks. But some parts of the world have a very limited range of materials with, for instance, heavy timber being in short supply. Similarly, some peoples are without the tools needed to work the materials: California redwoods were of limited used to Miwok Indians, who could only build with strips of bark and fallen branches before they had metal axes. To a great

transmit the gravitation 'loads' to earth while creating and enclosing the volume that is needed to meet the function of the building. Every dwelling has 'dead' loads which include the weight of the static elements, such as the roof, or of the walls which also carry and transmit its load. In addition, dwellings have to cope with 'live' loads—forces that are exerted inconsistently and at different times by the wind, the movement of occupants, the placing of furniture, the swinging of doors, or the pressure of farm animals against the walls. The unpredictability of the live

Shear failure caused by lack of jointing and of diagonal bracing of the wall frame, the omission of tie-beams to the roof, and by inadequate infill. The owner has buttressed the wall with poles and attempted to counter the roof-thrust. Lamu, Kenya.

extent the potential of a material can only be exploited when a society has the technology to work it.

Good builders know their materials and make the best of their properties. The 'elasticity' of a 'tensile' material to deflect or to stretch and to return to a norm is a property of green woods and saplings, which we have seen used in the frame-and-mat structures of the Kel Geres.

Deformation beyond a certain point however creates 'yield' where a material will not return to its former shape, as in the preformed ribs of the Rendille *min*. Bending is a combination of both tension and compression: a beam which is bent has its lower surface in tension and its upper plane in compression. Over a period of time poles and beams may deform permanently through being held in one position: this

is the phenomenon of 'plastic' deformation, or 'creep' which can even occur in a material which would break or fracture if subjected to a sudden blow.

It is the roof structure which usually causes the greatest problem, for the weight exerts thrusts on the walls which can force their centre of gravity to move outwards, causing curvature of the wall from bending stresses. In a conventional roof frame of 'principal rafters' meeting at an apex, a 'tie-beam' is frequently used to counteract this effect by triangulation. To stabilize the structure, buttresses may be used to create a counter thrust against a bending wall, to achieve equilibrium. Another way of avoiding the problem is simply to build an 'undifferentiated structure' where there is no distinction between roof and wall—the building is all roof. Two or more 'A-frames' of inclined straight poles tied at the apex support a ridge pole, the ground acting as the tie-beam. Additional poles or rafters may be laid along the length of the ridge pole and horizontal purlins may span the space

Shepherd's shelter in the Auvergne. A simple A-frame with rafters and battens takes roofing tiles.

Traditional dwelling of the Wichita Amer-Indians. An 'undifferentiated structure', it is thatched over a domical ribbed frame. Oklahoma.

between what are, in effect, roof trusses and rafters. Over this can be laid bark, or some other 'cladding' material which is not load-bearing but which keeps the weather out. Such undifferentiated structures clad with roofing tiles are used by shepherds in the Auvergne, who build them when tending their fields, and in Andhra Pradesh, where sprays of palmyra leaves are used for cladding. Easy to construct and effective proof against the weather, they are sometimes erroneously referred to as 'tents' though they are not covered with a tensioned membrane. Only the centre beneath the ridge gives adequate head-room which makes them inconvenient for permanent habitation.

A larger volume can be achieved by using curved poles set in a circle and lashed at the apex with bark strips, like the substantial dwellings once built by the

Wichita Amer-Indians of Kansas and Oklahoma, but now rarely seen. Horizontal poles were lashed across the main supports, providing fixings for the layers of grass tied to them. Often called a 'grass house' of the 'beehive' type, it was essentially a ribbed dome of pre-formed curved members which trace the 'meridians' through its apex. These are constrained by the horizontal poles parallel to the ground and as the dome at any meridian is symmetrical, it is held in equilibrium. The loads, however, are not equally distributed around the perimeter of the dome for the cladding is not load-bearing; they are carried by the poles to equally spaced points of contact.[2]

A ribbed dome can be conceptualized as a multitude of arches sharing a common centre. With a stone arch the vertical compressive action is exerted on the 'voussoirs' or truncated-wedge blocks which are shaped to bond together under the force of gravity. Each stone transmits part of the compressive forces to the stones adjacent to it, eventually transferring the weight of the arch to the supporting columns or walls when the 'keystone', the final and centre stone is put in place. Though a ribbed dome may be thought of as a rotated arch, a plain dome is special in that each layer of stones parallel to the ground may be conceived as hoops which can act as horizontal arches. In addition to the vertical compression loads there are compressive forces horizontally around the layers of the dome; this fact enables it to be built of successively smaller rings of stones, each carefully shaped on all faces in contact with other stones so as to produce rings of wedges tightly fitted to transfer the loads evenly. Among the many dwelling types using this construction are the *trulli* of Apulia in the southernmost 'heel' of Italy, where farms, villages, and the town of Alberobello employ this method extensively. Until the 1960s such domes were still being built from carefully trimmed pieces of tufa rock. Because of the horizontal compressive effect of the rings it was possible to omit the top of the dome and leave an opening, or to close it with a capstone supporting a *cucuerneo*, a lime-plastered decorative finial.

Apulian domes span rooms roughly square in plan. When commencing a new house the *trullisti* would

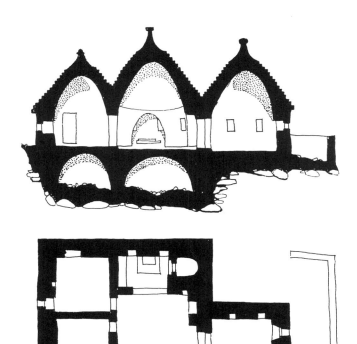

Section through a *trullo* showing relationship of chambers to excavated cellars, and corbelled stone roof.

often excavate the rock that was to be used *in situ*, then build a dome over the space to support the floor of the house and erect the walls. The space between the square of the top of the walls and the circle of the bottom of the dome was bridged at the corners by 'squinch' arches, which generate an octagon. As the corners were successively spanned a ring was formed from which the dome could rise. Two or more adjacent square cells would be domed to make a house and in the roof valleys between them rainwater collected which was stored in cisterns. Doorways were spanned with arches and conical chimney flues, ovens, and alcoves were built into the total structure with a satisfying unity of form and technical skill.[3]

Trulli builders overcame the difficulty inherent in extending a dome by building domes over each cell unit in a house and Eskimos overcame it by building

connecting tunnels. Basically however, the dome is not extensible without substantially altering its form. A simpler but more extensible structure is the vault, which can be visualized as an arch whose depth is greater than its span. Some vaults are ribbed structures, with the ribs as semi-circular arches at intervals or with opposing curved planes springing to meet at the apex. A timber truss would of course, span such a space equally well and this form of construction *is* more common in a region that has plenty of wood. Vaults made of a homogenous material have their loads distributed along the lengths of the supporting walls. As they still exert thrusts on the supporting walls, there are edge parapets, whose weight helps to contain them. These can be seen in the complex of stone-built and gypsum-plastered barrel-vaults and

Left A *trullo* built of volcanic tufa stone segments. The corbelled outer layer conceals the domed internal structure. Apulia, Italy.

Below Cluster of *trulli* at Alberobello, showing their relationship to the more recent, conventional buildings.

Berber village occupying a defensive position on the 'benches' of a rocky outcrop. The houses are barrel-vaulted, plastered with gypsum, with cross-vaults at the entrances. Beyond are fields and olive groves. Takrouna, Tunisia.

cross-vaults of the Tunisian Berber hilltop village of Takrouna.[4]

Many vaults in the Middle East are parabolic in transverse section, a form which corresponds to the bending moments of the arch. This parabolic profile counteracts the tendency to bend or shear and converts all the loads to the compression best suited to the stone or mud brick used in their construction. Arches and vaults are often constructed over 'centering', a wooden framework shaped to the profile of the inner surface which takes the loads until the 'keystone' is inserted and the arch is complete. It is possible to build a vault without such centering as the mud-brick builders of Nubia in Egypt have done for

centuries.[5] One end wall of the rectangular space to be spanned is built higher than the side walls which are raised to the level from which the vault will spring. A parabola is drawn freehand in wet mud against the end wall, thicker at the base and thin at the crest. Sun-dried mud bricks, some 10 inches by 6 inches by 2 inches which have been made lighter by adding more straw to the mix, are applied to the curve, grooves on their surfaces assisting the suction of brick to mud. The first layer of bricks leans against the thick, inclined mud arch scribed on the wall; subsequent layers also lean against each other, thus gaining support from their predecessors. Each inclined course is laid so that the joints are 'broken' and the interstices packed with dry earth. Whereas adjacent courses could be plastered with mud mortar so that each adhered in turn, the interstices at the end of the bricks within each arch layer are packed with

Method of laying parabolic arches of mud bricks against an end wall, employed by Nubian builders to produce a vault without supporting 'formwork' or timber framing.

dry earth; the shrinking of wet mud mortar would lead to distortion of the parabola and hence, weakness in the vault.

Such knowledge of their materials, and skill in the assembly of their buildings, was only acquired after years of apprenticeship and many bruised knuckles from the adze-handles of master masons.[6] With much practice and long experience, skilled craftsmen develop a 'feel' for their materials and a sense of appropriateness in their use which becomes almost intuitive. But it would be incorrect to believe, as many have, that vernacular forms are arrived at by evolutionary processes, in which the conscious decisions of their builders have played little part. The abstract structural principles may not be known to them but they are far from unaware of the expression of these principles in their work. They merely conceptualize them differently, basing their practice on their knowledge of what structures succeed or fail.

There is a considerable range of structural systems and building types within the whole compass of vernacular dwellings—a few have been mentioned here and others will be discussed in later chapters. But the questions of the basis of knowledge and the capacity of the craftsman to improve, to change, or to make design decisions need to be considered first.

NAMING THE PARTS

As much a stereotype of vernacular shelter as the 'beehive' is the 'cone-and-cylinder' hut. Describing the buildings in elementary morphological terms the phrase ignores the range of forms, details, methods, and materials which the multitude of dwellings with a circular plan represent. The Kipsigis, a people of the Kelanjin cluster of south-west Kenya, built a house which loosely corresponded to this type. It had a wall made from a ring of posts daubed with mud, and a thatched roof, from the peak of which a narrow pointed pole extended. Such a description is similar to those summarizing the dwellings of many other peoples, but it was the outcome of a process which had to be learned and whose details, each of which was named, were specific to the Kipsigis.[7]

A site was usually chosen close enough to water, but on the leeside of a hill-slope. The doorway faced downhill so that run-off water would not penetrate the house and, as neither rising nor setting sun should fall on the fire-place inside, the door normally faced south. After clearing and slightly levelling the chosen site a ring of posts, or *mugenik*, several inches thick and sharpened at each end and over head-height, was driven into the ground for about eighteen inches deep—enough to be rigid in the hard earth. Termite-resistant woods were preferred; when cedar could not be obtained, the red acacia thorn was chosen. Around the poles *mirotik*, or lianas, were interlaced in pairs at the top, centre and foot of the wall, held in place with *porinuk*, or thin creepers.

Long and slender poles, or *chagaiik*, were forced between the main supports and bent over to converge at the centre of the circle. A tight ring of lianas was tied around the ends, further strengthened by a ring bound beneath. As the chagaiik were held in tension the differentiation between wall and roof was not clearly defined but shouldered with the curvature of the poles. This meant that there were no projecting eaves to support the thatch that would protect the walls from rain. To provide the eaves, forked sticks were wedged from inside through the poles at the shoulder to produce a strong fringe.

As yet there was no door. The opening was made by cutting the lianas of the lowest ring and tying them back, and removing a section of side wall poles up to the second ring, strengthened by additional creepers bound round it to form the lintel. Two substantial posts were driven into the ground in front of those defining the doorway, producing a narrow slot through which the door could be slid to seal the entrance from within. Inside a large house as many as four substantial forked poles, called *tolaita*, were driven into the ground to take transverse joists, which in turn supported the attic (*tabot*) floor, and which was therefore a structure independent of the wall frame. A layer of narrow sticks was tied into position to finish the floor, and a trap left open for access.

Work on the house was by no means complete. More sticks had to be gathered for internal partitions, beds and bed screens: as many as 800 sticks and poles were used in the building of one large dwelling. Men carried the heavier poles and did most of the construction while the women obtained the sticks and long thatching grass, which was carefully laid from the eaves up to the apex in successive layers, over an underlayer of bush leaves. A central pole at the apex several feet in length, the *kimonjogut*, was tied in position above the loft floor to form a finial which was decorated with bands of colour. The thatch terminated at the kimonjogut to which it was tied over a thick layer of leaves; sometimes a broken pot, the *rokiet*, was slid over the pole to complete the crest. But the house was not finished yet—there were still the walls to be plastered by the girls with a mixture of cattle dung and mud, later to be decorated; the house to be smoked to inhibit rotting of the roofing leaves; the fire-stones to be put in place and so on.[8]

Further particularization here is unnecessary; the

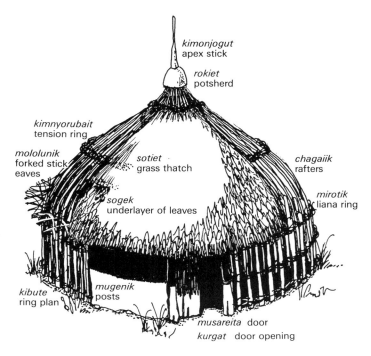

Cutaway perspective of the traditional Kipsigis hut. Some of the elements used in the construction are identified by name. (*Developed from Peristiany, Orchardson*)

precise names for all the component parts—which could be expanded by the terms for the techniques and methods employed in their use—are evidence enough of the deliberate nature of the building process. An established terminology ensures that the necessary materials are obtained and appropriately prepared in the required numbers as building components and that the methods used can be described and passed on to succeeding generations. Such detailed naming of the parts maintains the stability of the tradition; change in a particular element either requires the extension of the meaning of the term that describes it, or the need for a borrowed or adapted term to explain a new feature. Change is therefore slow, but it does occur. In recent years the traditional house type described above, which the Kipsigis shared with the Pokot and the Kuria, has altered in some respects. Interiors are now divided into two or three spaces, with the partition walls plastered and moulded; the roof poles have been differentiated from

Contemporary Kipsigis houses are similar in form to those of the Kuria and Pokot. Modifications in building are made possible by a precise terminology. Kenya.

the walls so that the shouldered profile is less evident. Today the roof has a conical form and the eaves may be supported and protected from fraying by sheets of metal obtained by flattening cans, each modification being reflected in their names.[9]

Accurate reporting of the terminology is therefore a key to building elements and traditions, and to the understanding of forms and processes. It is also an indicator of modifications and variants that have taken place and hence to constancy and change in building, which may reflect aspects of values and influence.[10]

But the question remains as to how the changes take place; how are innovations adopted, and how do tradition and standard practice meet with individual and family needs? For though it is customary to assume that in such contexts individual requirements count for little and tradition dominates, in fact most traditionally built forms appear to be modified in some measure by the owner-builders, to suit their own requirements. What then, are the design processes involved?

DESIGNING AND BUILDING

Acknowledged enemies of the Kipsigis were the Maasai, with whom there existed codified, but still lethal, rules of conflict. Whereas the Kipsigis were intensive agriculturalists the Maasai in the past have been cattle herders—although recent pressures have induced some to take up a measure of agriculture. Their respective societies differ in many ways. Kipsigis could build wherever they wished within the tribal territory, and their settlements were consequently dispersed; by contrast the settlements of the Maasai were always clustered round the hut of a headman. Low-lying, brown-coloured and appearing like a ring of loaves the Maasai *enkang* or domestic *kraal*, comprises a circle of dwellings. Each enkang may accommodate the members of one extended family or the combined homes of two or three. Another form, the *manyatta*, is constructed by the women for the *moran*, the young warrior age-sets at the time of their circumcision and initiation. Maasai move their locations every seven or eight years as the houses of the enkang rot or collapse from the attacks of the beetles and white ants which infest them. A site having been selected by the elders each wife of the headman was given her site for her own dwelling; the first wife to the right of the entrance to the enkang ring, the second wife to the left, the third to the right beside the first; the fourth second from the left. The enkang was approximately a circle some two hundred feet across, with a dozen or so dwellings planned to accommodate the headman, his wives, their children and elderly relatives. In accordance with Maasai custom the young men lived in an age-set manyatta on the plateau some distance away.

Women built the enkang, assisted in carrying the materials by the children. Leleshwa branches and sticks were used where possible, as the wood is relatively resistant to termites, ants, and beetles. Where the acacia predominates the women had to walk several miles to find suitable leleshwa and haul the branches back, narrower twigs and leaves being saved for later use in the building process. Before commencing the construction each woman was involved in the design of her house, its plan being defined with the aid of long, thin poles of the green wood. A wife would spend considerable time, even a day or two, laying out the poles to the plan of her hut, making decisions on the overall dimensions and access, the position of sleeping platforms, hearth and calves' pen. Maasai houses are about 5 feet (1.5 m) high, around 20 feet (6 m) long and half as wide. Usually, but not necessarily, the entrance is on the side facing the centre of the kraal, but the characteristic form has a snail shell entrance where the doorway is not in the same plane as the wall, but at right angles to it, with a projecting short porch or tunnel. Proof against fully-grown cattle wandering in, the form also puts an intruder in a vulnerable position should the enkang be raided. The position of the entrance in relation to the interior chambers is therefore important, and the internal plan has to be determined before construction can begin, so that the main support posts can be placed correctly. Designing the plan calls for much discussion with other women, and constant comparison with other houses. The leleshwa wands

Maasai *enkang*, within its encircling euphorbia hedge, merges into the landscape of the Rift Valley. Boys tend herds of cattle and goats.

were laid down on the ground to the proposed plan and adjusted until a satisfactory arrangement was arrived at.

Maasai have a distaste for cultivation, or even for digging; the position of the house was marked out with wet cattle dung which also served to soften the earth and permit the first ring of stout poles to be inserted. These were then stabilized by a 'ring beam' of twisted and interlaced wands some two-thirds of the height of the wall, a second or even a third ring

A new house being built in the Loita Hills, Kenya. The roof lattice of thin withies is fixed to the wall-stakes. To the left, women with sticks decide on the plan of another unit.

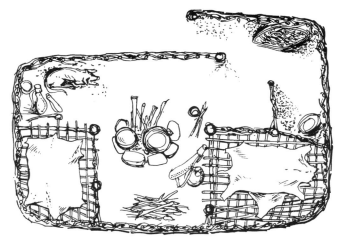

After the wall-stakes have been securely lashed with bark and the walls insulated with leaves, a plaster of cow-dung is spread over the structure.

Typical plan of a Maasai house. Though their general appearance is similar, each house is designed with partitions and sleeping platforms to meet the requirements of the woman builder/owner.

added below. While this was the general practice, a wife might choose to drive a closer ring of cedar stakes and place her entrance flush to the side wall. Other variants were common particularly in their internal arrangement. Slender leleshwa wands formed the roof of the hut and as with the earlier Kipsigis house these were forced into the restraining ring between the principal poles and bent over to produce a shouldered profile. Instead of meeting at an apex they were forced down into the ring on the opposite side of the hut. Gradually a lattice was created, affixed to the internal support poles and with all elements tied and bound with leleshwa bark strips to produce a mesh strong enough to stand on.

Some houses had a double skin of poles between which an insulating layer of leaves and thin branches was packed. The houses were now ready for plastering. A Maasai enkang serves as a corral and all the animals are herded back by the boys to spend the night in the enclosure. The ground becomes thick with cattle dung which, in the course of a few years is a knee-deep mire, providing a ready supply of material for plastering the walls, roofs and interior partitions. Pungent when wet, it loses at least some of its smell as the plaster dries becoming an effective protective layer for the house which somewhat repels insects. The plaster was generally first applied above the ring beam, though some women preferred to start with the internal partitions. Sleeping platforms were

now constructed against the internal posts, with a wattle mesh over which was laid a cow hide; there were no window openings but small vents, only a couple of inches wide, were opened in the walls, to give a glancing light across the sleeping platform. Three hearth stones were brought in and sited; a fire was lit and the smoke soon filled the interior, hardening the dung plaster. Store boxes of wattles, to take calabash vessels and tin cups, and pens for young goats or a child's pet dog were constructed in some huts. Within two weeks all were ready for occupation, and the old enkang was abandoned.[11]

Undecorated and gaining its only colour from the red blankets of the occupants the enkang is dull in appearance, the plastered walls hiding the care and craftsmanship that have gone into the making of the frame and the differing internal arrangements of the various dwelling units. On first glance the dwellings appear the same, but within the uniformity of the type each Maasai woman may design her house as she wishes. She may also adopt a new technique—the cedar stockade was almost certainly under Kikuyu influence. Changes and innovations will be observed, to be incorporated or rejected by her companions in future building.

This is the way with most forms of indigenous building: the tradition establishes a broad matrix, the individual builder designs and constructs to suit his requirements within it. Such dwellings are neither slavish copies of their predecessors, nor wilful deviants from them. Construction is not a matter of intuition as if the builders were like birds making their nests, but the result of deliberate decisions related to perceived needs.

A single tradition may be described in general terms, but it should be understood in specific ones; the differences are subtle but significant, eventually contributing to the slow changing of traditional form as innovations are introduced and influences assimilated. As design the process is different from that of the western architect, who may isolate problems and seek solutions to his brief through the abstraction of the drawing board and the building specification. In the indigenous dwelling there is design too, but it is carried out on a one-to-one scale; problems are perceived only as they affect the established norm and its suitability for the prospective builder and occupier. Nevertheless, cutting stone, moulding and firing bricks, working and carving timber, weaving mats, and laying thatch all have to be learned.

LEARNING THE SKILLS

Learning to build is part of the process of becoming a fully participating member of society, though the transition from imitative play to training in the craft may be a rapid one. Like children the world over, Ijaw children of the Niger delta mimic their parents, the boys climbing house posts as if they were coconut palms, the girls playing at fishing and cooking. They build miniature houses of their own from discarded slivers of bamboo, or from puddled mud but soon a girl is expected to weave mats from bamboo that she has herself gathered while her brother, though he may be still too young to obtain palm leaves from the treetops, learns to weave the leaves into roofing thatch. Boys are given toy machetes at an early age, preparing them to handle the full size blade. Small fingers may fumble at first, but they soon become adept. Ngoni girls in Malawi have been observed uninterestedly mudding the walls of newly built huts while older women and grandparents criticized and advised. They were inept at beating the floors hard

The 'shell' entrance of a completed Maasai house. The door is of woven wicker with an opening to permit some light. There are no windows.

Young boys in a Sumatran village weaving mats of split cane for use as wall panels. By alternating polished and smoothed surfaces a simple decorative pattern is achieved.

Refugees from Mozambique build traditional houses with
collective labour. All are fully familiar with the processes
involved in the construction of the dwelling. Tanzania.

cases, the whole village may be expected to participate in return for food or the exchange of labour. As
the ability to build a house, or at least to contribute to
the process, is required of every man in some societies, or of every woman and child in others, the
builder's craft often carries very little status. Because
each individual is required to build his own house the
capacity to do so is no more highly esteemed than is
preparing food, and often a good deal less than being
a successful hunter. Frequently, therefore, work on
house-building is relegated to the rank and file; even
among the Ngoni such work was considered too dirty
and exhausting for the 'women of good family'. This
low status has become institutionalized in some societies; in many parts of India house carpenters are of a
lower middle caste, above that of the *dhobis* (washermen) and the unclean sweepers, but below that of the
cultivators. Their relative status differs marginally in
every region, and often between villages. In the
traditional village of Madhopur on the Ganges plain
of Uttar Pradesh for instance the 'lords' or Thakur
families, are patrons to members of lower castes who
work for them, among whom are the *lohars*, the car-
penter-blacksmiths. But when brickmaking, house
building, or the digging of wells is required, a gang of
camars, or members of the lower caste, will be
recruited for the purpose. In the Brahman village of
Kumbapettai, (Tanjore district of Mysore State) on the
other hand, blacksmiths, goldsmiths, stonemasons,
and carpenters were all *kusavans*, or members of a
middle caste, who intermarried and were able to
choose which of these trades they wished to follow.
Yet the stratification of the castes is often much more
segmented and rigid: in the old city of Baghdaon,
(Bhaktapur) in Nepal, there are some nineteen castes
of which the brickmakers and masons rank seventh
with the potters, a level higher than the carpenters
and stonemasons, and five above the blacksmiths and
untouchables.[13]

The caste system inhibits any social mobility and
advancement through the acquisition of skills, though
it may be said to ensure employment for each member
within a caste and better payment for the good work-
man. What may be seen as a form of voluntary seg-

with flat flails, and found the polishing, with damp
ashes and cowdung finished with clarified fat, hard
work, but through this socializing process they
learned to develop their abilities.[12]

In such societies the skills necessary to build a
house are acquired this way, and all members of the
community are expected to have the knowledge and
the dexterity to be able to construct their own dwelling. When the help of several hands is necessary, as
for example in raising a roof, members of the same
lineage or clan may be called upon to help or, in some

mentation occurs in some societies, where particular families have secured for themselves the reputation for high standards of knowledge and workmanship in a particular field, and have made others dependent on them. In a society with a monetary base, skilled masons, carpenters, or housebuilders can sell their services, gaining employment and commanding more pay by the quality of their craftsmanship. This was the case on the Pacific island of Palau, where the people had a complex monetary system and a materialistic outlook. Persons of rank would not make their own canoes or build their own houses but employed specialists to do this work. Obligations to members of the same lineage to the community in, for example, the building of a communal meeting house, were exceptions to this principle of work for payment, but even in the latter circumstance the competitive spirit among the Palauans meant that craftsmen sought to outdo others and so improve their status. This would enable them to attract both more work, and the fees of apprentices anxious to learn their trade.[14]

Specialization leads to esoteric knowledge, which is available only to the in-group of workers; the naming of parts and processes becomes their property and the techniques and 'tricks of the trade' are carefully protected. Apprentices may be taken on to serve in a subordinate role for a number of years before being accredited and able to operate on their own. In such cases guilds may be institutionalized to guard the interests of the trade, to establish the levels of competence required, and to give status to the master craftsman. Guilds were established several centuries ago in Persia, each with its own *Ustad*, or master, craftsman. The *banna* or mason, the *kashisaz* (tile-cutter), and their fellow skilled workers in wood, mirror glass, and plaster relief were members of specialized guilds, which, in modified form persisted in Iran until recently.[15] But whether he or she lives in a society in which all people build, or in one where, as a member of a special group, lineage, village, caste, or guild he or she is associated with a particular craft, the vernacular builder has to know the properties of the materials with which he works and how to construct the forms appropriate to them.

Bricklayers of the seventh caste, building shop-houses in Kathmandu. Bricks are laid to the customary bond, but timber technology is imitated in the support of a concrete balcony slab.

Skilled stonemasons trim ashlar blocks and carve decorations. Guilds protect the interests of such craftsmen and control the training of apprentices. Delhi, India.

4.

BUILT FROM THE GROUND

Whether early man habitually inhabited caves, or whether caves afforded better protection for artefacts and detritus and so provided the best record of primitive culture, is still an open question. They may be the oldest form of dwelling, for even today uncounted thousands of people still live in caves, though most 'troglodytes' (cave-dwellers) have modified or adapted them for habitation. Many caves are still occupied in Europe, like those on the River Dronne. Their entrances are made trim with doors, the upper windows with shutters, while washing flutters on the rock-cut balconies.

CARVING A HOME

In Almanzora in Andalucia, Southern Spain, the rock faces of low and craggy hills open on to a tight amphitheatre of troglodyte villages. Honeycombed at many levels, the dwellings are often one or two storeys in height, ownership being proclaimed by limewashing the fronts. Internally, the rooms have been peck-carved back to claim more space, the ceilings barrel-vaulted to transfer the loads so that they are less likely to collapse.[1] Sixty miles further west along the sandstone escarpment is Guadix, where the ravine of the Rio Fardes and the slopes of the Sierra Nevada are sculpted into villages that accommodate twelve thousand or more people. White-capped chimneys are thrust through the shell of rock; extensions with tiled roofs and walls made from the rock spoil push forward from the rockface. Dry and comfortable, the interiors have tiled floors and limewashed walls. A large hearth serves for cooking and heating, the waste products of chaff and husks from cereal crops being used as fuel. In a few months two Guadix men can carve out a house of four rooms, with two at least fronting the rock face.[2]

It is a process that takes longer if they are peasant farmers who can work only at nights or in the slack periods of the farming year, as many have done for centuries in the bizarre landscape of Cappadocia, Turkey. Like giant sugar loaves, tufa pinnacles of ancient compacted ash from the volcano Erçiyas Dagi have weathered into shapes that recall a Flemish master's dream of mountains. Soft to carve, the tufa hardens on exposure to air, the calcium carbonate having a chemical reaction with carbon dioxide to produce a hard crust. In Ürgup and Göreme and numerous small settlements, peasants chip out multi-storeyed dwellings, honeycombing the rock with their narrow adzes. To carve an upper-storey room may take a peasant couple three months. To do so requires a mental map of the section of the rock pinnacle so that the sides are not breached, and of the position and number of a flight of steps as well as the thickness of floor above the room below, for there is little latitude for mistakes.

Most families carve out their rooms on the south or south-east face of the pinnacles, to get the benefit of any sun in the hard and cold plateau winters. Three or more rooms may be carved with inter-linking short passages and with balconied access to the outer faces, where steps lead down to cultivated plots.

Opposite top Cave dwellings of sedentary gypsies. Some have a simple shelter in front, others have a whitewashed rectangular facade. Cuevas de Almanzora, Andalucia, Spain.

Right Tufa pinnacles, Cappadocia, out of which thousands of dwellings have been carved. Rock spoil is used to build additional rooms or to make field and plot walls. Central Anatolia, Turkey.

Interior of a kitchen in a Cappadocian dwelling. Aspirations for a conventional house have led the owner to square off the corners.

Courtyard and entrance of a house carved in the thick loess of the Yellow River. A recess takes a store of maize corn. The vaulted internal form is defined on the facade. North Shenshi, China.

Cupboards, tables, benches, and sleeping platforms, even decorative imitation fireplaces are left in relief, the voids cut back beyond them to the wall plane. Niches for water pitchers and grain sacks may be cut deeper into the rock. Many peasants imitate conventional house interiors, squaring off the corners of rooms and carving flat ceilings. Smoke blackening on the ceilings is removed by chipping away the stone, threatening to weaken them. The rock spoil is used for internal walls, and for sealing the caves that are used as pigeon lofts, in which the nesting boxes are also carved into the rock. Successive generations, with faith in the strength of the tufa, have carved some pinnacles until they have become mere shells, perilously close to, and sometimes beyond the point of, collapse. But though many rocks have sheared

from excessive carving, the complexes of rock dwellings over some two hundred square miles still house many tens of thousands of people.[3]

Carving out dwellings is an excavating, hollowing process, essentially sculptural, but requiring that the carver works around himself, turning solid into void, rock mass into room. If the internal forms sometimes reflect those of constructed dwellings they are arrived at by a negative process, subtractive rather than additive.

Countless generations have riddled the thick loess reaches of the Yang-Tze river in China, where literally millions of people live in cave dwellings wholly or partially carved by man. In North Shensi, earth caves were cut into the hard yellow loess. After a vertical plane had been established as a facade, a slot which defined the entrance was cut back to wall thickness, before the inner rock was opened out to form a room some twenty feet deep, ten wide and ten high. Then the doorway slot would be enlarged, a window cut and the interior smoothed and plastered with loess mud. Several villagers might work on the same house but it would take some forty man-days to complete. After it dried out it would make a sound home for two or three generations, its life prolonged by springing curved planks to give tensile support under the roof.

Shenshi farmers excavated caves but they also *built* them; vaulted houses that were similar to caves, which took ten times as long to make but were even more durable. Deep foundations were cut and the loess tamped to support stone side walls, from which a barrel vault was raised over a wood centering frame, each voussoir being cut to fit. Beyond the barrel-vaulted shell secondary house walls were constructed some five feet away, the voids being filled with tamped loess, which was also used to cover the vault several feet deep. Finally, internal cross-walls were plastered with loess and whitewashed, and a window lattice with paper screen fitted. Soon the grass grew over the roof, the goats grazed on it and the constructed dwelling became a cave—a part of the hillside.[4]

STONE UPON STONE

Though the form of the 'built' cave in the end appeared similar to a carved dwelling, it was arrived at by the tight-fitting assembly of parts, an additive process. In some regions the tools have not been available to trim the stone, or the kind of stone available has not been suitable for fine shaping. From Tibet to Ethiopia or Italy, the stone is often utilized as it is found, large and small pieces interlocked, so that a tight, compressive structure can be made. Such mass walling can be held by its own weight and can take the thrusts of a timber roof, but problems arise when wood is scarce and the space has to be spanned with stone. Megalithic builders solved this problem by 'corbelling', slightly cantilevering successive layers of stone so that each overhung the layer below. When this was done from a circular plan an eggshell form

Tigre farmer's house, Ethiopia, constructed of rubble stone bonded with mud plaster. Internal floor joists rest on a course of large stones. Two-storeyed rural houses are rare in sub-Saharan Africa.

Diagram of the Shenshi 'built cave' dwellings, showing how the barrel-vaulted roofs are constructed with 'voussoirs' and how their covering of loess is held within retaining walls.

The principle of cantilever is applied to stone or brick in successive layers to produce a corbelled parabolic dome. This method is widely dispersed. Construction left, section right.

Bories, corbelled stone dwellings near Les Eyzies, France, survivors of a megalithic building tradition which stretched from Syria to Ireland.

was achieved. Because headroom is immediately restricted by the progressive inclination of the corbelling, many buildings had a corbelled parabolic dome springing from a thick walled cubic base. Often, as in the Ballearics the thickness of the outside walls and buttresses obscured the form of the dome. An argument can be made for the diffusion of this technique of corbelled stone building in an arc that sweeps from the Middle East to Iceland, while a connection with the distribution of Celtic peoples can also be traced.

In many parts of France different kinds may be found, with square plans and corbelled roofs with capstones. Some were used as field shelters or *cabannes* but the larger complexes of *bories* in the Vaucluse and Quercy were permanent habitations. Low walls and high vaulted roofs were built of layered slabs graded in dimension and selected so that any irregularities in the stone contributed to the runoff of rain water on the outside. Undulating over

dormer windows and entrances the vaults were bridged by monolithic slabs. In many cases a chimney flue was incorporated in the structure with, at an upper level, sleeping platforms made of juniper or liveoak inserted into the walls, to which access was gained by notched ladders.[5]

Stone building is by no means universal and even where rock is exposed it is not necessarily used. Some rocks are difficult to shape, or soon deteriorate; others are intractable. An igneous rock of a crystalline composition and no disposition to cleave, like granite, is hard to work even with strong and heavy tools. Millennia of weathering, and natural faults may cause granite to split into large slabs and the resultant monoliths have been used for house building. In Portugal for example, much of the country to the north comprises granite mountains and plateaux. Rough granite hills and rocky stream beds characterize the Beira Alta region. Arable land is scarce and jealously protected, the small houses clustered together to consume as little of the ground as possible while being close to the crops. Many of the houses are two-storeyed, the lower level containing the farm implements and housing the animals. Above is the single living space with a windowless alcove for sleeping, and a fireplace with iron cooking pots but without a chimney, deeply recessed into the floor. Massive granite blocks span the windows and doorway openings, and monoliths frame them; exterior steps and porches are constructed of huge granite slabs, levered into place. In some villages, such as Monsanto, immense boulders may be incorporated in the walls; in others the stones may be smaller, and the roofs are of thinner slabs, laid over rafters of fir from the pine forests to the west. Tough and uncompromising, it is an architecture with little room for embellishment, though the openings may be whitewashed following the shapes of the granite jambs and lintels, and the contrast of monoliths and smaller random infill has a rugged variety. It is the pervasive scale of the slabs, and the close affinity of houses, field walls, terraces and cobbled streets below the granite shoulders of the mountains that give the region a powerful unity.[6]

Apart from the availability of appropriate and

Monsanto, a village constructed of massive blocks of granite. Rock pieces are used in the houses of the peasants and Roman tiles are employed for roofing. Beira Alta region, Portugal.

workable rock, and access to suitable tools with which to 'dress' it, building in stone also requires time: time to quarry, time to carve and shape the blocks, and time to assemble. Time to build implies long-term residence; stone buildings are constructed by sedentary peoples and are extremely durable. Peasants do not necessarily have the time to spare on building and it is common to find that stone is reserved for the houses of the wealthy, for the palaces and temples. Or it is used for the engineering projects, road and bridge building, defences and fortresses where its strength can be exploited. Such major works have encouraged the emergence of specialized builders and craftsmen, whose skills have become both developed and protected. The imperious buildings are built in fine 'ashlar', cut square and laid in

Adjacent buildings in Linhares, a typical village in Central Portugal, include ashlar masonry (castle tower and rear facade), dressed corner 'quoins', and rubble infill (peasant house, foreground). Openings are spanned with arches with voussoirs or slabs.

well known, sections of the Great Wall built during the Ming dynasty having lime and sand mortars. The lime was burned in temporary kilns built on-site, a method which has survived in some parts of China to the present. Cones of clay and coal dust are layered with lime blocks and bound into a tapering truncated kiln, under which a fire is lit, the coal blocks producing an intense, slow-burning heat. Allowed to burn for a week, the lime is claimed after the kiln has been cooled and broken apart, the ash being re-used to form new fire cones.[8] Though some of the lime, gypsum, and pozzolan soils are to be found in many parts of the Third World they are often little used for building. This is due to many factors, but undoubtedly the lack of the necessary knowledge and technology for either the burning of limestone chunks to make the quicklime, or the slaking of this to produce hydrated lime suitable for mortars or plaster, has limited their use.

MOULDED IN CLAY

Whether it is bonded with mortar, or simply used dry, stone is not the most extensively used material for wall building, common though it is in Western Europe and parts of India and the Middle East. Throughout Africa, Central and South America, much of India, China, and south-east Asia the principal building material is mud. Soils are decomposed rocks and they occur over much of the world's land surface, being used for building in a variety of conditions. Chemically there are many soil types, and as any gardener or potter is aware, some soils are alkaline and some clays cannot be turned on a potter's wheel. It is this variability that makes it possible for multi-storeyed buildings to be constructed of earth in the High Atlas or North Yemen—but not in many other regions.

Podzolic soils cover much of Northern Europe, Russia, and Canada, but those beneath the fir forests tend to be extremely acid and unsuitable for building. Soils that were formed under deciduous forests on the other hand, as in Western Europe, or the grassland soils of the prairies and steppes of North America, are

regular courses, but the houses of the populace are typically in rubble masonry, held firm by 'quoins' or corner-stones and with dressed lintels or door jambs. Or the entire walls may be of random rubble, irregular pieces fitted together as best as possible and held with a binding material which, in the poorest dwellings, is mud.[7]

'Wet process' stone walling, which has been bonded with mortar, requires the mixing of lime and cement, or lime and pozzolana (volcanic soils) with sand. As pozzolan soils are often found close to limestones, tufa caves, dry limestone, and mortared building stone may all occur in the same region, as they do in Apulia. Lime mortar was known to the Greeks, and the Romans developed the construction of lime kilns as early as 300 BC. Countries that fell to the Roman Empire often retained the techniques, or regained them in medieval times. In China too, their use was

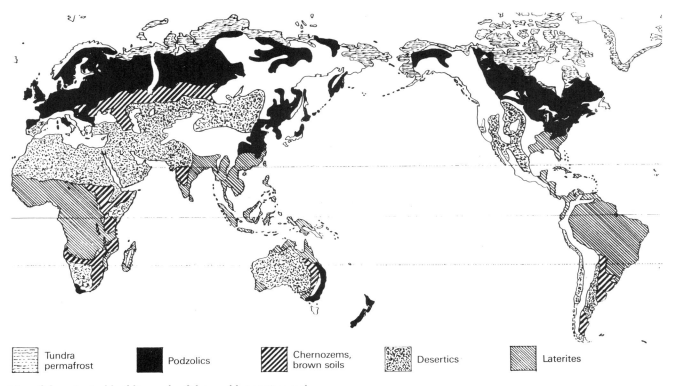

Tundra
permafrost | Podzolics | Chernozems,
brown soils | Desertics | Laterites

Map of the principal building soils of the world. Laterites and
sandy desertic soils are widely used; podzolics are also suitable.

widely employed. In thinly-watered areas, desertic soils of broken rock and sand have resulted in some of the most notable uses of earth for construction as have the laterites and red soils of India, Africa, and South America. Laterites are low in fertility—paradoxically, for they occur beneath tropical rain forests—and rapidly leach out when the tree cover is felled. They retain many of the characteristics of rock, becoming hard and encrusted when exposed to air. This makes them good for building, but poor for agriculture.

Building soils should contain large pieces of coarse sand as well as smaller sand particles, silt and fine clay. They do not all have to be present in one mixture, and other elements may serve similar functions, like the naturally-occurring shale fragments called 'shillet' which make the red clays of west Devon ideal for 'cob' construction.[9]

Mixed with water and with chopped straw or a similar building material, clay may be trodden in a pit until it is the appropriate consistency. But the method of preparation depends on the kind of soil, and each region has developed its own. In its plastic state mud is malleable, capable of being moulded to forms that are scarcely achievable with manual means in any other material. Close to the art of the potter, the huts and compounds of sub-Saharan West Africa sometimes display a remarkable aesthetic sense in the forms. From Senegal to Cameroon a wide variety of compound dwellings is built on similar principles.

Typically, a moulded earth dwelling in a West African savannah grassland village, such as may be found among the Gurunsi peoples of northern Ghana and Burkina Faso, is constructed by the men, women obtaining the water and mud from 'borrow pits' and doing the final plastering. A mix of mud and chopped straw is left for several days to cure. Later this is mixed with water to a plastic consistency and moulded into balls. The wall builder presses them obliquely in a spiral sequence, expelling the air and

Dwelling units, courtyards, steps, and workplaces are moulded in laterite clays in this Gurunsi compound. Beneath the decoration painted in earth colours, the layers of clay 'lifts' can be discerned. Burkino Faso.

compacting the material. A 'lift' of perhaps eighteen inches is completed and allowed to dry before another layer is added, often with a lapped joint between layers which assists the throw-off of rain and lessens the risk of cracking and penetration. The structure may be required to support transverse beams at roof level, which penetrate halfway into the wall; alternatively the beams may rest on forked columns which rise inside the dwelling independently of the walls. The roof of layers of sticks laid crosswise and plastered over with several inches of mud may have a parapet and often the entire external walls are rendered with a mixture of cattle dung and oil. A preparation made from the fruit pod of the locust bean produces an effective water repellent as do the juices of boiled plantain stalks, added to the earth mix. Though rain occurs only in brief periods it is extremely heavy and potentially damaging. U-section half logs are employed as gargoyles to drain off the roof water, and corn cobs or the fingers are used to produce looping or V-shaped markings on the external walls, which appear decorative but which have the important function of retarding water run-off and sheet erosion.

Because they have curved walls and are like segments of pottery, the compounds of many African peoples are structurally extremely efficient. They can be relatively thin because their curvature has the effect of transmitting along their length any external shocks, such as the swinging bulk of animals, and so dampening the impact. Fruits and cereals can be dried on the flat roofs of some of the dwelling units, but many have conical roofs, thatched with elephant grass, a store of which being kept for the repairs that are necessary after the short summer rains. In the living spaces where each woman has her hearth, granaries, and storage vessels, there are seats and thresholds moulded in clay; ziggurats of curved steps give access over the party-walls between huts, plastered and baked rock hard in the sun. Within the houses may be shelves with curving, crenellated edges for stacks of pots and gourds, while clay pens protect hens and guinea fowl. Moulded by the hands in convex surfaces, hollows, and runs as free of edges as the human form, the buildings have an anthropomorphic quality that is reflected in the names of the spaces defined.[10]

When the successive lifts, or layers, in an earth wall dry by evaporation, the soil shrinks and the particles are drawn closer together. As the plastic material becomes a dry solid it loses most of its elasticity. This means that earth is effectively used in compression: as for example, when it forms load-bearing walls. All techniques seek to compress the particles, and rammed earth, also known by the French term of *pisé de terre*, is an ancient method of doing so. Known by the Chinese for more than 3,000 years, it was probably brought to Europe by the Romans. All versions of the method are similar; an open-ended frame in the form of a box closed at one end is constructed, some eighteen inches wide with planks on the two long sides. These overhang that part of the wall already constructed to give stability. A frame is placed over the open end to hold the planks secure, and a spindle attached to the frame passes through the built part of the wall to lock it in position. With the 'formwork' in place the box is filled to a depth of about four inches with loose earth, which is then pounded or rammed with heavy poles. The compacted earth is further mixed with straw bonded by seed oil or with a loose strawpaper mixed with lime, which is soaked in water and pounded in with the soil. More soil is rammed until the top of the box frame is reached, the section of wall thus built being between one and two feet, according to the depth of the shuttering. It is left to dry, though not comple-

The anthropomorphic character of the moulded forms reflects the limbs of a mother and her children. Tallensi, Northern Ghana.

tely, before another layer is built on top; when it is finished the wall can be given a mud plaster or washed down to produce a skim, which, when dry, takes a whitewash or other suitable treatment.[11] Corners in a pisé building are either overlapped with successive layers, in similar fashion to the technique of building stone quoins, or lengths of board are embedded in the layers so that they make a firm bond. Such a method as pisé, though it produces strong and solid walls, is not usable as a roofing technique. A wooden ring beam, or fired bricks, can be inserted in the top of the wall to act as a wall-plate,

Rammed earth technique. Earth is broken up with a pick and wetted and the formwork box filled with it and tamped hard. After compacting, the box is moved along the wall for the next section to be made. Completed dwellings in the background.

were laid in bonds, to make a long building with a single dividing wall. Saplings or slats from a wagon would be used for a roof-frame, and the roof was covered with thin sods which sent up fresh shoots in the spring and bound it together. After a few months they had dried out and the walls could be plastered with mud. In the 1970s a few 'soddys' were still occupied, their owners complaining only of the maintenance against winter snows, and the fine rain of earth granules which persistently fell from the roof.

River bottoms generally have compacted soils, and the boggy river lands in New Mexico and Spanish America, where the root systems of river grasses have created a thick, matted texture, are cut out in blocks called *terrones*. Dried, they can be used as bricks. A similar method of cutting bricks directly from the soil is periodically used in Kiangsi province in China when the river silts become so deep that the depth of water necessary for rice to grow demands that the bed is lowered after the harvest. A stone roller is used to level the field which is then cut into bricks fourteen inches by nine inches and four inches deep. Cut in autumn so that the soil will not crack under excessive sunlight they are stacked in rows and covered in straw to assist slow drying. But though this is an effective form of brick making which is also found in West Bengal, it is extremely localized.[13]

Earth bricks are common in the Middle East, North Africa, parts of Europe, notably Spain, and in the Americas. In Iran the use of sun-dried mud bricks, or *khesht*, is widespread. Local desertic soils with their relatively high sand content make an effective material while the general heat and aridity greatly assist the drying of the bricks. These are moulded in a simple wooden form and are usually thin and square, around eight inches by eight inches by three inches. They are bonded by a mortar of wet mud of the same consistency as the bricks, which consequently dries and weathers at the same rate. Knocked into the hand from the mould, the bricks are stacked on end to dry in rows, or like dominoes in a continuous winding line. Laid with swift dexterity, with simple bonding or diagonal and herringbone patterns, the walls may be one brick in depth.

and the roof truss, with strong tie-beams to reduce outward thrust, is rested on it and made secure.[12]

Soils that are extremely dense sometimes occur naturally, and vernacular builders make use of them. Pioneer homesteaders in the Midwest States of America in the nineteenth century were short of timber but had prairie soils in abundance. Seeing the shoulder-high prairie grasses they turned the virgin land with their ploughs and used the sods to build their homes. Sods cut from the low ground where the roots were thick were some fourteen inches wide and two to three feet long. From a shallow trench they

Above One of a group of sod-houses. As much as four acres of sod, bonded with grass roots, was cut to make one house. Colby, West Kansas, USA.

Right Amer-Indians manufacture large quantities of adobe blocks by raking wet clay into 'gangs' of moulds. Finished blocks are stood on end in rows to dry. New Mexico, USA.

Arabs brought the technique to Spain where the word *atobe* was adapted to *adobe*, the term by which it is known throughout Latin America. Adobe blocks may be hand-moulded, but the use of a mould produces a sharper edge and standard dimensions and so facilitates bonding. Gangs of four or five moulds may be used though they are heavy to carry when the clay is wet. As they dry out adobes behave more like stone, though they shear and crack easily if they are not well-compacted. Consequently adobes are mainly used for load-bearing walls in compression, but it is not uncommon to see them employed in ways comparable with stone building, even to the construction of timberless domes by the corbelled technique. In northern Syria for instance, parabolic corbelled domes are constructed above cells of a square plan, with layers of sun-dried brick regularly laid and gently cantilevered to the apex. These domes have an egg-like section which efficiently distributes the stresses on the shell surface and is therefore very strong. One or two bricks may be omitted from the shell form to permit ventilation and the escape of warm air, and stones are inserted at points in the curve to facilitate climbing the dome for repairs. Finally, the whole dome is covered with a plaster of mud and straw to give a smooth, rendered surface which reduces wind erosion. A chain of half a dozen cupolas may run side by side beneath the unifying layer of mud plaster so that they appear as a continuous structure. However the cells are not linked internally; each opens separately on to an exterior courtyard space where other domes accommodate

Adobe blocks are used in Syria to make corbelled, parabolic domes, which may then be coated with a protective layer of clay.

animals and grain. In form and method of construction they are close to the French bories.[14]

Exposure to the weather necessitates that adobe is protected to prevent 'spalling', or the shearing of brick layers. In Iran, the adobe blocks are covered with *kar-gel*, a plaster made of mud and straw, sometimes with animal dung as an emulsifying agent, spread thickly over walls and roof domes. Some house roofs are so thickly protected with kar-gel that the domical structure beneath is scarcely evident, and a flat roof that can still drain is produced.[15] Details such as the edging of *ivans*, or closed vaults may be marked out in a light mud plaster. Elsewhere a gypsum plaster may be used, especially in the interiors, to give a smooth finish which can take painting and other decorative treatments.

Adobe blocks can be used for building a variety of forms, but the commonest use is for building with rectilinear plans. Where palm, bamboo, or timber are available they will be used to form the roof structure,

resting on the mass walls and often with a low parapet to give added protection at the meeting of the materials. For the problem of all earth construction is that it is subject to erosion, and is particularly susceptible to rain. Plasters of mud and dung, or mascerated okra and leaves, may repel water and protect the joints from seepage. It is the smooth surface of the plaster which alone is visible, softening the contours as successive layers are applied in maintenance. These weaknesses are considerably reduced or even eliminated when fired or 'burnt' bricks are used.

BRICKS AND MORTAR

Fired bricks are more expensive than sun-dried bricks; producing them is a specialized process and hence leads to craft differentiation, while the heat necessary to fire them consumes large quantities of fuel. There are other disadvantages—the physical change in the brick that firing creates means that brick, unlike adobe, cannot be reduced and the material reconstituted. But their durability, fire-resistance and relative imperviousness when used with suitable mortars, means that fired bricks are attractive to those that can afford them. This was evident in the early development of brick in England which, from the fourteenth century until the mid-seventeenth century, was exclusively used for the castles and halls of the gentry and a few public buildings.

Frequently, buildings of fired bricks are to be found in communities where mud bricks are generally in use, and are some indication of relative prosperity. They may also be a pointer to caste, as well as class distinctions. In many parts of India only the Brahmins and the Jats can afford *pucca* (or *pakka*) houses in brick, but the poorer members of even these higher castes may have unfired brick *kucha* houses which have been rendered with thick layers of mud to make them somewhat less vulnerable to monsoon rains. Kucha houses predominate; in some villages one in ten may be pucca, fired brick dwellings; in others none at all. Nevertheless, fired brick is distributed over the whole country, made in an estimated 10,000 rural kilns which account for all but one per cent of

Street in a small Dutch town. Both houses and road are entirely of brick. Roofs are covered with flat tiles or wave-like pantiles, and 'tumbled' (angled) bricks have been laid for a gable (right).

the nation's calculated output (1974) of 24 billion bricks. In all probability the estimate of the number of kilns was low; in 1978 there were some 3,000 recognised brick kilns in Sri Lanka alone, each producing an average 150,000 bricks a year, sufficient to build over 50,000 houses. But not without cost to the consumer, and a heavy one to the environment: even a firing of 25,000 bricks consumed some forty forest trees, a rate of deforestation in Sri Lanka alone of around three-quarters of a million trees a year.[16] Similar heavy consumption of fuel, in this case of palm trees, occurs in the Sudan where fired bricks were introduced by the British in the nineteenth century: what were once large groves are now almost totally depleted. In addition, the loss of bricks through poor firing or breakage is considerable.

One of the commonest forms of kiln is the clamp, or *pazawah*, where the bricks that are to be fired form their own kiln. They are stacked in ways that accommodate the fuel and permit igniting and stoking, and which circulate the heated gases. The entire structure is covered with a thick layer of mud which, after the firing, is broken off to expose the burnt bricks. Because of the heavy consumption of timber other fuels are also used: from large quantities of rice husks in Indonesia to a mixture of cow dung and coal cinders in parts of India.[17]

More efficient and much larger, the Bull's trench type of kiln is extensively used in India where as many as four million people are believed to be employed by the brickyards. Unlike the clamp type which often needs re-firing and which has to be totally dismantled to obtain the bricks, the trench kiln operates continuously. A deep channel, roughly circular in plan, takes the bricks which are stacked so as to permit the flow of air. Bricks are removed as they are fired, and fresh ones ready for firing are stacked in turn. Fuelled from above through holes in the covering clay layer, the fire travels slowly round the trench, a light chimney, made perhaps from oil drums, being manually moved above it. As the trench is in effect a ring, this can be an unending process. A daily output of 10,000 bricks is customary, and some brickyards in the fine clay areas of northern India cover many hectares.[18]

One of the attractions of fired brick is that as it does not need to be plastered it can be used decoratively. Brick walls are constructed by 'bonding' the bricks, laying them in arrangements of 'stretchers' (the long dimension) and 'headers' (the narrow dimension). They vary in size from two to four inches in thickness (thin bricks fire more easily) to eight or ten inches in length and sometimes half that breadth. By using thick mortar joints, contrasting horizontal courses with vertically-laid bricks, and the inventive use of herringbone and diaper patterns, diversity of bonds is possible, which may be enriched still further by the use of glazed headers, recessed bricks, staggered courses, and raked mortar joints.[19] Such virtuosity is occasionally displayed in vernacular traditions but generally the patterns are simple combinations of stretchers and headers. Though fired clays may still be porous, bricks are resistant to water penetration and erosion by wind and sand so that their use is particularly suited to regions where these forms of severe weathering are a problem.

Even more susceptible than the walls to the effects of the weather is the roof. Fired clay, in the form of tiles, is a widely distributed form of roof covering. It is believed that, like so much in building technology, the use of clay tiles stemmed from China, and that the Romans were responsible for their introduction into Europe. Roman tiling involved the use of flat, edge-lipped *tegulae* overlapped in layers, with half-cylinder *imbrices* covering the joints. A simpler version of the same principle employs half-cylindrical but slightly tapering tiles laid with the concave surface uppermost, overlapped by corresponding tiles with their convex surfaces visible, to give a ribbed texture to the roof. Being tapered they could slide over each other, but only so far; the close fit could even eliminate the need to use mortar, while the space

Spanish tiles roof a smallholder's dwelling, with stones along the eaves to prevent lifting by the wind. Note the clay oven, rubble-stone walls, pebble flooring, recycled stone column, and stone lintel used as a pillar. Mallorca.

between the curvatures inhibited creeping action. They can be thrown on a potter's wheel as a tall truncated cone which is then halved or even shaped, it is said, on the thigh of the maker. Such 'Spanish' tile roofs are used from China by way of India and the Mediterranean to the countries of Latin America. They are sometimes made of the yellow and red terracotta clays which are mixed with ground fired clay to reduce shrinkage when they are fired.

Like roofs that are clad in slabs of stone or slate, the clay tile roof is a heavy one, necessitating the use of substantial timbers in the structure, even if the low-pitched roofs of Spain, Italy, or Greece do not require the amount of timber that the steep pitches of northern Europe with their flat tiles demand. Many ingenious ways of spanning spaces with the same inert stone, clay, or brick of which the walls are constructed have been developed in vernacular traditions. However, the majority of dwellings are not built of a single material but of several, of which the organic, fibrous ones with their elasticity and tensile strength are especially important.

Opposite top Pazawah or 'clamp' kiln being dismantled, revealing the system of stacking. Women carry fired bricks in baskets; temporary shelters are made of unfired bricks. Terraces in the background result from clay-cutting.

Left A Bull's trench kiln which is continuously fired, the chimneys being manhandled round the trench. Stacks of freshly moulded unfired and fired bricks surround the site.

5.

RESOURCES THAT GROW

Though they do not reflect the evolution of architecture from a single source, there are marked correspondences between the architectural forms of many widely separated cultures. Sometimes these may be attributed to the dispersal of peoples and their carrying of building types and technologies with them; in other instances to the diffusion of the building forms themselves, through the influence of contiguous or dominant societies. But, as we have seen in the widespread use of corbelled stone domes, which can possibly be attributed to both of these forms of material culture diffusion, there is also evidence that like technological solutions may evolve from the acquisition of similar tools and the use of the same materials.

I do not wish to suggest that buildings *inevitably* take specific forms from the presence of common traits or resources; as any woodworker is well aware, there are many ways in which a couple of lengths of timber may be trimmed, fashioned, smoothed, butted, socketed, or jointed, and many ways in which the qualities of the material can be exploited. But while the nature and texture of organic materials may vary widely from soft woods to hard and from resinous to fibrous, and while the dimensions in which they are available also differ greatly from one context to another, certain characteristics may be found in common. These may be governed by the materials' growth, elasticity, mass and grain, not to mention their porosity or resistance to rot, heat or rain, and to the activities of fungi or animals. Ultimately, these properties will influence the materials' effectiveness in use and will help shape the ways in which they are employed to the best advantage.[1] As a result, there

are techniques of preparation and assembly that are to be found throughout the world, with many fundamentals in common, even when their details are localized.

That so much house construction is in timber reflects the widespread distribution of forests, which still cover a third of the land surface. Tropical hardwoods occur in regions with an annual rainfall in excess of 50 cm and a mean annual temperature of 24 °C or above. They are found in the Central American Amazon basin and the northern half of South America, the coastal rain forests of West Africa and western equatorial Africa, and extensively in India and south-east Asia. In some of these countries timber technologies have not been well developed for the lack of appropriate tools—as for example in the Amazon Basin, but in south-east Asia buildings of massive construction in tropical hardwoods are to be found throughout Malaysia, Indonesia, and Macronesia.

North of the arid zones temperate hardwoods, such as birch and hickory, are to be found in the eastern United States, in both western and eastern Europe and the Black Sea region and in Russia north of the steppes, thriving in areas of moderately high rainfall and a mean annual temperature lying between 39 °F and 65 °F (4 °C and 18 °C).[2] Coniferous forests lie to the north, in the colder zones of Canada and the northern Pacific coast of North America, central and particularly northern Europe where, in countries like Sweden or Finland some 60 per cent of the land is forested, and in a broad belt across Northern Russia to the Bering Sea. With immense stands of fir, pine, and larch meeting the birches at the southern limits, Russia has the largest timbered regions of any country.[3]

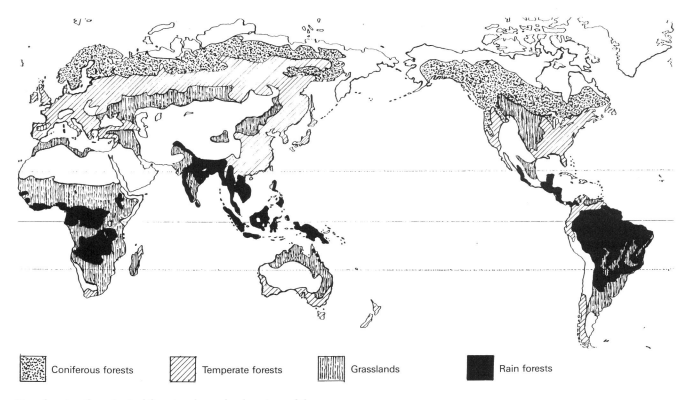

| | Coniferous forests | | Temperate forests | | Grasslands | | Rain forests |

Map showing the principal forest and grassland regions of the world. The use of hardwoods is partially restricted by the technology available. Bamboo is also used for building and grass is an important roofing material.

POLE STRUCTURES

Timber in its various forms provides one of the most important, longest-used, and most durable kinds of building material, which combine compression strength with elasticity and tensile strength. Many timbers are capable of being intricately carved and most can be worked with relatively simple hand tools. So we may find that the structural principles on which a building is erected in a remote island in the Pacific are not necessarily greatly dissimilar from those in other parts of the world. For example, we might take the tiny island of Vaitupu in Tuvalu (formerly the Ellice Islands) some seven hundred miles north of Fiji and a similar distance from Samoa. Here the principal building material is the pandanus palm, though milo and coconut are also employed. A house would be supported on six or eight pandanus posts, deeply bedded in the soil, with two corner posts at each end and the remainder at six-foot intervals on the sides; a typical house would be about twenty-four feet long and eighteen in width. Forked poles received the horizontal side members, or wall-plates but if the posts were not forked they were round-notched on the end to support the log; tie-beams and end-plates were then placed across to complete the framework and lashed securely in place.

Rafters, five or six on each side, were cut so as to meet tightly at a ridge angle of about 80 degrees; they were notched and pegged where they crossed so that they could rest on the wall plate and extend beyond the wall to produce deep eaves. A ridge pole, somewhat shorter than the full length of the house and held in position by temporary scaffolding, was lashed beneath the meeting of the rafters, and in the larger houses was supported by king posts resting on the tie-beams. The shortened ridge received a main rafter at each end, which consequently inclined inwards below the apex of the main rafters, and it was also

An early photograph of the traditional Vaitupu house. Pandanus leaf thatched-roof and gables with walls of woven coconut palm pinnules. Tuvalu (formerly Ellice Islands). (*Pitt Rivers Museum, Oxford*)

from the wall-plates and rested on the tie-beams; they provided valued storage space but reduced headroom at the sides.

Lashings were made from sennit twisted and plaited by the old men, as much as six thousand feet being used in the building of one house. Young men would cut and strip the poles of bark, while the women prepared the materials for thatching. Fallen pandanus leaves were gathered and pulled around a stick to smooth and flatten them. Coconut leaf ribs were then collected and split into wands to which the leaves were attached, by drawing the stem end of the leaf over the wand and attaching it to the leaf spear with a fine needle made from a coconut spine. Each leaf overlapped its neighbour and soon a deep fringe of pandanus leaves was fixed to the spine to make a *lau*.

Thatchers on the roof sewed the lau to the purlins with a barbed wooden needle. Working from the eaves in successive layers with their shiny and rain-repelling surface uppermost, the lau were laid over each other, the greater the overlap the denser and more durable the thatch. The end gables were similarly thatched and the roof ridge protected by plaited mats of coconut leaf pegged into position. Meanwhile the women gathered coconut palm branches with their leaves, or pinnules, attached. Split down the middle and laid side by side, they produced a double layer of pinnules which were then woven to left and right to produce a broad herringbone pattern. The woven mats were strung in several rows above each other to clad the external walls, low forked poles carrying internal members being used to brace the mats against the pressure of the winds.[4]

augmented by two short rafters, one on either side. The effect was to produce an inclined gable end. At intervals horizontal purlins were placed in position and a lattice of ribs of split pandanus laths was then affixed to the rafters with a continuous lashing. These were to take the roof thatch. To complete the internal fixtures, platforms were constructed which projected

Construction of the traditional Vaitupu, Tuvalu (former Ellice Islands) house. Under Tongan influence in the early twentieth century supplementary eaves were added to enlarge the internal space laterally. (*Developed from Kennedy*)

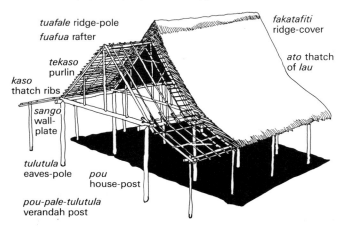

tuafale ridge-pole
fuafua rafter
fakatafiti ridge-cover
tekaso purlin
ato thatch of *lau*
kaso thatch ribs
sango wall-plate
tulutula eaves-pole
pou house-post
pou-pale-tulutula verandah post

We can compare the Vaitupu house with that built by the Maya Amer-Indians halfway across the world, in Yucatan, Mexico. The Maya build a dwelling that is supported by three or four pairs of substantial posts of *oxcitinche* or another Yucatan hardwood that is resistant to rot. These take the *pachna* or wall plates, and end-plates, and the principals of the roof frame. With its 'hipped' profile, shorter at the ridge than at the eaves level, it too has an inclined gable frame. A dozen or more common rafters on each side and six or

Mayan house under construction, showing the hipped roof frame, supporting posts and wall plates. A protective Cross has been raised on a thin wand (left of ridge) during house-building. Yucatan, Mexico.

Two Mayan houses showing side walls of *cololches* packed with earth. Corrugated iron covers the thatched roof at the ridge, which is vulnerable in rains. Yucatan.

eight at the ends are laid against the basic frame and supported by the purlins; these in turn are crossed by slender sticks tied into position with bark strips. In these respects the Mayan house is very similar in construction to that found in Vaitupu. But the final plan is deceptively different. At each end of most traditional houses a curving line of posts is driven into the ground and linked at the top with interwoven withies to produce an apse. In some houses these meet the end rafters, in others, poles converge on to the apse and are crossed with sticks to provide a support for the palm thatch. Along the side walls thin poles, *cololches*, produce a fence wall, made secure with horizontal poles. Packed with branches and leaves plastered over with red laterite it makes a sound wall, which however, is not load bearing. In the long wall on each side an opening is left for the doorway, which permits cross-ventilation, and hammocks are slung between the pachna.[5]

Vaitupu and Maya houses were not elaborated, the bamboo and raffia palm poles were not squared in section, trimmed down their lengths, or joined with precisely chiselled mortice and tenon joints. The nature of the building material inhibits such refinements, for the strength of the poles depends on their cylindrical section; trimming would have weakened the elements. Similarly, the poles were lashed, not jointed, though cusps and hollows were sometimes cut to receive the curved section of a pole cross-member. Lashings are strong and flexible affording some resilience in high winds without threatening the stability of the structure; mortice joints would weaken the poles, while nails would have split them.

Nevertheless, though details of the construction might be different, the builders of timber-framed houses all over the world would have found much in the building of these two dwelling types, particularly the structure of the roof, which echoed their own methods. The wall plates, roof trusses, tie-beams and collars, rafters, purlins, and ridge are the constituents of roof assemblies among hundreds of societies. Specific peculiarities, such as the shortened ridge and inclined end-gables have been developed as hipped roofs in some contexts, and as projecting peaked ridges over more steeply inclined gables in others.

To the casual observer the building might seem unsophisticated but building craftsmen would recognize the skill in optimizing the potential of the available materials.

TIMBER TECHNOLOGIES

Timber-framed dwellings are constructed on the 'post and beam' principle, in which the beam transfers vertical loads along its lengths to its supporting posts. Sometimes termed 'trabeated architecture'—from the Latin work *trabs* for beam—it exploits the tensile strength of timber. Doubling the length of the beam will halve the load that it can bear; doubling its depth will quadruple its strength. Hence, beams of considerable thickness are employed for larger spans, but these in turn need strong supports, either thicker and firmly connected with the beams, or braced to reduce the bending effects. Along the side walls of a framed house a number of 'studs' or intermediary vertical supports will often be placed, the spaces between the studs being spanned by shorter members. This can be seen in the houses of villages in many parts of South Germany where the timber-framed walls may have studs at intervals of a metre or so. These may be spanned with horizontal lengths of timber which together produce a regular cellular pattern into which the window frames fit.

Many fine buildings have been preserved, some dating from the fifteenth century, with tiers of floors each slightly 'jettied' over the level below. While the technique may have been one of cantilever on the ends of the floor joists where they rested on the wall plate, it also helped to protect the timbers and exposed wall surfaces. But apart from these grander

Top Post and beam construction of a large house at Manikan, Himachal Pradesh. All timber elements are squared, trimmed, and jointed.

Middle Detail of South German braced timber-framing with pegged joints.

Left Typical timber-framed housing in a South German village, showing a variety of framing and bracing patterns.

South German farm building showing evidence of wattle-and-daub and rubble infill. Joints were tenoned and holes augered to take wooden pegs which secured the joints.

examples, the humbler farmhouse dwellings offer many delightful and instructive examples of folk building, and are still used essentially for their original purposes, even though centuries have passed since they were erected. Large spans between thicker posts at wide intervals marked a succession of bays in many farmhouses. Horizontal elements linked the vertical posts and any tendency to lurch was counteracted by diagonal bracing. Often the brackets and braces exposed on the walls gave a lively sense of movement, and fanciful names such as the *Wilder Mann* or the *Schwabische Weible*, the Schwabian wife, were invented for the shapes they made. It is possible to see in these modest farms the eccentric or individual work of a carpenter who had devised a system of his own, sometimes including curving braces,

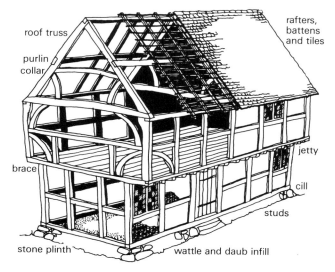

Diagram of timber-framed construction (South-east England) showing roof truss, wind-braces, purlins, battens to take roof tiles, jettied upper storey, and brick infill.

Half-dovetail notching of a horizontally-laid timber wall; a full dovetail would be chamfered at the top and bottom of each plank. Many forms of notching are to be found in Europe and the United States.

apparently employed for their aesthetic effect as well as their functional purpose. Joints were frequently 'halved' (lapped), especially in Schwabia, but tenon joints were common in other parts, and in both methods the timbers were secured with wooden pegs. Left to project, they were driven further into the joint as the timber shrank, so as to keep the structure tight. With these systems the load-bearing structure is the frame and the building will stand, and can be roofed, even without solid walls.[6]

Of itself the frame provides support, but no screening from wind and weather; the spaces between the framing elements must therefore be closed with an 'infill' which may be made of wattles, interlaced around slender poles and strained against the frame, or inserted into specially cut grooves and drilled holes. A wattle infill can be made weather resistant with mud 'daub' forced into the interstices or the spaces may be packed with adobe and clay lump, the gaps that open in the drying process being filled with wet clay and the whole mud-plastered over. Again, random rubble-stone or brick can be stacked in the boxes, sometimes laid in short courses, but often diagonally or in 'herringbone' pattern so that the settlement of the stone only leaves a space at the top of each box to be closed with clay or pebbles. Alternatively, the building may be 'clad' with an external covering of slats or planks nailed on to the frame and, when time and materials are available, over the interior also. Cladding is often applied, though with less reason, to timber-walled buildings as well, so that external appearances are sometimes deceptive, the surface treatment not necessarily being an indication of the structural system.

Timber-walling, or horizontal log construction, is the other main tradition in building in wood. Unlike timber-framing it uses the mass and dead weight of timber and does not exploit its tensile properties. As a technique it also consumes much more wood than timber-framing, in terms of the quantities of timber used relative to the volumes encompassed. On the other hand, it makes use of the insulating and defensive advantages of solid wooden walls. It is not surprising to find that timber-walling methods are to be found in countries that are heavily forested, often mountainous, and with low temperatures. From Scandinavia to the Balkans, through vast regions of Russia, and as far east as Nuristan and northern Pakistan, timber-walled houses are numerous.

Whether of logs with or without the bark, or lengths of heavy worked timber, which have been sawn into thick, broad planks in the saw-pit, or split lengthwise along the log with wedges and finished with broad-axe or adze, essential to the system is the principle of 'locking' the layers of timbers so that they are not thrust apart by the pressure and weight of succeeding layers. Each timber baulk is 'notched' at the ends, above or below (or sometimes both) making a 'halved' joint which receives the planks placed at right angles to it, the ends of the baulks pro-

Above Peasant house with shingled roof (right) and thatched store made of horizontal baulks on stone plinths. Entry to the house is by the short stone ramp; there is no chimney but the roof opening is covered with a wooden cupola. Central Serbia.

Right Cutaway perspective of a traditional Serbian house of trimmed horizontal log construction notched at the corners, and raised on a stone cellar-plinth.

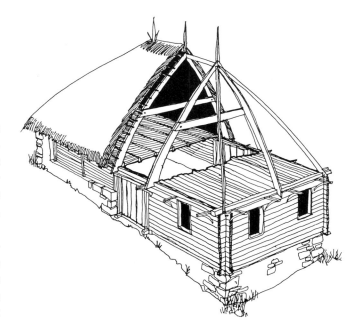

jecting and crossing at the corners. The halving of the timbers permits a tight joint, and if the notch is literally half the width of the log—which cuts into the heartwood—the planks, baulks, or logs fit tightly together. Farm buildings of the Balkan plank house type in Central Serbia, though smaller than many, combine the features of this form of construction.

Houses are frequently sited south-facing on a hill-slope, with the long dimension at right angles to the incline and access ramps banked to the entrances, the main door facing east. Because the bottom timbers may rot if they are placed directly on the ground it

Serbian farmhouse with planked timber *ajat* (verandah) supported by bracketed posts. The walls have been painted to simulate stone, and pantiles have replaced shingled roofs.

The stock sold by a Bombay timber merchant is entirely of bamboo. It will be used for the dwellings of the poor and for scaffolding in the erection of high-rise buildings.

was customary for the house to be built on a stone plinth which, in this mountainous region, also took up the irregularities of the ground. Often enclosing a basement store or byre, it took the *podvale* or heavy timber sills, over which were locked the massive floor joists. Trimmed some 150 mm thick the wall logs were square-notched, interlocked at the corners and mortised into the substantial door frames. With this structural system all walls had to be constructed together and only after they had been completed to a height of some two metres were the ceiling beams, the *nastavnice*, notched over the wall plates and the principals of the steeply-pitched, hipped roof raised into position. Deep overhanging eaves were constructed on many houses and the roofs were covered with large shingles of split timber, held in position over the purlins and laths with carved wooden pegs. At the ridge the roof was slightly peaked to permit a protected opening for the escape of smoke and in some cases an additional roof cowl with a carved finial was centrally placed.

Divided in two by a timber screen wall, a typical peasant house has one room, the *soba*, for sleeping and a larger room, the *kuča*, onto which the doors open where all domestic activities take place. Above, the ceiling may be partially planked and a secondary soba or store made in the loft space, with a forked wooden ladder for access.[7] A larger farm may have a two-storeyed plank house sometimes with an *ajat*, or verandah, supported through two floors by posts with carved wooden capitals and with an external staircase.[8] Wood technology is almost total; granaries and stores of similar timber construction, sometimes with thatched roofs held down by poles, separate dairies, and wattle-clad, timber-framed and single-roof corn cribs constitute the peasant homesteads, their small-holdings defined with wattle fences.

Theoretically, organic materials are renewable, stocks to replenish resources being grown with good management, at a rate that will ensure a continuing supply. Many of the earlier techniques have declined in the industrialized countries; coppicing for example, in which small woods of young trees—hazel, oak, chestnut, or ash—are planted closely so as to produce long straight poles, cropped, cut, sorted, stacked and carted for different building purposes. Though the practice has declined in Britain, coppices are carefully nurtured in eastern Europe and the forested parts of the Middle East.[9]

There are however, many desert, steppe, prairie, and veldt regions where there are few or no trees, yet they do not constitute the only organic and renewable natural resource for building and many societies have discovered the structural possibilities of the grasses.

BUILDING IN BAMBOO

Popular usage distinguishes bamboos from grasses or palms, but they all have fibres embedded in pithy tissue, the bundles of tissue developing from the growing tip. Nevertheless for practical purposes, the bamboos constitute a recognizable group notable for the convenient size and weight of the 'culms' or natural lengths, that are divided by nodes making cross-walls which give them a high strength-to-weight ratio. The hardest tissues are on the outside, producing a strong, cylindrical shell which can be cut up, sawn, or chopped into suitable lengths, but which can also be split to produce half culms, and split-peeled to make strong binding materials. There is no bark to remove, virtually no waste, and bamboo can be worked with a machete. But bamboos vary: there are some 700 species throughout the world—over 200 in Latin America alone, and they may grow in tropical and temperate climates from sea-level to over 13,000 feet (4,000 m). The range means that some are stronger than others.[10] Generally the thicker culms are good for compression, while the thinner culms have moderate elasticity and considerable strength. Starch and moisture on the inside pith layer tend to be subject to rotting fungi and attract damaging insects like the so called 'shot-borer' beetle in India, or the 'powder-post' beetle in Puerto Rico. But this is not always the case; a giant bamboo which grows up to 90 feet in height in Colombia, Ecuador, and Peru, is very resistant to both. The six-inch diameter culms, with their nodes at frequent intervals provide a substantial building material for supporting house posts; narrower bamboo culms are used for the rest of the construction of houses.

Half sections of culms can be used in a fashion similar to that of Spanish tiles. It is customary to lash the joints, passing the rattan or bamboo strip splines

A common bamboo detail. The supporting post has been cusped above the culm to take a roof purlin. Rafters are held by the ridge of thick bamboo lashed above.

New houses in a refugee camp, with bamboo frame and mats of diagonally woven bamboo secured by a lattice of split poles. Dacca, Pakistan.

through holes bored just beyond the node; nails can be used but are inclined to split the bamboo lengths; pegs and dowels of narrow-gauge bamboo or sections of thick culm-walls are also used in jointing; harder woods may be used for the flooring as they are less inclined to spring, but they are more liable to attack by insects than the bamboo which, in some houses, may last thirty or more years.[11]

Though bamboo houses can be plastered with a mixture of mud, dung, and chopped grass, in many

Village houses, Bafut, Cameroon, showing the high pyramid roofs, vertical box frame and diagonal bracing of raffia poles.

parts of the world the side walls are of woven bamboo splines, which have been split from the culm and then beaten flat before weaving. Extremely strong, bamboo makes for a relatively light construction and, where other available woods permit, it may be combined with a basic frame of heavier timbers. This makes for a more durable structure and one which can assume greater height, the bamboos or raffia-palms being used as studs, cladding, or bracing, and stiffening the structure in the process. Among the hilly slopes and grassland pasture of Western Cameroon which rise from a plateau region some 4,500 feet above sea level, live a complex of related peoples numbering well over half a million. Efficient farmers, they raise small livestock and grow a wide variety of

food crops including yams, okra, watermelons, millet, bananas, and more recently potatoes, maize, and beans. Bamboos, raffia-palms, and many slender types of tree provide the materials for the substantial houses built by most of these peoples. Many live in compact villages, often centred about the courts of divine kings. Typically, the Fon of Bafut, chief of some 20,000 subjects, lives in a large compound with his many wives each having a separate dwelling house. In the main village and in others nearby, the inhabitants live in similar houses, square in plan and with tapering roofs.

When a new house is to be built the male head chooses a site on his land and seeks the assistance of others in his lineage in clearing the land and preparing a twelve-foot square platform for his dwelling. This is dug over with hoes, rain water pools indicating where undulations need to be levelled. Raffia poles are brought from the bush and are trimmed with a cutlass to nine-foot lengths for the uprights and twelve-foot lengths for the horizontal members. A notable feature of the buildings is the extensive use of prefabrication or the individual construction of component parts of the building prior to assembly. Walls are preformed on the ground with a double layer of vertical uprights at intervals of a few inches clenching the five or six horizontals which are drilled, pegged, and lashed with raffia into position. Substantial corner poles are erected and the wall panels raised by communal effort and lashed securely.

Above the walls a large platform or ceiling is placed, which is similarly prefabricated on the ground and which has deep eaves extending two or three feet beyond the walls. To raise this substantial platform into position requires a team of eight men. An opening is cut into the eaves to permit access to the loft space, which is later used for storing fuel, the ceiling being solidly packed with bamboo poles to provide a firm flat surface. Four triangular elements are next constructed on the ground, with sides of some 16 feet (5 m) poles tapering to the apex with purlins threaded between two layers of rafters. With men on both the roof platform and on the ground the triangles are hoisted into position and lashed securely to make a massive pyramidal roof which is further supported by perimeter poles. Other members of the lineage are invited to participate in the gathering of grass and the making of sheaves for thatching the roof, though the thatching process itself, with the sheaves packed tightly in layers between the purlins in a process which may take three days to complete, is done by a professional thatcher. The grass is beaten and flattened until a thick watertight shield is ensured and against a pole used as a straight-edge, the edge trimmed with a cutlass. With the roof thatched and the structure completed the walls are heavily plastered with puddled mud packed into the interstices of the bamboo framing. The heat from a central fire in the house dries out the mud walls during which time the owner builds pole-frame beds and storage shelves; eventually a second, lower ceiling

The triangular elements of the Bafut roof frame are prefabricated on the ground and raised into position by a team of men.

Securely lashed and pegged, the roof frame is thatched by a specialist. In this example adobe block walls have replaced the pole structure.

Houses of *qasab* reed on the artificial islands made by the Ma'dan marsh dwellers of Iraq, seen here with a number of water buffalo.

will be constructed on which can be placed dried corn and palm kernels. Throughout the process of building, the house-owner plies the helpers from his lineage with food and palm wine and holds feasts for the thatch-gatherers and for the blessing of the house when the work is completed.[12]

The grand, even extravagant buildings of the Bafut, the Bamiliké, Bamoun, and other related peoples of Cameroon's grasslands and highlands, are only possible because there is an abundance of suitable resources. The layers of vertical, horizontal, and diagonally-lashed bamboos and raffia poles, together with the carved timbers and deep thatch on the buildings consume considerable quantities of materials. These ensure however, the relative durability and stability of the structures; rebuilding at frequent intervals is not necessary.[13]

Fast-growing reeds, canes, and bamboos are readily replenished, some bamboos growing at the rate of as much as 12 feet (3–4 m) in a *day* while most will grow two or three feet daily in the wet seasons. Bamboos are widely dispersed throughout the world, with high concentrations in Central and South America and in India, Burma, China, Japan, and Indonesia where stands of 100 feet in height (35 m) are far from uncom-

mon. Villagers may grow on their own plots sufficient bamboo for their building needs and with yields of as great as twenty tonnes a hectare the problems of durability and maintenance are largely offset by their fertility.[14]

REEDS AND GRASSES

Because of their attenuated form and length-to-width ratio, grasses alone are not suitable as structural materials. They have great flexibility and elasticity, but little compression strength and, when severed from their roots, insufficient rigidity to support their own weight. Bundled and tied, however, certain grasses can be used structurally when other materials are not to hand, as the reed dwellings of the Marsh Arabs dramatically demonstrate.

Technically and botanically part of the grasses, reeds which are water- or marsh-growing have strong straight stems and are used at least for temporary shelters in some parts of Africa, India, and Bangladesh. In the broad marshes between the confluence of the Tigris and Euphrates north of Basra in Iraq the *qasab* reed grows to over twenty feet in height. Qasab provides the basic building material of the Ma'dan, whose tribes are scattered through some six thousand square miles of marsh. Though building techniques differ to some extent with the various tribes over the central and eastern marshes, a house might be raised on an island if the builders were fortunate, or on an artificial one if they were less favoured. A stockade of high reeds would be forced into the area of marsh water chosen for the site, and more reeds and rushes gathered and transported in the ubiquitous high-prowed *mashaf* canoes. As the water rises, reeds, sometimes alternated with mud gathered at low water, are packed into the space until the water ceases to rise above the reed mattress thus formed. Then the reed fencing is bent over to form a further layer, and other trampled layers of reeds and mud laid across. Eventually a firm base, or *dibir*, for the dwelling is established and fresh, golden-hued reeds of 20 foot length (6 m) secured to form the basic structure. These are inserted singly at an angle of 30 degrees away from the intended enclosed area, forced into the reed mattress until secure. Clusters of reeds are bundled together by binding them with straw ropes at frequent intervals along their length.

An irregular number of the bundles, from five to as many as thirteen, are arranged at around 4–6 feet (1.5–2 m) intervals, like the ribs of a skeleton. The differing lengths of the reeds produce a natural taper in the bundles which are now ready for drawing together. Starting at one end the bundled reeds are drawn into the centre, producing a graceful parabolic arch held in tension. Standing on a tripod of reed bundles, one of the three or four men constructing the dwelling ties the overlapping bundles with straw lashings. When the row of arches is complete, further but more slender bundles of reeds, tied at one end for ease of handling, are bound to the arches to act as horizontal rafters; on a 12-foot high arch some 9 rafters a side might be used. Straight columns of bundled reed, two or four in number, may stand across the openings at each end, not to provide stability so much as to offer a secure base for the hanging of the reed mats that close the gables. Large woven mats made from split qasab stalks clad the whole structure, overlapping each other with three or four thicknesses, and secured by narrow bundles tied through to the purlins. The house is now complete but some may have more elaborate doorways which always face Mecca

Reed bundles are inserted into the base mattress, brought together in an arch and tied with straw to hold them in tension.

and open screens to admit light but retain privacy. However a much larger *mudhif*, or guest house, will be built in the village settlements. Some of these reach considerable proportions; an 18-foot (6 m) high mudhif of 11 arches and 60 feet (18 m) in length would be common but Wilfrid Thesiger reported a 21-arch mudhif 120 feet (36 m) in length. Such mudhifs may be fastidiously built, with as many as seventy rafters and over fifty overlapping covering mats, the ends elaborately patterned with open weave mats.

Tending their herds of water buffalo, raising cereal crops of rice, making reed mats for sale in the markets of Basra, the Marsh Arabs have maintained a way of life that has lasted millennia; a tradition now threatened by the Iraq-Iran war and by plans to drain the Marshes. The *sitras* or winter shelters for their buffaloes, the *raba*, part dwelling, part guest-house, the merchants' houses and other temporary or permanent structures of the marshes are among the most striking examples of ingenuity and skill in building developed in the face of the severest limitations of resources. Their marsh settlements are not without problems; the lack of sanitation has meant that their water is

Horizontal straw bundles are lashed to the arches to stabilize the structure. The woven mats of *qasab* stalks with which the house is covered are fixed to them. River Euphrates, Iraq.

contaminated and that dysentry is rife. Bilharziasis affects most of the population, and rising flood waters which may even come up within the houses add to the discomforts of a hardy but independent people.[15]

Living at a very different altitude but in equally harsh climatic conditions the Aymara Amer-Indians of Bolivia make their living from fishing in Lake Titicaca, at 13,000 feet (3,800 m) the highest lake in the world. Best known for their banana-shaped boats made from tapering bundles of *tutora* reed, skilfully bound together with grass ropes, they also make reed dwellings in the dense tutora beds. A few supporting poles hold up the roof, which is spanned with wide mats of reed stalks, and takes a keel-like shape over which the cold lake winds blow.

Reeds grow in marshy, well-watered places and can only be used in limited circumstances. Grasses, however, are to be found in profusion in many, even most parts of the inhabited world, luxuriating even where other vegetable materials that could be utilized for building are in short supply—the veldt, steppes, pampas and savannahs among them. Grass, like reed, is an excellent cladding material which can be bunched or sewn, or even pulled up by the roots to provide a thick cover. In consequence, it is probably the most extensively used of all roof cladding materials, thatch being relatively light to handle, resistant to water penetration, and cool because of its poor conduction of heat. Changes in rural technology have adversely affected the production of by-products used in building in western Europe, thatch being a case in point.

Until the 1950s the cutting of wheat by hand with

Aymara Indians, on Lake Titicaca. Both their boats of bundled reeds and their houses of woven mats are made from *tutora* which grows in the lake marshes. Bolivia.

Interior of the Zulu/Nguni hut showing the close mesh of overlapping arches of thin poles. The posts support an internal platform and are not necessary to reinforce the dome. (*Pitt Rivers Museum, Oxford*)

sickle and scythe, and its threshing over a frame so as not to flatten and bruise the straw, ensured that it could be used for thatching. But, with the extensive, and eventually universal, use of mechanical and combine harvesters the wheat straw was broken and of no use to the thatcher. Nevertheless, in peasant societies in Europe and in many other parts of Africa, the Middle East, and Asia, cereals and grasses are carefully grown, harvested, and stored for roofing while marsh reeds are widely used.

In Rajhastan and Uttar Pradesh in northern India temporary shelters are made by grass and straw gatherers who supply materials for the thatching of mud-built houses. By bundling and tying canes and thick grasses a light framework is constructed against which thatching grass is secured with straw.[16] But for any more durable structure thin sticks or light poles are obtained to provide the necessary rigidity. This is the case with the domical 'grass hut' of many of the Southern Bantu peoples, among them the Zulu, Nguni, and Xhosa who migrated south from the Lakeland regions in the sixteenth century.[17]

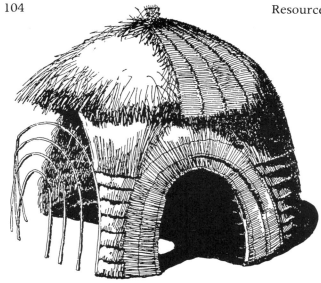

The Ngwame house, a variant of the Zulu and Nguni type, showing some of its successive layers of frame structure, overlaid mats, insulating grass layers, further mats, and finally grass rope net. (*Developed from Knuffel*)

The upper storey of this house near Kumbakonam is made entirely of woven and plaited palm leaves used both structurally and decoratively. Tamil Nadu, South India.

The Ngwame, a Natal Nguni sub-group living in the foothills of the 'Little Berg' close to Lesotho, are cultivators of mealies. Living at an altitude around 4,500 feet (1,400 m) and in extremes of temperature that range between 95°F (35 °C) to below freezing, they endure a difficult climate made more hazardous by sudden gales. Their huts are therefore very expertly, if laboriously constructed. In summary, the hut comprises a close framework of overlapping arches, a layer of mats which keeps the inside clean, an insulating grass layer, another layer of mats, a water-repelling layer of grass thatch and a protective net.

The structure, whose external appearance gives little indication of the complexity of its manufacture, is not made without cost in time. Knuffel, who carefully recorded the whole process, calculated that the building took sixty-five work days to build, two-thirds of the work being done by women, and the remainder shared by four men. Of this, thirty days were spent in weaving mats, braiding the ropes for the tying and roof nets and for the ornamental stitching—in all nearly 9,000 feet of grass rope were used.[18]

Few techniques of building so ingeniously exploit the potential of the available resource as does the Ngwame grass house. In the detailed description of the building process the knowledge of the potential of the limited materials, and the skill and craftsmanship involved in the construction are readily apparent. But it is also evident that the considerable time spent on building is in large part due to the problems encountered in a moderately high altitude, wind-swept veldt, subject to extremes of temperature and seasonal heavy precipitation. Within, the spaces are ordered and given value, but the first function of the structure is to provide protection from the weather, thick enough to keep out both sun and rain.

Opposite Building a 'Nubian' vault without using centering. Inclined layers of parabolic mud brick arches are placed against an end wall.

Hand-hewn dwellings in a tufa rock pinnacle, a balcony off the upper-level living space to the right. Rock spoil is used for walls and additional rooms. Cappadocia, Central Anatolia, Turkey.

Opposite Berber cave dwellings off an excavated shaft; a cistern in the centre. Matmata Mountains, Southern Tunisia.

Interior of a Tallensi compound. The phallic form is an ancestral pillar to which libations are made daily. Tongo, Northern Ghana.

Opposite Maya Amer-Indian single-cell house with earthen side walls and *cololche* apsidal ends of slender poles, Yucatan, Mexico.

A street of *trulli*, with domical, corbelled stone roofs,
Alberobello, Apulia, Italy.

Opposite Interior of the *kuča* or kitchen living-space of a peasant
house, Central Serbia. A ceramic stove in the adjacent bedroom is
stoked from the *kuča*. The forked pole ladder leads to the loft.

6.

COPING WITH CLIMATE

Dwellings are built to serve a variety of functions, but one of the most important is to create a 'micro-climate' acceptable to their occupiers. Buildings do not *control* climate which, apart from the wind or sun shadow that they may cast, remains largely unaffected by them. But within, the dwelling does *modify* the climate, creating internal conditions that come closer to those which the occupants find most comfortable. When we light a fire or, if we are among the privileged minority, turn on the central heating, we are in one way or another, responding to the prevailing climatic conditions. Our response is sometimes to repel the effect of the weather, cladding the walls with a water resistant material to keep out the rain, building a roof with a steep pitch to shed the snow; sometimes it is to accept or welcome the weather, or an aspect of it: when we open the windows to 'let the fresh air in', or, on a bright, cold day we sit by a glazed window to enjoy the warmth of the sun's rays.

TAKING THE TEMPERATURE

Though we spend much of our time literally 'out of doors', outside the dwelling, we also spend a great deal inside; more in some weather conditions than in others, for the climate changes not only seasonally, but daily, even hourly, in some regions. Seldom are both night temperatures and the day temperatures equally to our liking: the evenings get chilly, the mornings are fresh, the noon sun too hot. Virtually every type of dwelling serves the function of assisting

Opposite Single-direction wind-catchers mounted on rooftops direct breezes down air shafts to cool the rooms below. Sind, Pakistan.

us in adjusting to one or many aspects of the climate. One type is effective in keeping the wind off us, another for keeping the occupants cool in blazing heat. They may not always be equally good at coping with a variety of climate conditions; when they do we may emphasize that the house is 'warm in winter and cool in summer'. Often we describe internal temperatures or relative humidity in terms of 'comfort'; though comfort values differ widely between cultures. Some arctic or desert peoples survive, apparently contentedly, in conditions which would be exceedingly uncomfortable to a Southern European. Immigrants from the Caribbean or East Africa may take a long time to adjust to the 'damp cold' of northern latitudes. These differences in attitudes to comfort

Climate modifiers in this Mombasa house-row include a verandah with pierced railings; a shaded loggia, windows, curtains, and awnings permit fine adjustments. The corrugated iron roof may be hotter, and noisier in rain, than a tiled roof, but it is cheaper.

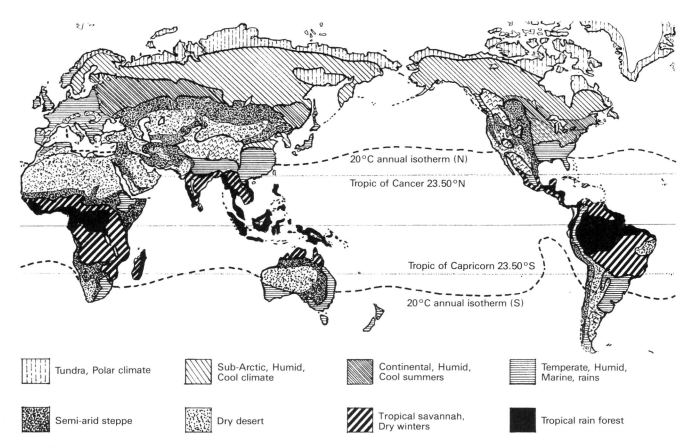

20°C annual isotherm (N)

Tropic of Cancer 23.50°N

Tropic of Capricorn 23.50°S

20°C annual isotherm (S)

Tundra, Polar climate	Sub-Arctic, Humid, Cool climate	Continental, Humid, Cool summers	Temperate, Humid, Marine, rains
Semi-arid steppe	Dry desert	Tropical savannah, Dry winters	Tropical rain forest

Map of the principal climate zones of the world. Also indicated is the 'tropic' region as defined by the 20 °C isotherms, North and South.

are partly physiological, but they are also psychological and cultural. As cultures change, attitudes to comfort conditions change also: today's descendants of the nineteenth-century pioneer families who braved the rigours of a Kansas winter or the stifling heat of a summer on the great plains, insist on centrally-heated and air-conditioned offices and houses.

Such mechanical and energy-consuming devices are effective, but in most dwellings of the world, 'climate modifiers' must be installed, or be a part of the total design, with the minimum of cost. Secondary service industries for the provision of air conditioning or the installation of double glazing cannot apply; the means of cooling a building and maintaining an acceptable temperature and quality of air for living, or the insulation of the dwelling needs to be a part of the original design and structure. It is not merely a question of the cost of installations, it is also, with regard to cooling or heating, the costs of the fuels needed to provide the requisite energy. Wherever possible therefore, 'passive' systems which, in effect, have no running costs, are desirable.

Forms of building which have already been discussed with regard to the materials used in their construction may also be examined from the point of view of the climatological performance: the corbelled stone dwellings of Europe and the Middle East, for example. In the hills of Judea and Samaria 10,000 stone huts were reported by Zvi Y. D. Ron, who measured the climatic performance of a number of them. In this region daytime highs may be as much as 95 °F (35 °C) but the nights are cool dropping to 66 °F

(18 °C), so the 'diurnal-nocturnal temperature range', or the extremes within 24 hours, lies between 54 °F (12 °C) and 59 °F (15 °C). Humidity, which affects comfort conditions, may range from as little as 30 per cent during the day to as much as 90 per cent at night. After summer readings were taken in the huts and then analysed it was found that the daytime internal temperatures were much lower than outside—as much as 52 °F (11 °C) difference in July. But at night the temperature was higher than that outside with a nocturnal range of less than 36 °F (2 °C) in some cases and not higher than 50 °F (10 °C), because of the transmission of heat through the mass of the stone walls. In daytime the humidity levels were 30 per cent or more higher than outside, but they were lower at night, becoming uncomfortable only in the high summer. Then in July and August, many farmers raised thatched, open-sided shelters to sleep in *on top* of their corbelled stone huts.[1] In this, as in the other examples, the typical shelter performed well climatically for most of the year, but in the extreme periods beyond its range, an alternative structure was built. It is analogous to a temporary change in one's customary clothing—the wearing of a balaclava helmet perhaps, during a bitterly cold spell in an otherwise temperate climate.

Unlike hats or gloves parts of buildings cannot easily be donned or doffed to suit climatic changes, though there are plenty of examples of temporary appendages which meet occasional needs—the awning over the shopfront or window, the curtain hung over the inside of the door to reduce draughts. Most structures are too substantial, and often too permanent, for major changes to be practicable; instead, the buildings are made to respond to the demands of the particular climate to which they are subject. This, of course, varies throughout the world and specific solutions to climatic problems are often extremely localized.

Tents and shelters of the nomads may seem elementary as structures and spartan as dwellings, but in terms of climate they are often very effective. Part of their suitability is related to their impermanence; as a tent is pitched or a brush shelter constructed it can be

'Passive' cooling system in a Swahili house. Hot air escapes through the open gable end, but the extended roof keeps out the rain. Palm thatch lowers the temperature several degrees. Lamu, Kenya.

Corbelled stone dwellings and stores 'perform' well under intense solar radiation, with internal temperatures much lower than outside. Huran, Turkey, Syrian border.

placed to exploit to the greatest advantage the prevailing conditions. It can be placed under trees for additional shade, sited to make the best use of breezes, or tucked in the lee of a hill to evade fierce winds. This flexibility, which can make the best of the slightest undulations of landform also extends to the structure itself—tent walls can be raised or removed, openings can be made in brush shelters and others closed, a new site can be selected if a change of conditions warrants it.

Tent of Kababish nomads, Sudan. Brushwood filters windblown sand and affords additional shade for a cooking area. Such tents and shelters are sited to take advantage of prevailing conditions.

Nomads may have a high tolerance of extreme conditions out of necessity, for there has to be a 'trade-off' between their freedom to move and the portability of their dwelling types. Many such peoples have more than one dwelling type according to the season, though in the transitional period between the change of seasons the shelter may become unpleasant to inhabit. As we have seen, nomadic economies do not support very large numbers of people though, in the environments where they live, nomads are often the only kinds of social group that *can* survive. These interesting and instructive exceptions apart, the world's populations are sedentary. How then, do peoples living in permanent dwellings cope with climate?

LIVING IN COMFORT

Comfort conditions, or the thermal balance between the body and that of the environment in which one finds himself, depend on many factors. Some of these are biological, such as the metabolic rate, the skin temperature and the capacity of perspiration to bring down body heat.[2] Others are to do with the variable conditions of a given environment, such as the temperature of the air, its humidity, the radiant temperature of the sun, the ground, or buildings, the movement of air, and so on. Generally, however, when the skin temperature rises above 93 °F (34 °C) or

drops below 84 °F (29 °C) we begin to feel discomfort;[3] a moderately clothed individual in humid conditions who is not engaged in physical activity and who has a skin temperature of 85 °F (29.4 °C) is likely to feel comfortable, but in an arid area with low humidity his tolerance may be higher. These, however, are figures for skin temperatures and not for the environment; what has been termed the 'effective temperature', takes into consideration the combined factors of air temperature, humidity, and air movement in determining the limits for comfort. Experiments in equatorial regions have indicated that above an effective temperature of 79 °F (26 °C) some discomfort can be felt, and that human efficiency drops noticeably in higher temperatures.[4] Above 104 °F (40 °C) discomfort is experienced though much higher levels are endured by the Australian aborigines who adjust themselves to the heat by wearing virtually no clothes, building *wiltjas* or sideless shelters to provide shade, and remaining inactive in the hottest parts of the day.[5]

Clothing is, for many societies, the first defence against the weather, shedding the rain, keeping the feet dry, and affording insulation with layers of wool or fur. But in the African Sahel with daytime temperatures around 81 °F-85 °F (27 °C-29 °C) clothing is often minimal because contact with the skin causes discomfort and interferes with the process of sweating by which the body temperature is regulated. Where clothing is worn in the desert as it is by Bedouin peoples the white *burnous* reflects the rays of the sun and the looseness of the garment assists air circulation.[6] This would be an argument for the use of white tents, but as we have seen, tent strips woven of goat hair are left unwashed and unbleached so that the water-repelling natural oils remain within them. This property is considered to be more important than reflectivity.

Many factors influence the world's climates: the angle of the earth's axis to the sun, the direction and speed of its rotation, the irregular and unequal distribution of land masses and oceans, the differences of atmospheric pressure, the energy received from the temperature from solar radiation and that radiated

Australian aboriginal *wiltja*. An open-sided shelter through which the breeze passes easily, it is covered with paper-bark and scrap materials. Wet season camp, Mulyununuk, Arnhem Land Reserve, Northern Territory.

into the atmosphere, the types and density of vegetation, the patterns of precipitation, prevailing winds and ocean currents, among them. Though each region within each continent has its own complex climate, broad generalizations can be made, and some measure of agreement reached among climatologists as to the major climatic zones. These may be summarized as 'polar', including ice cap and tundra; 'cool', sub-arctic, or humid microthermal climates; 'temperate' or humid mesothermal and sub-tropical; 'dry' semi-arid steppe and desert; and 'tropical' savannah and tropical rain forest zones.[7] Each zone has a multitude of dwelling types that reflect these general as well as specific conditions but for our purposes one tropical region may serve to illustrate a few of the forms they have taken.

Theoretically, 'the Tropics' refers to the belt between the Tropic of Cancer, 23.50 °N. and the Tropic of Capricorn 23.50 °S., the limits of the overhead noonday sun. But for reasons such as those summarized above, the climatic tropics do not directly corres-

pond with this; they are more effectively defined by the 20 °C (approximately 70 °F) isotherms or mean annual temperature, north and south. This broad band embraces Central and most of South America, virtually all of Africa, part of the Middle East, the Indian sub-continent, Southern China, south-east Asia, and much of Australia.[8] Included within it are some of the most densely populated parts of the world and in the Amazon Basin, the Sahara, and the Australian desert, many of the least populated regions. The dry desert and semi-arid steppes, and the tropical savannah and rain forest regions largely fall within this belt, but for illustrative purposes I intend to discuss here some aspects of houses within the desert regions of the Middle and Near East.

In actuality the hot arid desert zones of the world lie mainly between 25 °N. and 15 °S. (though in Australia and the Namibian desert, 30 °S.). These areas are exposed to extreme conditions with 98 °F (38 °C) annual mean maximum day temperatures in the shade, rising in some instances to 113 °F (45 °C) and even more; night temperatures average 68 °F (20 °C), dropping as low as 50 °F (10 °C) in the cool months which, in the northern hemisphere are in December and January, and in the southern hemisphere, June

A *haush* or excavated shaft off which are dwelling units, stables, and stores. The haush acts as a 'thermal lung'. Matmata Berber, Tunisia.

approximately circular, sometimes more square in plan. A curving flight of rock-hewn steps or a ramped tunnel off which are stores and donkey stables, leads down from the desert surface to the bottom of the shaft. The haush usually has a cistern to one side and some have a well; cess-pits are also to be found, serving several families. Openings tunnelled into the haush walls open out to bottle-shaped, barrel-vaulted chambers. Often at two levels, the upper chambers are used as cereal stores. Further tunnels have sleeping recesses and niches to accommodate personal belongings. Inside, the room temperature is pleasant and though the desert sands become cold at night, within the chambers there is little fluctuation. As the sun passes over, the shading on the walls travels round the rough textured surface. The shaft acts as a 'thermal lung' exchanging warm air with cool air in the course of 24 hours. Sun-heated surfaces act as a heat-store slowly transmitting their warmth to the rooms within so that at night the interiors are kept at an ambient temperature. This principle, arrived at by excavation in Matmata is also the principle behind the courtyard house.[9]

Desert settlements tend to be clustered together and urban forms of compact housing are common throughout the Middle East, as well as in many parts of the dry savannah regions to the south of the Sahara. Muslim preference for domestic seclusion, particularly of the women, plays an important part in the organization of the villages and towns, but the climate exerts powerful constraints on building. Defence against solar radiation starts with the orientation of the building which is sited so as to expose as little as possible of its external surfaces to the intensity of the sun. This is particularly the case with the roof, which receives the highest levels of solar radiation and so should have the minimum surface commensurate with the necessary spans of the internal spaces. Flat roofs or shallow domes are usual, the former built in several layers of pole, mats, and palm fronds and covered with a thick dressing of compacted earth so that the heat gain is only slowly transferred to the interior. Dense, thick walls of stone and mud are invariably built, and houses are constructed

and July. Generally the humidity is low and rains are few, occurring in the space of a few weeks. Overhead the skies are bright and the solar radiation intense, though dust storms and haze often obscure the sun. There are hot seasonal winds but the climate is bearable because it is dry and sweat evaporates rapidly, and because men have developed house types that temper its effects.

In some areas where nomads move with their flocks other peoples are sedentary farmers: this is the case in the Matmata mountains of Tunisia, North Africa, where Bedouin tents are sited in a rough and scorched terrain that is dotted with depressions—the subterranean dwellings or *haush* of the Matmata Berber. Essentially, these are shafts some 35–50 feet (10–15 m) in diameter, excavated into the red sandstone and marl to a depth of 16–20 feet (5–6 m), sometimes close together, casting deep shadows over passage-ways and lanes, and on the walls of adjacent buildings. There are few openings in the outside walls, and the houses frequently face inwards to courtyards.

Courtyard houses have an ancient history: examples have been excavated at Kahun, Egypt, that are believed to be five thousand years old, while the Chaldean city of Ur, dating from before 2000 BC, comprised houses of this form. Essentially, the courtyard house, which consists of rooms on three or all sides of an open atrium, is associated with Arab culture, but its distribution extends between Salé and Marrakesh in Morocco to the west, and India to the east where the *haveli*, or atrium house, is common in the cities developed under Moghul influence such as Haridwar, Jaipur and Ahmedabad. Others are to be found as far south as Dar es Salaam and north in Bukhara, Russia.[10] Rural houses of the Egyptian *fellahin*, or of peasants in Central Iraq for example, reveal the basic forms of the courtyard plan: long, single-storeyed rooms on three sides of a yard, the fourth being closed by a wall as high as the buildings. Constructed of mud, the walls are thickest where they are exposed to the sun.[11]

Much attention has been given to the elaborate houses built around the *riad*, or garden court, of the wealthy merchants of Baghdad, for whom the most lavish forms were developed. But the *dar*, the paved court of the house of the working people, is not only more numerous but displays the essential elements of the courtyard type and its efficiency as a climatically appropriate building. To the visitor, the narrow and angled streets and alleys of the older quarters hide the houses beyond the blank brick and timber walls, only the decoration and scale of the upper-storey window bays, and the elaboration of the portals indicating the relative status of the occupants. Entry is gained through a heavy, carved door which opens on to a reception corridor. This turns through a right angle, concealing the courtyard beyond. A guest room off the entrance corridor is sited over a basement, the *sirab*, which is used as a summer room. Service rooms, a kitchen, and a large domed and vaulted living room also surround the open space. Opposite the guest room the courtyard flows into an *iwan*, or covered

Open courtyards, high, shading walls, flat roofs or shallow domes, and few exposed surfaces in relation to the volumes covered make these houses comfortable. El Oued, Touggourt, Algeria.

dining loggia. Columns support the *tarma*, a balcony room above used for light meals and sleeping, which sometimes has an additional *salon* which may overlook a street. Around the courtyard at the upper level runs a gallery with ornamental balustrade which acts as a communication between the stairs and the bedrooms. Often constructed with a timber-frame system these rooms are segregated on one side as quarters for the male members of the family, on the other as a *harem* for women and children.[12]

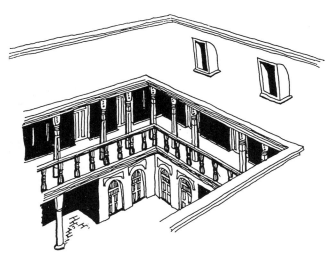

Diagram of a traditional Baghdad house, showing the covered loggia, or *iwan*, the balconies at first floor level around the central courtyard, and *badgirs* on the roof.

Rowshin or boxed lattice frames which project from the windows of old houses. Their lattices admit light while keeping the interiors private, shaded and cool. Jeddah, Saudi Arabia.

Baghdad houses are closely packed together presenting few surfaces to the outside. Facing the street at first-floor level the tarma may have a *shamashil*, a wooden boxed-screen over the window, supported on brackets and with a projecting, shading cornice. The degree of carved embellishment on *ursi* (sliding shutter) and shamashil, and elaboration of ceiling and wall surfaces with faience and mirrors in the building are an indication of the owner's prosperity, but they are also functional: the tiled surfaces are cooling and the carved decorations in bold relief add to the shade.[13]

Atrium houses with local variations are to be found in Arab and Persian communities throughout the Middle East; but their plans and space use may vary considerably. Some are single-storeyed, some are several storeys high, but in principle the atrium performs a climatically similar role. At midday the sun may reach the courtyard floor but the thickness of the walls and the adjacent buildings prevents excessive solar heating. Cool air in the rooms is drawn into the courtyard, and warming, begins to rise causing convection currents. Though these continue to circulate during the afternoon, the lower angle of the sun creates deep shadows. By the time the sun sets, the temperature drops rapidly and air currents circulate within the courtyard and filter through to the rooms, which remain cool until the following afternoon. As the warm courtyard floor and the flat roof radiate heat at night they are often used for sleeping in the summer, but in the winter shutters are closed and the storage effect of the walls is utilized to raise by re-radiation the internal temperatures of the rooms.[14]

MODIFYING CLIMATE

Because of the intense heat in the Middle East desert zone, devices that add to comfort are introduced in house design. Among these are the shamashil and the ursi mentioned above, which have geometric lattices designed to filter cool air into the house while minimizing the direct play of sunlight into the rooms and reducing glare. In Jeddah, Saudi Arabia, the *rowshin*

Mashrabiya or window lattice, made of hundreds of turned wooden pegs locked into each other and assembled in frames. Cairo, Egypt.

A *mashrabiya* seen from within, showing the large open surface and the decorative effects of the turned pegs. These disperse the light, the curved surfaces further diminishing glare.

box-frame equivalents of the Iraqi shamashil are of great variety and, projecting well beyond the wall surfaces, offer additional cooled spaces in which it is possible to sleep. In the simpler form the rowshin may be a framework with panel infills and windows, but without carving; elaborate forms may be richly detailed with projecting and decorated canopies and carved supporting brackets. Often they may be stacked on the facade in a complex assembly or *mashrabiya*. Additional screens, or *shish*, which in the poorer houses may be an alternative to rowshin, may be affixed over side wall windows, and 'magic eye' windows which open downwards and have openings that collect rising currents of air are also used. Jeddah houses tend to be high, with airshafts but without courtyards, and hence the use of rowshin is extremely important for the cooling of the buildings. In Egypt the *mashrabiya* is made from hundreds of small, turned wooden pegs assembled to make lace-like lattices whose decorative geometric patterns are enhanced against the external light, the repetition of small elements contributing to the reduction of glare. Balconies and carved or assembled lattice screens performing similar functions are to be found in countries widely dispersed in East Africa, South America and south-east Asia.[15]

Section through a *badgir*, or 'wind-scoop', showing how breezes are 'caught' and deflected down a ventilating shaft to cool lower rooms.

Wind-scoops take a variety of forms. The traditional *malqaf* channels cool air to ground floor rooms. Cairo, Egypt.

One of the most ingenious and widely-used climate modifiers is the wind-scoop, which collects breezes above roof level and transmits them to the living quarters. In common use from North Africa to Pakistan, wind-scoops take a variety of forms. Those in Hyderabad are of stretched fabric over a cruciform frame adjusted to deflect breeze down a ventilating shaft; a cover can be lowered to close off the shaft if there is too much dust or cold air admitted. On the evidence of papyrus drawings found in Egyptian tombs, wedge-shaped inclined scoops were used 3,500 years ago; today the roofscape of Old Cairo still reveals the use of a similar *malqaf* in numerous houses. Its equivalent, the *badgir* ('wind-catcher') of Iraq, Iran and the Gulf states, is often a more sophisticated structure. Of unknown date, but described as early as the fourteenth century, badgirs of immense proportions have been built on the roofs of some mosques and the houses of the wealthy. But they are used in more modest scale on the village houses of the general populace, whose dwellings are orientated to make the best use of shade for the summer room. The Iranian badgir is a tower with a row of tall slots, or vents, which admit the prevailing wind, generally from the north, and deflect it down the shaft. High pressure on the wind side and low pressure on the leeward side of the house ensure the movement of the air which is channelled to an opening at the bottom of the shaft. Though it is cooled by the side walls of the shaft the air may be warmer than the air within the room, but its movement assists the evaporation of perspiration on the skin surface, and hence the reduction of body temperature. Through-draught is effected by corridors into which the exhaust air is directed. To assist the cooling process, water vessels may be placed in the shaft at the opening into the room, or straw matting, soaked at intervals in water, may be hung over the vent opening to cool by evaporation, and trays of charcoal, wetted at intervals, may be placed at the bottom of the shaft for the same reason. Deflected into a basement, as in the Baghdad house, the draught from the badgir moves stale and humid air within the room, bringing down the night-time humidity which may reach 75 per cent, to a pleasant 35 per cent; a factor that seems to be more significant in terms of comfort than a reduction of the air temperature.[16]

Evaporative cooling is achieved in other ways: small pools in courtyard gardens both cool and humidify dry air passing over them, while mats of palm fronds, hung over windows and kept moist by intermittent soaking, can cool and humidify the air in the same way, with the additional advantage of filtering desert dust. The cleansing effect of sprays or fountains, which trap dust particles as well as cooling the air, is also considerable, but normally only the wealthier families can indulge in this luxury and fountains are seldom seen in ordinary dwellings. Trees, however, are important modifiers of climate and as well as providing shade are efficient in cleaning the air. Moisture in plants, shrubs and trees helps reduce air temperature by the process of evaporative cooling while the transpiration of the leaves also assists in lowering the temperature while increasing the humidity. Shade trees can substantially cool the air beneath them and trees near houses allow the heavier, cooler air to pass to the buildings while intercepting the hotter air at foliage level.[17]

In courtyard houses trees are therefore valued and, similarly, trees along a street add greatly to comfort conditions. That villagers in north India are well aware of this is evident from their careful planting of young saplings, their protection of them from cattle and goats with cylindrical, perforated walls of mud bricks, and of course their cultivation of them to produce fruit. Vines, likewise, provide both fruit and shade when trained over a trellis, pergola, or a window opening. When grown beside a house, as

An alternative type of wind-scoop to the *badgir* with its tower structure, is common in Oman. Water jars may be placed within to assist cooling by evaporation. Sohar, Batinah Coast.

they are frequently in Greece, Sicily, and other Mediterranean countries, they contribute to thermal regulation by reducing the radiant effect of stone walls, and by creating a cool space between foliage and wall surface. It should be added that in more temperate climates deciduous trees intercept the sun's rays in the summer and conveniently permit them to pass through the leafless branches in winter; in hot and dry countries evergreens are favoured precisely because they do not have this seasonable variability.[18]

Many measures that contribute to an improvement of comfort conditions in arid climates are even simpler than the planting of vegetation, and more immediate in their effect. Cross-ventilation is necessary to create a through passage of air; it is not sufficient to have one side of a loggia open if there is no means for the air to escape or be drawn through the space. In village homes openings are often to be seen in the wall which allow air to pass through and which are situated at levels where the draught is most convenient for occupants sitting or at rest. Such openings can be an inducement to thieves, even where there is

Trees provide shade, filter dust, and bear fruit. In this Indian village trees along the street are carefully protected from cattle. Saraisahara, Uttar Pradesh.

Whitewashed walls deflect the sun's rays and greatly reduce solar gain. Vines, trained near windows and doors, assist in cooling. Ibiza.

little to steal, so that 'hit and miss' brickwork, where bricks are omitted alternately or in successive courses, can have the same ventilating benefits but create openings that are too small for wayward hands; in many instances the technique has led to inventive decorative brickwork, which is also to be seen on parapet walls where roofs are used for sleeping.

One of the most widespread and economical techniques for arid climate modification is the coating of walls with a reflective surface. Ground chalk mixed with thin glue size (whiting) or a solution of quicklime and size (whitewash) painted over walls and roofs can have dramatic results in reflecting the sun's rays. Experiments were conducted in Khartoum on a mud layer roof 17 cm thick, and on an identical surface painted with several coats of whitewash. When the solar incidence reached a maximum of 131 °F (55 °C) and the air temperature was 92 °F (33 °C), it was found that the maximum surface temperature of the exposed mud roof reached 145 °F (63 °C). The effect of whitewashing on the internal temperature was to bring it down some 10 °C.[19] This accounts for the habitual whitewashing of walls in the valley towns of

the Mzab, or in the Greek island villages where the practice at times seems obsessional, but which, by frequent overpainting increases the density of the reflective area and contributes to its efficiency.

DWELLINGS AND DISASTERS

Even if many of the effects of climate extremes upon houses can be substantially reduced by building form, details, and modifications, there are some which are difficult to control. In differing circumstances damp may penetrate from outside the walls, or rise from the foundations, walls may be prone to condensation, timbers may rot or decay over time. Some of these problems have to be endured; others may be overcome with skills which may be introduced from other cultures: trenching around walls to inhibit creeping of moisture, laying of damp proof courses of slate slabs, protecting the exposed ends of timber joists. Remedial actions can be taken when necessary, such as the replacement of weak and broken timbers, or the repair of mud walls which have been cracked from the strains of expansion and contraction caused by high diurnal range and extremes of humidity. Many of these conditions are recurrent and dealing with them becomes a part of the annual cycle of work: elephant grass is stored for thatching in the African Sahel after short seasonal rains have brought about the almost inevitable collapse of the cover; stone rollers are kept on flat mud roofs in Turkey or Afghanistan so that weaknesses and cracks may be rolled out. These problems the indigenous builders has learned to accept; their periodic occurrence is anticipated and there are measures that he can take to deal with the inconvenience or damage caused.

But disasters are another matter. Drought, such as the Horn of Africa experienced in the mid-1980s, causes great hardship, starvation, and considerable loss of life. But it does not seriously harm buildings, though long term drought may affect the resources such as grasses which might be used for their repair, and it saps the energies of those who would build or maintain them. Floods are far more devastating, especially those that occur as a result of the movement of tropical cyclones (typhoons or hurricanes) over the sea and towards land. Atmospheric pressure drops as a storm gathers, causing the sea to rise, while the wind draws up the waves still further to cause penetrating inundation of low-lying lands. Torrential rains which accompany hurricanes can have other devastating effects, saturating the soil on hill-slopes which have been deforested and cleared for farming, swelling rivers that flow to the flood plains where the alluvial soils make them attractive to the poor farmers, and creating immense mudslides.[20] Though the deaths from the inflow of high seas are relatively

In damp climates plastering over stone walls can cut moisture penetration through joints, and exposed beam ends of a jettied storey may be covered, as here with slates, to lower the risk of rot. Brantôme, France.

few, 8,000 people were killed and over 140,000 rendered homeless when Hurricane Fifi struck the Choloma district of Honduras in September 1974. Damage to housing alone was estimated at $30 million. Gigantic mudslides set in motion by the rains loosening the soil contributed substantially to the loss of life and homes, as structures were destabilized or submerged in liquid mud and torn apart by the winds. Hurricanes may reach speeds of 300 k.p.h. at the 'eye' of the cyclone and tropical cyclones cause damage to buildings by virtually exploding them: the increased loads of the wind speed on one side of the building create low-pressure areas on the side and opposite walls, the roof rips off, and the suction pulls the building asunder. In areas where buildings are of light frames, fatalities from the damage to buildings may not be high though flying debris can maim and kill. In some instances devastation and loss of life on an almost unimaginable scale have occurred as a result of cyclone, like the terrible 'storm surge' that devastated the Chittagong region of East Pakistan in 1970 by inundating the islands and the vast delta of

Stone houses, such as these, reduced to rubble by an earthquake in 1968, are vulnerable because they have little elasticity. Falling masonry caused many casualties. Gibellini, Sicily.

the Ganges river; half a million people died and untold numbers of homes were destroyed. The inactivity of the government of West Pakistan in providing relief precipitated a civil war which ultimately led to the establishment of the independent state of Bangladesh.[21]

Some regions are notoriously subject to disasters: Kingston, Jamaica, for example, or Manila in the Philippines, which are prone to hurricanes, floods, and earthquakes. Earthquakes are not hazards that can be directly attributable to climate, but as environmental catastrophes they can cause immense damage and casualties. Like most other cataclysms, earthquakes occur largely, though not wholly, in the tropical zones, their incidence primarily related to the periphery of the continental plates. Movement of the plates builds up massive pressures which are released through earthquakes, often along fault lines on the earth's crust. But seismic hazards are unpredictable and such methods as there are of ascertaining the potential danger spots and predicting the possible time that a new disaster may occur are unreliable. Moreover, earthquake shocks may be felt at irregular

distances from the epicentres and the transmission of seismic shocks through the mantle is affected by geological factors that may be highly localized, often resulting in tremors being felt from different directions. Buildings that may shake, but remain standing when struck by shocks in one direction, are likely to collapse when multiple movement is experienced, as walls are pulled apart and roofs cave in. Casualties from disintegrating masonry and collapsing mud and adobe walls are likely to be high, exacerbated by the falling of roof timbers and mud layers, while the self-same stone rollers used on roofs to smooth out and seal cracks become instruments of death in earthquakes.[22]

Fatalities can be on appalling scale: in the 1970 earthquake at Chimbote, Peru, 50,000 people were killed, four-fifths in the landslide that engulfed the town of Yngay, half a million were rendered homeless and 100,000 houses were destroyed; precise figures for the 1976 earthquake in Tangshen, China, are unknown but it is believed that 650,000 people died and the number of houses demolished ran to millions.[23] It is the poor who suffer most from the effects of floods, windstorms, and earthquakes; theirs are the houses that are likely to be built on the least stable ground, like the ravine and hill-slope dwellers affected by the 1976 Guatemalan earthquake; they are the cultivators of the low-lying lands prone to inundation by the *tsunami*, the terrible ocean waves travelling at hundreds of miles an hour and rising to thirty metres in height, that are generated by earthquakes in the Pacific.[24]

People who are obliged for economic reasons to build on unstabilized land, or whose houses are built of earth, stone, and timber which are notoriously dangerous in disasters, might be expected to have developed structures which were resistant to such cataclysms. In the face of high winds many dwellings in south-east Asia and other hot-humid tropical regions can afford at least some protection. Roofs are built at pitches steep enough to deflect prevailing winds without their behaving, through too shallow a pitch, as aerofoils that lift off in a gale. Light frames of bamboo and roofs of palm leaves are not essentially

Homes of *campesino* ravine dwellers which were swept away by landslides in the 1976 earthquake. Over 2,000 people died. Guatemala City.

dangerous, though typhoons may tear down palm trees and rip leaf cover to shreds, greatly limiting the materials available for rebuilding. With the resources available to them and in conditions as unpredictable as earthquakes, builders in stone and adobe have not been able to develop earthquake-resistant structures; timber frames are safer if well-jointed, though wall infill is still likely to collapse.

Against the annually recurrent rigours of the tropical climate most building techniques are a defence but earthquakes are likely to recur at intervals of between fifty and a hundred years, often not in any one person's lifetime. To the indigenous house dweller, concerned as he may be with the more immediate risk of crop failure or declining job opportunities, unpredictable 'acts of God' are of such a magnitude and often of such a rarity that they cannot enter his reckoning; for him it is far more important and more realistic to get on with the daily business of living in the dwelling; problems that are beyond his powers are 'as Allah wills'.[25]

7.

LIVING SPACES

That a great many dwelling types that were built for living in also succeeded in being good to look upon, may well be the outcome of their clarity of form and directness of purpose. This, at any rate, was one argument for functionalism in modern architectural design.[1] But what is good to look upon is still within the eye of the beholder, and what satisfied the criteria of being good to live in may only be known to the occupier. Modernist architects were contemptuous of suburban housing, and had little interest in the ordinary dwellings of Western Europe, the United States or elsewhere in the industrialized 'west'—a term loose enough to embrace Australasia—when they developed their functionalist theories.[2]

Yet the chances are that the majority of readers of this book live in just such houses and, preferring their use to their uniformity, still find many good to look upon. This kind of house, in very general terms, might well be on two, or perhaps three storeys, with 'living' space on the ground floor comprising a hall, a parlour or living room, a dining room or dining area and a kitchen; on the floor or floors above are to be found the bedrooms of parents and children, bathroom and water closet. Even when we have a 'bungalow' or 'ranch-house' style single-storey dwelling, it is likely to have similar spaces. Though the form of the dwelling may differ in a great many other ways—as row or terrace, semi-detached or detached houses and, according to our economic status, may have from two to four or five bedrooms, with additional utility room and toilet—our expectations of the kinds of space they offer and the relationships of these spaces to each other, are broadly similar. It is easy for us to consider this to be the norm, and to regard all other kinds of dwelling as either meeting or failing to meet

these 'standards'. But each culture has different expectations of its dwellings, and makes demands on them which are related to its social structure and to the ways in which its members organize their daily lives. So the internal plans of dwellings and their space use can be indicative of dissimilar value systems. A single-celled dwelling with no internal partitions to differentiate its spaces and their use may seem, from the perspective of the western suburban house, to be a materially impoverished one. Yet the quality of a dwelling is probably best considered in terms of the environmental conditions and cultural requirements that it meets.

DEFINING SPACES

Waitabu is a village on the tiny island of Taveuni in the Fiji group, which shares the typical Melanesian hot-humid climate. Rainfall is moderate but Fiji is subject to tropical cyclones which sometimes reach hurricane force. For this reason traditional houses have steeply-pitched roofs which deflect the winds— if the roof *is* lifted off in a hurricane it is customary for the family to take refuge under it wherever it falls until the storm is over. Taveuni has a subsistence economy and there is no money exchanged in Waitabu—wealth is measured in whales' teeth which are also used for gifts. Consequently, community labour is by obligation—Tuesday is set aside for work within the village. When a new *vale*, or dwelling is needed it is built by the young men of the *tokatoka* or lineage group, assisted sometimes by other members of their *metaqali*, the larger exogamous kin group. A raised *yavu*, or dwelling site is traditional to a family and remains its sole property. Here are inserted the corner posts on which rest the wall plates, to form a box frame. On this are raised the principal rafters and the ridge pole, significantly called the 'rat scrambler'. Vertical bamboo splines bound with coir to horizontal bundles of reeds, line the inside walls, which have an outside layer of woven coconut fronds. Bush vines are used to lash the members but interior exposed fixings are decorative and elaborately lashed with sennit. Recent houses tend to have lower-pitched roofs and corrugated iron is replacing palm and other forms of thatch: more durable, but potentially lethal in a hurricane.[3]

The main entrance in the gable wall facing the sea opens onto the interior space which is notionally divided into four zones, two more public, two private in the long dimension. First of these is the female area, formerly used for cooking, but now closest to the kitchen which is situated on the fringe of the village. Beyond this is the men's section, of somewhat higher status, where the household head sits at the top right, with any guest opposite him. The pandanus eating-mat spans both areas when the customary meal of taro, vegetable, and fish is consumed, but each sex keeps to its zone. Beyond, there is a change of level, marked by a plinth and by entrance doors on either side and seldom used except by the family head and special guests. The front zone of this higher level is a private area where chiefs and honoured guests may be received with appropriate ceremonial. At the back is the *loqi*, the totally private zone where the members of the family sleep and household effects are kept.

The people of Taveuni are staunch Wesleyan Methodists and many villages have a church. Nevertheless fear of magic is real. Formerly a fire was kept burning in the vale to keep away malignant spirits and witchcraft. The fire also indicated that a household was in residence and the vale well looked after, and had the additional advantage of hardening the thatch and to some extent repelling insects. With the moving of the kitchens—from within the house to the edge of the village—under missionary influence, kerosene lamps are now used to meet some of these problems and exorcism is called upon to repel evil spirits.[4]

Spatially the house was divided by custom in ways

Completed and thatched *vale*. The off-centre doorway recalls an earlier type when central poles supported the ridge.

Vale interior showing headman's plinth and *loqi* or private area beyond. Note elaborate lashings and locally-made fabrics. (*Pitt Rivers Museum, Oxford*)

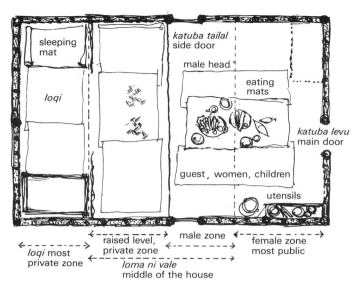

Spatial differentiation within the Waitubu, Taveuni (Fiji) *vale* or dwelling. In former times the hearth was close to the door in the female area.

that are commonly found, differentiating the area occupied by the men from that occupied by the women and children, giving a place of importance to the household head. When spaces are differentiated within the dwelling there are alternative ways of defining them. Subdivision of a circular hut, though not infrequent, can create rather inconvenient and often unventilated spaces; the alternative, common in much of Africa, is to build huts for particular functions within a defined compound. Each unit is in effect a room, and the whole compound constitutes the dwelling. This is the case with the Tswana of Botswana, for an instance among many.[5] The Tswana dwelling may comprise three or four huts within a yard which is bound by a hedge of rubber plants or poles. Within this is a carefully maintained and swept area of beaten earth, *lolwapa* (lelapa), with its opening facing the main entrance to the yard. It acts as a forecourt where guests may be received; an apron to the main sleeping hut whose entrance faces it. Other huts may also open on to the lolwapa or be dispersed within the yard.

Tswana huts are circular in plan and built of mud, often of wet brick, raised by the women in layers that are sometimes reinforced at intervals with poles. A

Coir string, widely used as a binding material, is made from coconut husk fibres. Here it is being twisted by a Swahili craftsman. (*AMCAS*)

ring of fifteen or so forked poles encircles the hut to take a circle of beams on which are rested and lashed with bark string the converging rafters of the conical roof, over this the battens and grass thatch is laid. As the wall is not load-bearing a space between the wall and the roof gives ventilation. The outside walls may be lightly decorated with finger markings in the mud plaster and painted in earth browns, red, or light orange, perhaps with an upper band of white. Inside, the hut may also be painted and the floor may have a

Huts, shade tree, and *lolwapa* of a Tswana homestead.

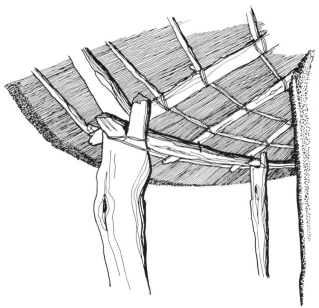

Diagram showing the ring of forked posts taking the roof structure in the Tswana dwelling.

mud plaster finish topped with cow dung and polished as a hardening layer.

The main hut may be occupied by the parents, or, if the husband is working in South Africa, by the mother with her young children. Older children or unmarried daughters may sleep in other huts which can be built as the need arises. Absentee sons may also build a hut within the yard, frequently favouring a modern style with rectangular plan and hipped roof, covered with corrugated sheeting. Also in the yard an open kitchen is usually to be found, with nearby storage spaces for spare building materials, grass, feed, chicken pens, a small kraal for calves, a vegetable plot, and perhaps a covered granary with deeply-shaded eaves. Any trees are retained for their shade.[6] Additional structures in the compound may include a pit latrine within a wooden shelter, a fenced ablutions area for older women and daughters, and sometimes a shelter for beer-making and selling, or for some other modest enterprise. Not all the family may reside at home; sons and grandsons may be at the cattle post or in the huts at the family fields where sorghum and maize are grown.

Inside, the huts are furnished with wooden beds, a platform for storing sorghum sacks, wooden or cardboard boxes for additional items, a shelf or two for the cups, buckets, pottery or plastic bowls that make

up the domestic utensils and, if they can afford them, a table, one or two chairs, and even a small wardrobe.

Maintaining the house requires repainting once or twice a year, frequent resurfacing of the floors with cow dung and polish, repair of erosion cracks in the mud walls, and every few years, replacement of the thatch, jobs that are undertaken in the quiet period after the gathering of the harvest.[7] They are the responsibility of the wife, who swiftly invites censure from other women if the huts and lolwapa are not kept in good repair.

Though the compound system of individual units dispersed within a defined open space is extremely flexible, the majority of peoples prefer 'living under one roof', an indication perhaps, of close familial relationships and mutual dependence. For instance, in the verdant green, undulating but rough landscapes of Ireland the houses lie low beneath their thatched roofs. The poorest and simplest houses have only two rooms, but three or more ranged in line are common. Varying in depth from as narrow as ten feet to twice that, the houses are rectangular in plan, with the kitchen and hearth both physically and symbolically

Traditional Irish farmhouse. The kitchen at the centre with the principal door opening on to it; the parlour to the right.

Interior perspective of an Irish farmhouse showing fireplace with beam supporting a projected hood, 'scroop', and an outshut extension with bed space close to the hearth.

at the centre. The broad hearth is set in a transverse wall, often with a smoke canopy in the form of a truncated pyramid made of wattles built above it. The front plane of the canopy may rest on the brace-tree, a cross beam which runs from the back wall to a wattle-and-daub 'jamb-wall' or *scroop* set at right angles to the fire, giving protection from draughts coming from the front entrance, and providing a back support to the bed settle.[8] A small peep-hole was cut into the jamb-wall, so that incoming visitors could be observed. In some regions of the north-west of Ireland an 'outshut' extension under a sloping roof which could take a bed was added to give greater width, which permitted sleeping within reach of the warmth of the open turf fire.[9]

Behind the cross wall of the hearth a door led to 'the room' or parlour, considered to be 'above' the kitchen, generally placed to the west of the building. This was little used in practice; like many parlours and salons it was primarily for 'best', for Christmas and other special occasions, and for laying out the dead. Recently, many parlours have been partitioned off to make a second bedroom. Once the old habit of sleeping by the fire and on the bed settle had given

way to the use of conventional beds the room 'below' the kitchen—generally on the left of the principal entrance—was used as a bedroom or, divided in two as most are in the Ulster farmhouses today, and used as a store or 'larder' at the rear and a small bedroom at the front.

Over the years most houses have had additions, including a porch to keep out the draughts at the front of the house, and a stable or a byre, and sometimes both, each under its own roof extension, built against the end gable. Often a house built in turf or clay would have a stone extension, or in recent years, one of concrete block under a corrugated iron roof. The spaces were therefore differentiated by both subdivision and addition, or sometimes by alteration, with the closing in of part of the roof space with a ceiling to make a roof in the half-loft above. Today the heart of the house and the focus of all its life is still the kitchen. Any tables are small and placed against the wall, often beneath a window or even, as a 'falling table' folded up against the wall. The middle

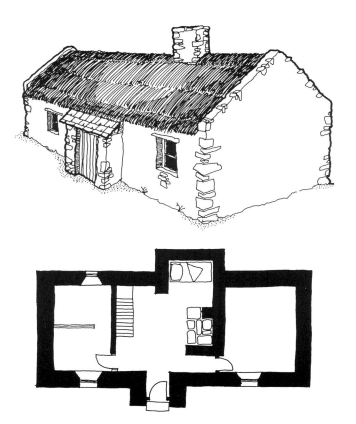

Kampung (village) house in Pahang State, Malaysia, showing the traditional construction, with *atap* (palm) thatch roof and bark panels. The main structure is the *ibu ramah*. The *ruang tetamu* or social space is to the right.

Perspective and plan of an Irish farmhouse. The room 'below' the kitchen is divided to provide extra sleeping space.

space of the room is left clear of chairs until they are needed. This allows the housewife free movement to and from the hearth, and also permits easy access when the family gathers for evening *ceilis* or song and storytelling sessions. The kitchen and its furnishings are the woman's domain, scrubbed, swept, and polished as evidence of her caring.

Opposite the fireplace was customarily situated the dresser with its display of glittering china, cups, and ceramics. When the stairs to a half-loft were installed against the down-side partitions,[10] the dresser would be placed against it, still opposite the hearth, sometimes providing additional support for the half-loft floor; or it might be placed next to the box bed, on the same wall. Traditionally the butter churn was placed beside the hearth and the 'boles' recessed in the wall beside the fireplace for the safe-keeping of personal articles: knitting for the women on the left of the hearth, pipes of the men on the right. A huge pot

for hot water is always over the fire for washing up the china for the succession of meals and teas; often it hangs from a chimney crane suspended so that when swung out it follows the arc of the sun. New houses are built only when marriage makes them necessary; inheritance confirms the continuity of the buildings which are, in many cases, centuries old.[11]

In contrast with the slow accretions of the Ulster farmhouse, the dwellings of the jungle regions of the West Malaysia peninsula are in a continuous state of evolution and alteration, as new sections are added to meet changing family needs. Traditionally the Malay house was a timber-framed structure which, in the older examples, was often made of teak; other woods such as *chengul*, which is resistant to termites, or bamboos have been employed as teak has become more scarce and expensive. Raised on piers which rested on blocks of stone or hardwood, the house consisted of several elements linked together in various arrangements. The basic unit was the *ibu ramah* (literally, mother house) with a steeply-pitched roof thatched with *atap*, or palm leaf. The floors and walls were of split bamboo in woven panels, sometimes stained and oiled to bring out the pattern of the

Interior of the *ibu dapor* or kitchen of a Malay house. Utensils and stores line the walls, but the room has no furniture.

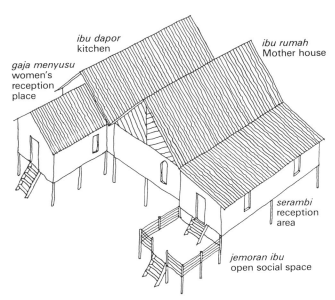

The process of developing the Malay house. Further living spaces may be added to the *ibu ramah*, their status marked by variations in level. A diversity of configurations is possible.

weave; corrugated iron sheeting and timber plank walls have largely replaced the traditional materials. More resistant to the monsoon rains they have often meant a considerable loss of internal comfort conditions, where temperatures with a marginal diurnal range averaged 82 °F (25 °C) and with humidity of 80 per cent. The ibu ramah is the main sleeping space for the parents, the unmarried daughters sleeping beyond a screened partition or in the attic which was ventilated by the gable ends. Off the ibu ramah and slightly below it and beneath broad eaves, is the *serambi*, or partially open platform with a lean-to roof which acts as a reception area for guests, a place for feasts and prayers, and a sleeping area for the male children. When it is walled in to become part of the living space, a further *ruang tetamu*, or railed entrance platform and social space might be added. On the other side of the house and at a lower level the *ibu dapor* or kitchen platform was built off the ibu ramah; covered by a lean-to roof it was known as the *pisang sa-sikat* (literally, 'bunch of bananas'), or when it was attached to the gable end, as the 'suckling elephant' (*gajah menyusu*). Other lean-to or pitched roof elements might be added over the years, and there is considerable variety in the combinations used.[12]

Young couples are not obliged to live near the parents of either side but, with the inducement of land on which to build, and help with the materials, most would settle close to one or other. Most households consist of the nuclear family (parents and children) but two or three households commonly live near to each other; even more if they are cultivating rice.

Though the Malays are Muslim they retain many practices and beliefs of their former animist religion, including the propitiation of the spirits of earth, water, and jungle into which the *kampung* (village) and the house intrude.[13] A *pawang* (magician) would build a ritual hut and perform rites to drive off malignant spirits when new ground was being cleared for building. When the first pillar was positioned on the south side of the house, offerings of iron, copper, and hardwoods were placed in the hole; the 'Soul of the House' or house spirit would reside there.[14] Raised, as it was, above the ground and situated in a defensive clearing, the house was separated from the dangerous spirits of the jungle. Even so, charms and spirit traps were hung round the building as further protection from their power.

A recent kampung house with boarded walls, partly roofed in sheet metal. A skeletal *ruang tetamu* leads to another extension, while a vehicle store has been added to the left.

SPATIAL RELATIONSHIPS

Adaptable and extensible single-storey or split-level houses can be economical to build, being added to when resources permit, provided that sufficient land is available. Yet houses of more than one storey have a number of advantages: where agricultural land is scarce they consume less of it; where timber for roofs is limited in quantity, length or strength, they require a smaller external surface to protect the house. There are fewer external walls relative to the number of rooms through which to lose heat, and upper-level rooms can benefit from any breezes. But these advantages may be offset by the greater technical problems involved in their construction, often requiring the assistance of specialists, while more floors require more internal timber to span rooms. Status and fashion play their part; tall buildings are often esteemed merely for their scale and are sometimes built high in a spirit of competition with other builders and fami-

lies. As is so often the case in the dwellings of the world each culture develops a trade-off of benefits against costs.

Kütahya province in western Anatolia, Turkey, is a hilly, and in some parts mountainous region, relatively well-watered, and with extensive forest cover which supports several hundred villages of peasant farmers. In this region the dominant house type is of two storeys under a pitched and tiled roof. Rather roughly made, the walls have either timber frames with adobe or stone infill, or the lath-and-plaster construction of Iraqi origin still known as *bagdadi*. The living space is on the first floor; below is the stable for wintering the cattle whose body heat helps keep the rooms above warm, and storage rooms. A broad ladder leads to the centrally located *salon*, a large communal space, with a balcony open to the weather at one end. Used as a reception area for special guests (casual visitors are often not invited even into the ground floor), it is also the place where shoes are left, grain sacks are stored, hand tools are kept, food is prepared, and often, much of the cooking is done. The salon has rooms on either side, each taking a corner of

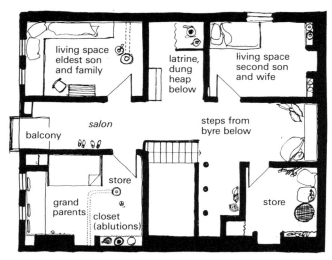

The basic Western Anatolian house plan with central *salon* and corner rooms over stores and byre.

the building; a transverse corridor extension of the salon has a storage closet at one end and a *garderobe* toilet closet at the other.[15] The toilet is as private as possible; no doors open on to the corridor in which it is situated. Excreta falls to the animal dung heap below; the mixture is considered to be excellent and inoffensive manure.

In this officially secular state the people are devoted Muslims with an 'extended family' structure. In one room lives the patriarch and his wife; his eldest son, his wife and children in another; perhaps a second son and family may occupy another, or if too young for marriage the sons and daughters sleep separately in other rooms. What appears on first sight to be a large house has often more than a score of occupants. Privacy is valued and the doors close on the rooms of each family, and are so arranged that no door overlooks the doorway of another family room.

Village houses are built where possible on a south-facing slope, for though it is hot in summer the winters can be bitterly cold. They are situated so that no windows overlook those of another house, and there are none in the backs of the buildings. Beneath the windows on two sides of each living space runs a wooden box-couch where the men sit and sleep; women and children sit on the linoleum-covered floor where the whole family takes its meals. In one wall is a central fireplace and flue, flanked on either side by a recess covered with curtains or doors. One is used

for storage of bedding, the other for ablutions. A few houses may have iron beds and an iron stove may replace the fire in the rooms but other furniture is minimal, save for a lavish, plastic-veneered, glass-fronted buffet, the modern equivalent of the dowry chest in which family treasures and souvenirs are kept.

The pattern of life is unchanging though its timing is influenced by weather, resources, and prices at the market. With the spring the family may make essential repairs to their dwelling, even to dismantle a substantial part, or all, of the structure to rebuild it. Building skills are expected in everyone, even if some villages are noted for the quality of their timber framing. As in many extended family systems where the sons bring their wives and raise their families under the same roof as their parents, the region has a system of partible inheritance; the property being shared among the sons on the death of the family head, and the fields being similarly divided. It is a system which over the generations leads to decreasing farm units and necessitates the purchase of more land, but which means that the property stays within the family.[16]

Western Anatolian houses of the Kütahya type are spatially differentiated laterally through the depth of the building, longitudinally through their width, and vertically through two floors and the loft space. As two-storeyed buildings they are not exceptional and in a few parts of Turkey, in particular the well-known conservation village of Safranbolu, some houses are three storeys in height. But this *is* unusual: only 1 per cent of Turkey's rural houses are of three storeys or more; of the rural houses as a whole six in ten are on one floor. Statistics are lacking but it is very likely that this is lower than the world averages; single-storeyed dwellings probably represent over 70 per cent of the total.

Given space, there are ways in which even larger populations than the extended family can be accommodated under one roof: the longhouse is one. Distributed discontinuously through south-east Asia, from Miri in Assam through Malaysia and Indonesia, what is generally termed the 'longhouse' is a community dwelling type of impressive proportions. It shares

Part of the village of Eski (old) Muhipler, Kütahya Province.
House with ground floor stable and stores, and living spaces on
either side of a central *salon* above. Women gather at the well;
electricity has been brought to the village.

little but the classificatory name with the longhouse
of England and Wales. Asian longhouses are not only
much wider but are also of far greater length. Structures that are over 300 feet (100 m) are common; some
have been recorded that are over 1000 feet in length.
They find their highest concentrations among the
diverse peoples of Borneo and Sarawak, though in
some areas they have all but disappeared. Longhouses
of earlier times were massively built, some raised on
ironwood piers that weighed up to three tons each.
But there are many regional and local types, from the
umu of the Kenyah of Borneo which was constructed
with a stepped succession of roofs, or that of the
mountain-dwelling Kelabit, whose longhouse is not

Interior of a family room in a farmer's house, Eski Muhipler. An
'ottoman' runs beneath the windows; an iron bed stands in one
corner. Meals are taken on the floor.

Section of a Sarawak Dyak longhouse raised on stilts. Bamboo walkways link with other sections, the whole long-house accommodating 160 families. Benuk Sega, near Kuching.

divided, the many families living in noisy contiguity within a single space.[17] Such variants are indicators of social and cultural distinctions between the various peoples and are a reminder that in all examples cited in this book there are types and sub-types with specific characteristics that reflect small, but in local terms, significant, differences between broadly-related peoples and communities within a culture area. Most numerous of the peoples of Sarawak are the Sea Dyaks who number in excess of quarter of a million. Formerly they were ocean-going, but the Sea Dyaks, notably the Iban of the central Third Division, are mainly river-dwelling, using their boats for communications. Cultivators of wet and dry *padi* (rice) the Iban also grow rubber, and many collect and sell rattan or other jungle products.

An Iban village will normally consist of two or three longhouses ranged along the river. Whether a longhouse is constructed of timber or bamboo, or whether the boards that form the walls are slats or of sawn wood, the Iban longhouse takes a consistent form. Raised on piers with its main supports raising to the ridge which may be 24 feet (7 m) above the

sadau loft, used for storing padi

dapor detached kitchen

bilek family living space, with sleeping mats, storage jars

tempuan through passage

rusi common work and social space

pantai sleeping space for guests

tanju outdoor platform, used for drying padi, woven cloths. Pigs and fowl below

An Iban (Sea Dyak) longhouse, Sarawak, with the end wall removed to show the relationship of an internal living space or *bilek*, to the communal spaces.

ground, the structure consists of a platform with a long pitched roof over differentiated spaces. Through the centre of the longhouse, with one edge beneath the ridge, is the *tempuan*, a broad passage which runs the whole length of the building. Apart from being the principal circulation corridor it is used by the women for pounding padi with poles and mortars. Off the tempuan on one side are the living spaces or apartments, each *bilek* with its own door opening on to the corridor, lined with sleeping mats and large jars. A notched log ladder leads to the *sadau* or loft storage area above, where the padi is kept in large baskets, spare mats and containers are rolled, and hunting equipment is stored. It may also be used as a sleeping place for the young girls. Behind the bilek is the *dapor*, or kitchen, which may be attached or be under a separate roof. Because of the risk of fire the dapor is sometimes to be found detached from the main dwelling spaces, but still on the raised platform. Opposite the apartments and across the tempuan is the *ruai*, a broad boarded work space, where looms are set up for weaving of the intricately patterned and dyed *pua* cotton cloth; here too, mats, fish traps, and rattan containers are made. It is also used for ritual dances and the playing of the gong sets at night as

well as for meeting and conversation. At the outer edge and under the eaves of the covered part of the structure is the *pantai* where guests and the young unmarried men retire. The pantai opens at many points on to a broad verandah, the *tanju*, which is used for drying padi, and where the whole longhouse community gathers in the cool of the evening. Rain occurs in the afternoons of most days—an annual rainfall of 150 inches is common and daytime temperatures are high.[18]

Membership of the longhouse community implies the meeting of many social obligations, acceptance of the rule of the *tuai rumah*, the headman, recognition and respect for the rights of others, and appropriate usage of the internal and external spaces. It also means observing the correct rites as decreed by the ritual head of the longhouse, the *tuai burong*, the 'bird elder'. To the Iban certain birds are incarnations of gods. When seen they are believed to be giving warnings or counsel and it is the role of the tuai burong to interpret them and other auguries of the success of every activity, including the building of a new longhouse. From the cries of the *nendak* bird he decides whether a selected site is auspicious. As the moon is waxing, women beat gongs and other lineage members repel evil spirits with omen sticks. In the centre of the site the hole for the first housepost is given offerings of river stone and the blood of a cock,

Interior of a typical longhouse showing the *bileks,* or living apartments, off the *tempuan* main passage. Stores, equipment, and utensils are kept above; outboard motors lean against house posts.

and with further ritual objects attached to it the house post is raised: parallels with Malay practice are clear. Other posts are similarly ritually sited and as each bilek-family continues to construct and clad its section of the longhouse it must observe other rituals and prohibitions. When the time comes for occupation, offerings, sacrifices, and the consumption of specially-cooked rice must be performed to ensure ritual security for the community in the future.[19]

Though it is likely that in the past, all the occupants of one longhouse were members of the same clan or lineage, it is possible now for members of others families to join a longhouse, or to leave one as they will, subject to the agreement of the tuai rumah. If a family wishes to move it is required to leave the main structural members, but cladding materials, including roof covering may be removed for use in another structure. A young family may set up and wish to be independent while remaining in the longhouse. Additional living quarters may be built at the end, increasing the length by a bay, or the width of an apartment. This also requires additions to the tempuan, verandah, and other balancing elements, and the moving of the access ladder at the end of the building. Beneath the longhouse the space between the pillars is used for pig pens, for keeping fowls, and for threshing padi. Iban longhouses are therefore spatially differentiated along the length of the building on one side by apartments, in depth by functions, and vertically by making spaces above and below accessory to the living level.

FAMILY HOMES

These few examples of spatial organization could be the first sketch for a basic taxonomy of house plan types. If it were to be developed the immense variety of plans within vernacular and indigenous buildings would become apparent. Such a typology might also reveal important aspects of spatial articulation, from the significance of entry and departure points, to the movement between—and turning of spaces through the placement of—doors, corridors and stairs.

Considered in their sections, the relative importance placed on volume and vertical dimensions would also be evident. Such an exercise would be formally interesting and revealing of the complexity of spatial disposition and integration within buildings, when compared with space use. Utilization of spaces in dwellings throughout the world has many aspects in common. Sometimes the spaces occur within a single volume, sometimes, as we have seen, differentiated with walls, screens, curtains, or changes of level and surface. Some societies demand less of their houses, some require more: rooms for bathing or excretion, lobbies or halls in which to receive visitors, private spaces in which to work or public ones in which to conduct a trade, special rooms for ceremonials or prayer.

A typology of dwellings that compared built forms only, and which identified spaces according to designations within the structure could well overlook the spillover of uses into external space. Flat roofs, for example, are used for drying fruit, for airing the domestic washing, clothes and bedding, for sleeping, or even for movement from one dwelling to the next. It might similarly ignore the claims made on external ground by some societies for space uses which, among others, are found within the building—particularly the outdoor hearths and cooking facilities, the separate structures for stores and granaries, the yards used for sleeping on hot and sultry nights, the use of fields and bush in lieu of latrines, the drawing of water from a well, fountain or standpipe, and much else.

In fact, the dwelling is not isolated from its surroundings but is a constituent part of its environment, sometimes territorially determined by walls, hedges or thickets, sometimes by the sweeping or maintenance of adjacent space considered by the occupants to be part of its domain, or simply as acknowledged by custom. How societies regard their relationship to external space is often a measure of the importance that they place on privacy. For many the threshold marks the limits beyond which the visitor may enter only by invitation; for some there is a transitional zone between the public and private

The family of an Agra rickshaw man in their small, one-roomed *bustee* home. *Charpoy* string bed at right, another stowed beneath it. Recesses take cooking vessels and a sewing machine. Agra, India.

spaces, for others relatively free movement between and within spaces is acceptable, though it may change at different times of the day or night, or freedom of access may be permitted only to a specific sex, age group, or members of the same lineage.

Internal and external space relationships when considered in the context of use are indicative, therefore, of much more than the functions to which the spaces are put. As we have seen in the examples cited not only in this chapter but elsewhere in this book, the ways in which dwellings are organized and used, and the forms and plan types which they assume, are expressive of the specific cultures which have developed them and whose life-ways they accommodate and serve.

In many societies much of the domestic life takes place outside the house. Ashanti women care for their children while making pots (without a wheel) prior to firing.

Such ways of life commence with the daily cycle of fire-making, food preparation, cooking and eating, the fetching of water and fuel, the care of the dwelling, work at home in the practice of crafts and light industries, and the periods of leisure spent visiting and entertaining, in sexual relationships and sleeping. In their various ways they all have a bearing on the dwelling, as the centre of the daily activities, or the home to which those engaged in working outside it return. Frequently the domestic space is defined in ways which reflect this—male and female areas, related, by no means always equitably, to their respective roles within the family. In many societies the responsibility for the domestic tasks, the bearing and raising of the children and often, an inordinate share of the productive work, falls to the women, though this does not necessarily, or even frequently, bring equivalence of status.[20] As the traditional male roles of hunting, aggression, or defence have diminished at local levels leisure or unproductive time has increased, with the men relinquishing neither the decision-making nor the status that these former activities had secured.

Varying from one society to another according to its priorities, the daily round is modified by the cycle of the year as the months flow into seasons, marked perhaps, by considerable changes in temperature, length of days, and exposure to sunlight or precipitation of rain and snow. In regions where these seasonal phenomena are less distinct they may be subject to regularly recurring rains, monsoons, searing winds or periods of stationary temperatures and high humidity. The annual cycles of different parts of the world influence the nature of the economies they support and in turn, the utilization of dwellings. As we have seen, the shelters of the pastoral nomads, or of farmers on marginal lands, differ markedly from those of sedentary agricultural peoples in temperate climates.

Between harvest and planting, old houses may be repaired and new ones built; when the crops are nearing fruition field huts may be built and occupied; when the need for fresh fodder makes transhumance necessary, secondary seasonal dwellings may be occupied; when the climate is too severe for all but the hardiest or hungriest hunters, families may pass the season by drawing upon the stores of food laid down when the hunting, the gathering, or the harvesting was good.[21]

For every individual in society the cycles of the day, the months, or the seasons are embedded in the cycle of life itself, but whereas the days and the seasons are shared as they recur, the life cycle of the individual overlaps the different stages of maturity of the other members of the family and the community. Some societies have institutionalized the unfolding of the years through an age-set system, where groups of approximately identical age progress through life together, sharing their activities, rituals, and their habitations. Almost all have institutions of marriage whereby the union of husband and wife is formally recognized through ceremony and perpetuated by obligations, and by the bearing and raising of children. For the family the focus of its identity as a collective unit is the dwelling.

But what constitutes the family? The biological relationship of parents and their offspring is expressed in the nuclear family, which all over the world constitutes the basic domestic group. Often,

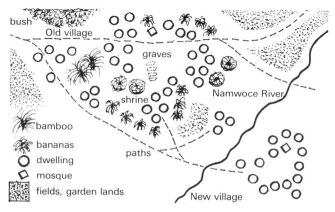

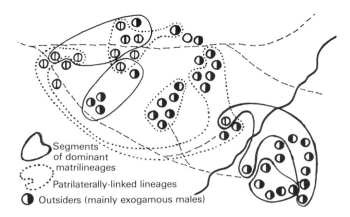

Cikoja, a Yao village in Malawi. The Yao are matrilineal, generally uxorilocal, the men living exogamously in the villages of their wives. Patrilateral links exist in the maternal village through the descendants of the slave wives of former chiefs. *Left*, Cikoja settlement pattern. *Right*, dominant matrilineages and patrilateral lineages overlaid on the village plan. (*After Mitchell, adapted and simplified*)

however, it is projected back to one set of the grandparents, to form a stem family of three generations living together. Brothers or sisters of the parents with their spouses and children may expand the unit to an extended family which can easily result in a score of adults and children living in one dwelling, and may often include many more. Generally such an extended family is related to a lineage or line of descent which is traced back to a common ancestor. This may be on the male side of the family (patrilineal) or on the female side (matrilineal) or, with some complications, through bilateral descent. Descent lines are an important aspect of inheritance, including the passing on of the dwelling.

Lineage members frequently live in close association, if not together in one building, at least in the same village or locality, and may be called upon to assist in house building and other corporate activities requiring many hands. A lineage is not the same as a clan, which may include a number of lineages who believe themselves to be related and who share their origins in a common, but often mythical, ancestry. Clans may again live in proximity, but even if they are dispersed individuals may retain their identity with the clan of their birth.[22]

It may be seen that the complexities of kinship could result in considerable pressure on settlement

and dwellings of great size. Moreover, incest would be inevitable if there were not other measures to control marriage and inter-breeding. Some societies are 'endogamous', requiring that an individual marries within a specific group, but 'exogamy', or the system that obliges individuals to marry outside the group (though often within specific limitations of village or ethnic identity) is a safeguard against inbreeding. It may apply to one sex only—a daughter is expected to marry into a family within, say, a particular village. A newly-wedded couple is by no means always free to decide on where they wish to live: some societies are 'virilocal', expecting a son to reside close to his father or his male relatives on his father's side; others are 'uxorilocal', requiring that the couple live near, or with, the wife's mother or matrilineal kin.

Monogamy, the union of a single male and a single female, is the commonest form of marriage, but polygamy, or plural marriage is also widespread. Generally it takes the form of 'pologyny' with a man taking a second wife who will be separately provided for, though often within the same dwelling unit. Some may take a third wife, the attendant problems of many children and mouths to feed being offset by the increase in the domestic labour force. Nevertheless, relative wealth and large dwellings are the inevitable implications of such multiple unions.[23]

All these and other systems of kinship have far wider implications in terms of hierarchies and authority, of political systems and ideologies of social organizations and community interactions, of class

Multiple wedding among the Ayt Hadiddu, held in winter. After three days veiled, the young brides wear elaborate head-dress and appear unveiled in the marriage ceremonies. High Atlas, Morocco.

and caste and much else, which are ultimately relevant to settlement, but which are beyond the scope of this book. Nevertheless, it is evident that they have a bearing on the physical form and spatial organization of the dwelling, of which some examples have been summarized above.

With the growth of families, the addition of newly-wedded couples and young children, and the care of the infirm and the death of the aged, the demands on the dwelling to meet a changing family size and structure are considerable. There are various solutions but they can be summarized as the capacity of the compound type to respond to fluctuations in family numbers by the addition or demolition of individual domestic units, as in the instance of the Tswana; the large-scale, multi-celled dwelling which accommodates the maximum anticipated growth of the family with the likelihood of redundant spaces at various

times, such as the western Anatolian house; the medium-sized, basic structure of the nuclear family which is adapted or extended to meet family growth, like the Malaysian dwelling; and the selling of a house as it becomes unsuitable, and the purchase of another, with increase or decrease in family size. Of these systems the latter is the most common, and probably the least immediately responsive, in western technological countries: selling and repurchasing being the most expensive option and requiring loose kinship ties and greater mobility. In societies where attachment to ancestral lands and close kinship ties are customary the other options are the most appropriate.

Whatever the plan and utilization of the internal spaces might be, and however the dwelling is made to adapt to family structure and evolving needs, the dwelling embodies the values of the group to which it belongs. At certain stages in the life cycles of the occupants and in the life of the dwelling itself, these are frequently given special emphasis in meaning, ceremonial, symbolism and aesthetic enrichment.

A Tswana woman stands proudly in the *lolwapa* or apron court, of her home at Lethlakane, Botswana.

Malay house near Temerloh, Peninsula Malaysia. The bark-walled *ibu ramah*, or 'mother house', has been extended at both front and rear.

Opposite Gable end of a Tukanoan community house. The wall of flattened bark is decorated with motifs derived from 'phosphenes', or drug-induced visual images. Vaupés, Colombia.

Preparing *Tjok Putri*. These offerings of rice and flowers, in palm leaf baskets,
are laid on the house shrine for the festival of Galungan. Bali, Indonesia.

Opposite Decorated gable end of incised and painted wood on a Toradja house at Lemo, Sulawesi.
The spiral and interlacing motifs may derive from fabrics and are widely distributed.

Facade decoration of a house in Kano, Northern Nigeria. The design in moulded mud plaster includes a sword, a rifle and a *dagi,* or 'endless knot'.

Opposite Street in Paroikia, on the Greek island of Paros. A section of the cul-de-sac has been made into a living space. The white walls and green paint are probably of Islamic origin.

Brick is used decoratively on San'a houses, and details are
emphasized in gypsum plaster. Some windows have fanlights of
coloured glass. Smoke holes indicate the kitchen. North Yemen.

8.

VALUES, SYMBOLS, AND MEANINGS

It is the sign of the intruder that awakens in many of us in the West an awareness of the values we place on dwellings. But the pleasurable satisfaction of being at home after a vacation or period away is also a reminder of how we identify with our houses. Conversely, the inhibitions that we experience at a friend's house in going into certain parts without specific invitation, are indications of our recognition of the close association between dwelling and occupier. Of course, such inhibitions can rightly be ascribed to the persistence of parental training and formalized polite behaviour.

We have here a number of closely related aspects of the dwelling: as symbol of the self, as physical encoding of many of the values of a society, and as an indication of the processes by which these have been assimilated. In a sense the latter is the most significant, for it is by the socializing of succeeding generations that society perpetuates and inculcates its value systems. Through guidance and correction, children acquire the domestic behaviour patterns appropriate to their culture.

Training in living under adult guidance may be customary, but the values of society are deeply implanted in children through their own creative play. By mimicry of their parents and kin children act out relationships, imitate work and social activities, and learn the values of the home. 'Playing house' may well be a universal phenomenon; it allows, within the perceptions and understanding of children, the first essays in the patterns of behaviour, the first attempts at the explorations of domestic rituals, of spatial relationships, or of recognizing the values of their parents with regard to the dwelling.

In the process of learning through play the children enlarge their vocabulary and learn the spatial concepts important to the community. Words are symbols, and language is a symbolizing process; ideas of space are wholly symbolic. Observed over an extended period Amer-Indian children at New Oraibi, one of the Hopi pueblo villages of the northern Arizona desert, repeatedly made play houses out of compacted sand; interestingly, these were excavated rather than constructed and in the process the children would have had to communicate their spatial intentions, even though the Hopi have no words for specific building types, rooms or spatial concepts.[1]

SUNWISE PATHS

Diamond-shaped, the Hopi Indian reservation is situated within, and surrounded by, the vast 25,000 square mile Navajo reservation which is mainly in the high, desertic north-east of Arizona and spills over into adjacent states. Navajo residential patterns and lifeways are very different from those of the pueblo desert farmers; they are mainly sheep-herders and small ranchers. Largest by far of the Amer-Indian nations (over 125,000) they are dispersed over the reservation. The majority live in modest 'outfits', with a loose grouping of habitations, smallholdings, and corrals. While not being strictly-speaking, nomadic, they may move to another habitation for part of the year when taking their animals to winter grazing. Some log cabins and single-storey houses are to be seen on the reservation, but the fundamental dwelling which is the focus of Navajo family life is the *hogan*. It is present in every homesite, even if other buildings are erected nearby, and is the centre of family and spiritual life. Like their counterparts in other societies

Navajo 'forked stick' *hogan*. A smoke hole above the fireplace is partially protected against rain. The entrance faces east. Near Betatakin, Arizona, USA.

Interior of 'forked stick' *hogan* with store made from oil drum, and sheepskin bedcovers.

Navajo children build 'play-house' hogans, often on a toy scale and with *ramadas* or unwalled shade shelters of sticks, grass corrals, and clay sheep and horses. But though the play hogan helps reinforce the behaviour patterns and values that they are acquiring, the Navajo children learn most from being within the single-celled hogan itself and through being the centre of important elements in the religious life.[2]

Oldest of the hogan types is the 'forked stick' structure constructed from a tripod of forked poles against which others are laid. A porch extension to the entrance with smoke-hole opening facing forwards above it, is not uncommon. The pole frame was thickly plastered over with mud. Though rarely made now, the basic form of the type is still used to make the small 'sweat-house' in which ritual cleansing sweat baths or hot-stone saunas, are taken. A large number of other hogan types has been noted built of horizontal logs, or planks, vertical poles, coursed and uncoursed sandstone, and more recently, cinder blocks. To the observer the structure often seems crudely made, especially when compared with the fine quality of Navajo woven blankets and rugs, and turquoise and silver jewellery.[3]

When the hogan is built it is consecrated with the Blessingway Chant which evokes the first hogans built by the Holy People Hastyeyalti and Hastyehogan, gods of Sunrise and Sunset, the words indicating that the symbolic connotations are very different from the physical reality:

> Built of afterglow
>> Standeth his hogan
>> The hogan blessed
>
> Built of yellow corn
>> Standeth his hogan
>> The hogan blessed
>
> Built of gems and shining shells
>> Standeth his hogan
>> The hogan blessed
>
> Built of holy pollen . . .
>
> Evermore enduring . . .

Interior of a contemporary *hogan* showing a small number of traded, store-bought, or donated articles. Traditionally, the north side is used by the women. Arizona.

Blessingway rites occur at least twice a year in most hogans, and often more frequently, as for example, when a member of the family leaves for a long period. Within the hogan the space is physically undivided, but to the Navajo it is symbolically an interpretation of the world as he perceives it: the floor, slightly dished, represents the earth (female), the roof, slightly concave, the sky which is male. Sacred pollen is smeared on the house posts which symbolize the four poles that support the sky. The entrance pole is always to the East, and the east post is dedicated to the Earth Woman deity; that to the west to Water Woman, divinity of the Water World. Corn Woman's pole lies to the north; the south hogan pole is dedicated to Mountain Woman. Many Navajo divinities are women, and even though the household head is male the people are matrilineal and matrilocal. On entering the hogan men are expected to sit on the north side, facing south, and women on the south side. The woman's loom and her cooking utensils are kept on the south side. Belongings are hung on pegs and notches or are placed in crevices and ledges in the

Navajo *hosteen* (medicine men) make a 'dry-painting' with coloured sands for a curing ceremony. The sick person will sit within it and absorb its power. *(Pitt Rivers Museum, Oxford)*

Hogans are built of any available materials. The roof of this stone hogan is of diagonally-placed logs, covered with earth. On the north side an opening has been made for the removal of the body of the deceased owner. Near Holbrook, Arizona.

structure. In the middle is the hearth, which symbolizes the nadir and the centre of the world. To the west of the hogan is the place of honour for the patriarch or matriarch, and for visiting medicine men, or *hosteen*. Movement through the hogan must follow the 'sunwise path'. On entering, one encircles the hearth on the south side in a clockwise direction and exits by the north. Behaviour within is marked by prohibitions—one may speak loudly or vociferously

outside the hogan, but not inside; one must not look into the hogan without permission, but once invited may inspect every detail. No matter how crowded the hogan is with sleepers the reclining bodies must never be stepped over, nor the hearth crossed.[4]

When a curing ceremonial takes place such as the Beauty Way or Mountain Way Chant a smooth sand floor in the centre of the hogan (normally the hearth) is prepared for the rituals and the making of *likaah*, or symbolic 'dry-painting', in coloured earths. Lasting several days it culminates with the sick person, often a child, sitting in the centre and infusing the healing powers of the Holy People invoked. It is possible that children have a psychosomatic disposition to be ill, in order to experience the unity of kinship among the witnesses of the chant, and are similarly disposed to get better after. But in any event the hogan is the centre of the ceremonial and the place from which all good emanates to counter the hostile spirits that exist in the desert. Solidly built and lacking any apparent aesthetic merit, the hogan is at the heart of much of the people's spiritual and behavioural values. As the symbol of life it is also witness to death; when an occupant dies the body is taken out through an opening made in the north wall, and the hogan is abandoned and allowed to collapse; with death the spirit and material of the hogan rejoin the earth.

Like other single-cell dwellings the hogan is spatially differentiated through custom by gender, by hierarchy, by ritual and by symbolic association, and not by physical partitions. Spatial organization of a similar kind is not only to be found among many other Amer-Indian nations, but also among peoples of Asia.[5]

Spread over a vast territory stretching east more than two thousand miles from the Caspian Sea to central Mongolia, the *yurt*-dwelling peoples include the Turkomen, Uzbeks and Kirghiz of Afghanistan, the Russian Kazaks, and numerous Mongol tribes. Some herd Bactrian camels, and in the mountains, yaks, but all are fine horsemen. They depend largely on sheep for milk, wool, and to some extent meat, owned either by themselves or by wealthy families. Their ties to lineage and clan are strong, western

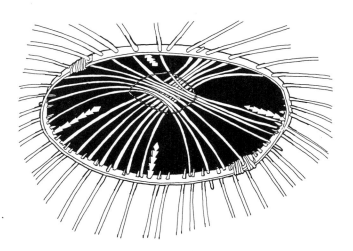

Above and top right Yurt and *ger* built from diagonal lattices, used in sections to make the walls. The centre 'crown' is raised on poles, its opening symbolizing the eye of heaven.

peoples being formerly politically organized in 'hordes'. Adapting the yurt to the harsh climatic conditions of steppe, gravel desert, or mountains several million people still follow the traditional nomadic pastoral way of life in spite of governmental attempts at implementing resettlement schemes.[6]

The yurt—a Turkish word for 'dwelling'—is known to Afghan peoples as the *kherga*, in Russia as *kabitka*, in Mongolia, where it achieves its most remarkable forms, as the *ger*. Among all these peoples the structural principles underlying the yurt are basically the same: the dwelling is circular in plan with walls made of an open, loose lattice frame of willow wands which may be expanded to build the house and contracted for carrying to the next site. The lattice is lashed at the cross-overs of the wands which are lightly thonged with rawhide. Each lattice or *khana* is made up of some 33 wands, and half a dozen khana will produce a yurt about 16 feet (5 m) in diameter. Light poles that have been preformed into an arc by steaming are lashed to the frame, which is further stabilized by webbing tension bands, and the poles inserted into a centre ring or crown. In Mongolia the poles are straight and the crown is a heavy structure with mortice and tenon joints, but elsewhere lighter crown hoops are used. Juniper wood

Though all *yurts* are structurally similar they differ in their details. Most are covered with felt or reed mats which may be decorated with appliqué. Kirghiz near Urumchi, Djungaria, China.

door frames provide a secure fixing for the khana; the door may be a felt mat which can be rolled up, or a solid carved wooden door, or a pair of doors with leather hinges. Once the frame is in place the yurt is covered with thick woollen felt mats made by the women, which are secured with webbing bands or ropes. Kirghiz yurts of white felts may be decorated with appliqué designs in brown felt, while Turkomen yurt walls are covered with reed mats, held in place

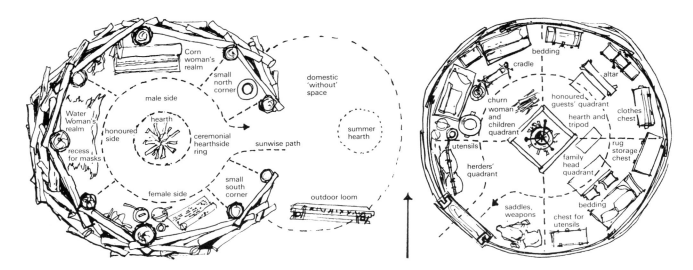

The spatial organization of the *hogan* and the *ger* compared.
Differentiation by gender, symbolism of internal spaces, and
movement around the central hearth have many points in
common. Other arrangements have been recorded.

and enriched with a broad, patterned tension band.

Spatially, yurts are strictly divided by systems
which strongly recall the Navajo organization, though
sometimes with different orientation; Turkomen
entrances, like hogans, face east, but other yurts customarily face south-west. The transition from exterior
to interior of the yurt is also symbolically important
and inside a sunwise path must again be taken. The
interior is divided in quadrants, the south-west
entrance zone being that of the herders, of lowest
status, the position opposite on the north-east quadrant being for a shrine and distinguished guests. The
quadrant on the right-hand side from the entrance is
the male domain of the family head, with saddles,
weapons, and hunting gear, the women and children
sleeping opposite with cradle and churns. Chests for
rugs and clothing, boxes for valuables and utensils,
small tables and vessels for food and mare's milk have
their assigned positions.[7]

In the centre of the yurt is the fire, regarded by
many Mongols as a protective deity who must not be
disturbed. The 'square of the hearth' within the circle
of the yurt follows the Buddhist principles of male
and female symbolism of square and circle; the five
eastern elements of Earth, Wood, Metal, Water and
Fire are symbolized respectively by the earth floor,
the wood hearth frame, the iron tripod, and the kettle

of water over the fire in the hearth. As with the
Navajo the roof of the dwelling symbolizes the sky,
the open smoke hole being seen as the Eye of Heaven.[8] Yet the *ger* embraces other values as these
extracts of a song collected from a nomad woman in
the Central Gobi desert illustrate:

. . . Although the lucky thread-shaped lattice
    was made of criss-crossed willow wood.
Happiness and joy are in it.

Although the firm smoke hole of the tent was
    made with many gaps
It looks like shining precious stones . . .

. . . The felt is beautiful, it looks like a white
    sunflower,
Printed letters are decorated, creation of a
    Goddess.

I am holding a long pair of scissors in my skilful
    hand;
I was taught by my mother and directed by my
    elder sisters.
Regarding my skill and knowledge, I was
    educated by the Nation;
Regarding the structure and shape, I have built
    it better than anyone.
Heart and mind have been satisfied with the
    structure,

Covered it with the best felt which flaps like the
King Bird,
The Tent is protecting the people from the
world's powerful winds.

The hair rope was made of the mane of the wild
chestnut horse,
And the long hair of the mating bull camel.

The hair ropes were nicely reinforced and tied
down firmly;
The twelve leather ropes are like the People's
Hero's bow strings.[9]

Interior of a *yurt* showing the lattice structure of the *khana,* the placing of domestic items and traditional seating positions. Inner Mongolia.

Chanted in a wild, strained voice the song was redolent of pride of workmanship, joy in the creation of the dwelling, and an appreciation of its beauty of form and fabric. Her song is a window on the aesthetic of a nomadic people, and an indication of the significance of myth and legend in confirming indigenous values.

Though the time-spans implied are immense in terms of human history, the correspondences between the symbolism of the hogan and that of the yurt, let alone those of many other types of Asian and Amer-Indian dwelling are at least, highly provocative. But we may note that Navajos speak an Athapaskan language, having broken away from the main cluster of Athapaskan speaking peoples who inhabit northern Canada, Yukon, and Alaska, close to the Aleutian 'land-bridge' by which the Mongol peoples many millennia ago are believed to have crossed into the Americas.

SYMBOLIC OPPOSITIONS

Societies of all kinds and in every part of the world need to account for the evidence of the nature of their environment and their perceived place in the scheme of things, in order to give meaning, purpose, and structure to living. The origin of sun, moon, rain, and earth, of animals and plants; the mysteries of conception, birth, life, and the destiny of the souls of the departed, are commonly at the centre of man's religious beliefs and practices. Fearing the unknown,

mastering the known, the world is made somewhat more comprehensible by bringing such observed phenomena within a system. Correspondences are perceived, influences deduced and similarities made apparent. Forms are modelled or carved in ancestral likenesses, dances are patterned on the movements of animals and birds, devices are painted and masks worn to tap the spiritual essence; voices are masked and hallucinogens taken, rituals are performed, trials endured, and ceremonials observed to make contact with the supernatural. And the contexts for so much of these are man's constructed symbols of the cosmos, the foci of ritual and reverence in the stupa, the temple, the shrine, the mosque, the church, the chapel—or, in its human-scale simulation of his universe, the dwelling.[10]

Signs are used to *denote* something—an object, a situation, an event, specifically and unequivocally, and they do not under such circumstances carry any additional associations. Symbols are used to *connote* meanings in addition to those which they may depict; they have associative meanings. In this kind of usage signs are distinct from symbols, but it should be noted that a sign may be a symbol as well. As the

Bull's horns hang with popular religious prints in a mixture of superstition and Catholicism above the altar in a peasant home. Tarasco, Oaxaca, Mexico.

doorway denotes the entrance it is a sign, but it is also a symbol of entry or privacy, and may have many additional symbolic meanings of, say, sexual penetration or birth. As a sign it has only one specific meaning; as a symbol it may have a much larger sphere of associations. Both sign and symbol, to be recognized and understood, must exist within systems. The doorway exists within the sign system of door denoting entrance, window denoting opening, roof shape denoting house. But as symbols the windows may connote release, broadening perceptions, eyes of the spirits; the roof may connote protection, the sky, the deities in their celestial abode. Again, signs exist effectively in the present: they denote here and now. Symbols exist in the past, the present, and may imply the future. In a sense symbols are timeless, though being non-specific over time their meaning may change, gaining or losing in force or effectiveness,

and taking on new levels of connotation.[11]

It can be seen, therefore, that a people may develop a symbol system which includes virtually all their experience of the present and embraces their history: myths are symbols of their unknowable past. Through the myths and legends, lore, and customs of a society its values may be transmitted, communicated, repeated, and learned. As the roof under which so much of this is acted and re-enacted in the daily, yearly, and life cycles, the dwelling readily becomes the symbolic model of the greater universe of time and space in which they are seen to exist.

A number of studies have been made of the religious concepts of different peoples which have revealed the importance of the dwelling as microcosm, such as Lebeuf's research on the Fali of the highlands of Cameroon. Better known and frequently cited is the work of Marcel Griaule and Germaine Dieterlen and their colleagues concerning the culture of the Dogon people who live on, or near to, the Bandiagara escarpment in Mali. This work is remarkable for

Kabylie dwellings are simple stone buildings with low-pitched tiled roofs. Theoretically, the east wall is male, the west, female; in practice the terrain necessitates a variety of orientations. Kabylia, Algeria.

The profound symbolism of Dogon dwellings is seldom explicit. These granaries contain chambers for the eight seed types given by God, each also symbolizing the organs of the Spirit of Water. Beyond, men sit in the *togu na,* its columns carved with female symbols. Near Bandiagara, Mali.

having been conducted over more than three decades; even so it was some fifteen years before the Dogon revealed the essence of their cosmological ideas.[12]

In the complex Dogon mythology the Creator God Amma generated within infinite space a primordial egg with a double placenta in which were the Twin Nommo, sons of God. One being broke from the egg, Yurugu the fox, bringing with him as he fell a piece of the placenta which became Earth. Eventually in the creation myth Yurugu came to stand for the dry, the uncultivated, the uninhabited, the night, and disorder, while his counterpart Nommo became the symbol of the ordered world, of the day, the sky, fertility, the cultivated, and the inhabitable. The con-

cept of twin-ness, essential to Dogon mythology is a recognition of the duality of so much in the world of experience, which in many other societies, has become a fundamental ordering principle in their created world, including their dwellings.[13]

Male and female, left-hand and right-hand parts of the house have been noted in several examples in preceding pages. Sun and Moon, night and day, good and evil, life and death are dualities within the experience of all of us. So too are the spatial dichotomies of earth and sky, above and below, front and back, inside and outside and, as we have seen, these are often related symbolically.[14] This 'binary principle' may be extended in numerous ways: by comparisons, contrasts, antinomies, homologies, parallels and polar oppositions which are nonetheless on the same metaphoric 'axes'. How such dualism is manifest in the dwelling was demonstrated by Pierre Bourdieu in his analysis of the Berber houses in Kabylia, Algeria.

A simple structure, the Berber house consists of one rectangular room divided a third of the way along its length by a cross wall to make a dark, flagstoned stable at a lower level and a higher, better-lit, living space with a floor polished with black clay and cow dung. A main ridge beam which spans both spaces is supported at the dividing wall by a pillar; in Berber

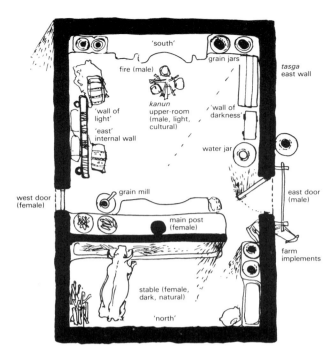

Plan of the Kabylie Berber house. The woman's loom stands by the 'Wall of Light' illuminated by the 'male' door in the east. Interior benches and details are moulded in clay and richly decorated in white and terracotta. (*After Bourdieu*)

In the plan, labels read: 'south', grain jars, *tasga* east wall, fire (male), *kanun* upper-room (male, light, cultural), 'wall of darkness', 'wall of light', 'east' internal wall, water jar, west door (female), grain mill, east door (male), main post (female), farm implements, stable (female, dark, natural), 'north'.

Corner of a Kabylie room where the 'Wall of Light' (left) meets the hearth wall. Grain jars with quern below, to the right of the upright post of the woman's loom. Maatka, near Tizi Ouzou, Algeria.

symbolism the protecting, strong beam is male, the pillar is female. The dark end of the house is where the water vessels are placed and, in the stable, where the animals are kept; it is associated with sexual relationships, birth, sleep, and death—with what is 'animal'. In contrast, the higher living space is associated with all that is noble: the honour of the household head, his protection of his wife's virtue. As a symbol of his patrilineal kin his rifle is by the hearth at the north gable wall, where there are recesses to take household utensils and grain vessels.

In the long wall on the east facade is the main entrance, which is male: opposite is the female entrance, smaller but set in the wall and illuminated by the main entrance. Called 'the Wall of Light' it is where the loom is situated, the symbol of woman's creative and domestic activity and of the values that her husband protects. It is before the loom that a bride is presented, behind the loom where she sits after marriage, there where the umbilical cord of her child is buried. Opposite her is the front wall, dark against the light of the open east door, and literally termed the 'wall of darkness', which is associated therefore with the dark end of the house, the stable. The interior of the house is the woman's domain and men are expected to leave it at first light. Man, the Kabylie say, is the light of the outside (the true light) and women the light of the inside. It will be seen that the light, illuminated end of the house and the 'wall of light' are linked with all that is 'cultural', transformed, created; it is where the meals are cooked, the cloths are woven. *Haram*, that which is forbidden or taboo, is the sacred aspect of the interior, the secret and the female. As the dark, lower, animal, 'natural' end of the house is female, so the light exterior, the world proper, is male.[15] The dark side of the room and the dark end of the house are symbolically connected with all that is natural but also secret, so that the house represents a natural/cultural dichotomy,[16] the 'raw and the cooked' in Claude Levi-Strauss's memorable phrase.

THE COSMIC DWELLING

Part of the appeal of the Dogon conception of both village and dwelling was its anthropomorphism. The parts of the *ginu da*, the big house of a lineage cluster are related to those of the human body. So the head is associated with the kitchen, with the hearth stones as the eyes, the *dembere* or central room with the belly and the flanking goat houses and stores culminating in towers, with the limbs. The breasts are symbolized by jars of water, the sexual organs by grinding stones, and the whole, graphically expressed by Griaule, represents a man lying on his right side in the act of procreation.[17] Dogon compounds do not correspond in plan to Griaule's much reprinted drawing, it is the anthropomorphic symbolism of the entities that matters and not their placement in figurative terms.

Zoomorphism, or the employment of animal forms and metaphors may also be found, even in combination, as is the case with the Tukanoans, one of the Amer-Indian peoples of South America. Though many tribes have been assimilated into the new Latin societies of mixed race, in Amazonia and the remoter regions of South America tribes of Indians retain their identities, their lifeways, and beliefs. A territory that

Entrance to the Kabylie house. The stable entrance (right) is to the dark, lower, symbolically female and 'natural' end of the dwelling. Maatka.

Idealized plans of the Dogon homestead having symbolic parallels with the human body. (*After Griaule, Dieterlen*) compared with actual plans of homes, Lower Ogol Village. (*After Parin et al.*)

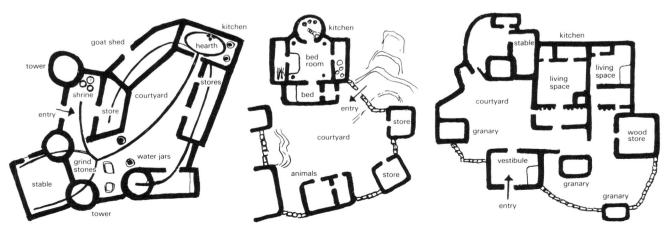

The east, male end of the Tukanoan *malocca* or community house. The decorations depict patterns perceived under the influence of an hallucinatory infusion. Vaupés region, Colombia.

stretches between Brazil and Colombia is the home of many Indian tribes, among them the Tukanoans, manioc cultivators who live in patrilineal and exogamous groups on the banks of the Pirá-paraná river. The complex ritual and spiritual life of a group of these Indians has been examined in detail by Stephen and Christine Hugh-Jones.

Tukanoan community houses are of considerable dimensions, thatched with palm leaves on palm slats, with eaves that sweep close to the ground. Each roof-frame is supported on eight major house posts placed on either side of a central male/female axis. The male end of the house, which is also where visitors are received, faces east and is clad with bark paintings; the female end is apsidal with a central door and faces west. Inside, nuclear families of the male lineage occupy walled-off rooms on either side and towards the rear, female, end. In each compartment hammocks are slung around cooking hearths and doors open both to the central space and to the manioc gardens outside. In the centre of the longhouse is the main social area which is embraced by a ceremonial dance path. Here, the men gather nightly, young male initiates sleep and ceremonials are held. When major ceremonials, such as the initiation rituals *He wi*, take place, they are hidden from the women by a rattan screen.[18]

All Tukanoans believe themselves to be the children of the Primal Sun, but each group traces its origin to a mythical ancestor, one or other of the largest species of snakes, the anaconda. In mythical time Anacondas swam west up the rivers from the Water Door of the Milk River (the Amazon) stopping at the 'waking up places' where the ancestors of the Tukanoans danced and their homesites were established. The Anaconda journey east to west, corresponded to the path of the Sun, and accordingly, the male entrance, facing east, represents the Water Door by which the ancestral Anacondas entered. The house

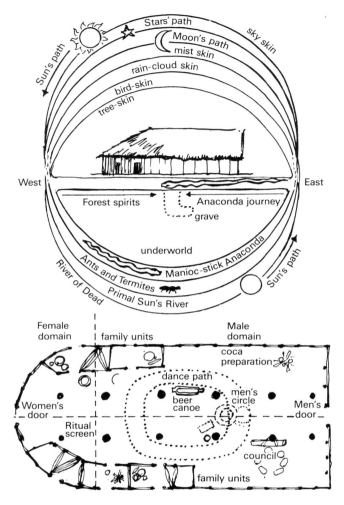

The Tukanoan concept of the multi-layered 'cosmic gourd', and the plan of the Tukanoan community house showing spatial differentiation. (*After Hugh-Jones*)

as body has the entrance as mouth, but it is also perceived as the entrance to the womb; the rear doorway is regarded as the anus. Birth is associated, as might be expected, with the ancestral 'waking-up houses' but also with the manioc gardens where birth literally takes place. The gardens are reached through the family doors and the woman's door, but the womb interior of the house, the family apartments, the heat of the cooking fires (which is associated with female sexuality), the nourishment of the gardens and of the forest beyond, are all seen as female and the source of

the creative power of women. The practice and locations of ritual and ceremonial, the rectilinear structure of the front of the house, the phallic form of the Anaconda, the men's door as Water Door and symbol of sexual penetration, the river landing and the path that links it with the dwelling are all male and associated with the origin of the patrilineal group.

Vertically the dwelling is also perceived symbolically; the roof as sky, the house-pots as mountains, the floor as the Earth and the grave the Underworld. The upper half of the multi-layered cosmic gourd with its arboreal 'tree-skin' and successive 'skins' of birds, rainclouds, mist, moon, sun, stars, and 'sky-skin' of the First Being, which the shamans, priest-healers, pass through on their trance-travels to the supernatural world, lies above the plane of the Earth. Below it is the Underworld of negative forces, of the River of Death, but also of the Sun's River by which it travels to its daily regeneration in the East, and of other mythological associations. When a member of the group dies the body is placed in a coffin made from the halves of a canoe and is interred in a chamber off a deep hole below the floor of the house. While the spirit of the ancestor remains in the house, the body decays in its grave, but the soul enters a beautifully painted ancestral longhouse, visible only to the shamans and the dead, where the ancestors perpetually dance. When the name of the deceased is given to a newborn child the spirit is happy for it lives again, the soul thriving in the continuing ritual of the ancestral house.[19]

ORIENTAL ORIENTATION

Many other kinds of symbolic system related to the house exist, some peculiar to one culture, others borrowed or assimilated. Among the Sakalava, a tribe on the west coast of Madagascar who, like other Malagasy tribes may be of Indonesian descent, use the plan of the house as an astrological calendar—which is of Chaldean origin. The terms used are of Arabic extraction but to confuse the issue of its source further, connections have been noted with some aspects of the

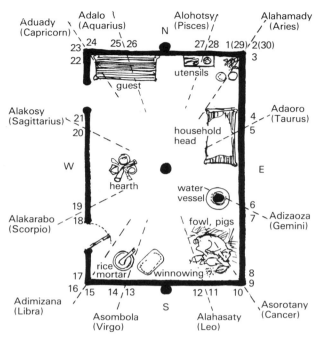

Aduady (Capricorn)
Adalo (Aquarius)
Alohotsy (Pisces)
Alahamady (Aries)
N
23 24 25 26
22
27 28 1(29) 2(30)
3
guest
utensils
Alakosy (Sagittarius)
21
20
Adaoro (Taurus)
4
5
household head
W
E
hearth
water vessel
Alakarabo (Scorpio)
19
18
6
7 Adizaoza (Gemini)
fowl, pigs
rice mortar
winnowing
17
16 15 14 13
S
12 11 10
8
9
Adimizana (Libra)
Asombola (Virgo)
Alahasaty (Leo)
Asorotany (Cancer)

The dwelling as calendar and zodiac: plan of the Sakalava, Madagascar house with zones of activity, defined by their astrological associations. (*After Dahl*)

Houses at Waltair. The short ridge is supported by a central pole and the corner posts are placed according to the rules of the ancient sastras. The doorway, hidden by the deep eaves, is central. Andhra Pradesh.

Japanese house. A simple rectangular plan house with a central pole supporting the ridge, the Sakalava dwelling is oriented north-south. The months are identified with the corners and two points on each side of the house, commencing at the north-east with *Alahamady*, or Aries. Each corner has three days associated with it; each wall point has two, (twenty-eight in all) so that the zodiacal calendar is also a daily one. The points of the zodiac determine the position of household articles: *Adaoro* for example (Taurus) is the household head's sleeping place; *Asombola* (Virgo) is related to the Arabic *as-sumbula* (grain) and is the site of rice mortar and winnowing pan.[20]

We can only guess how old such symbolic associations with the building may be in these and other societies; there is reason to believe that many may link with the remote past of tribal peoples, and have been passed on orally by successive generations. In societies where a literate tradition developed, and where mystic rites and observances became increasingly esoteric and the province of a learned priesthood, traditional customs were written down. In the process some may have become less flexible, entering the canons of religious doctrine, and by application, of building. This appears to have been the case with Hindu architecture, where ancient practices were noted, especially from the members of the guilds, and as early as the sixth century AD recorded in the *sastras*, or manuals of the *sílpins*, the temple craftsmen. One of the *Vastu Sastras*, the *Manasara*, laid down the proportions for temples and towns and the rules of building in the finest detail.

The sílpin sastras gave rules governing the plan of the house, recommending positions for the courtyard, the respective rooms of men and women, the room for receiving guests and storerooms, the kitchen and cooking space, and the bathing place. The house was interpreted anthropomorphically, conceptualized in human terms as the organs of the *Purusha* or the Primal Being, whose head, arms, legs, stomach, and sexual organs had their parallel in the organization of the dwelling.[21] Such treatises were directed mainly at the temple priests and at the wealthy and literate, often being passed on, many times removed, through the assimilated knowledge of the craftsmen and the propitiatory practices of the village priests, to influence the dwellings of ordinary people.[22]

Building a house in Andhra Pradesh today involves religious observances which commence with the selection of the site. Having divined the most auspicious time and day for building, which is generally considered to be between February and April, the *pundit*, a Hindu priest, enjoins the family in prayers at the site. There he marks the positions of the corner poles and coconuts are broken in a ritual intended to ensure the safety of the building. The householder digs the hole for the centre post and the coconut milk is poured into it. Nine coloured bean seeds, signifying the planets, are buried in the hole, invoking the protection of Vishnu, Lord of the Universe. Evil spirits are warded off with bunches of sacred mango leaves tied to the top of the house post, so that they protect the dwelling and ensure the prosperity of its occupants. The rules of the sastras are followed by the unlettered village craftsmen who build the houses and raise the steeply pyramidical bamboo roof frames. A house is required to be symmetrical with a central doorway and well-made door. From one to three poles should support the ridge, and the plan must theoretically conform to specific measurements: 12 feet (4 m) square, 12 feet by 19 feet (4 m by 6 m), and so on. Village craftsmen generally adhere to the canon of the sastra, though with variations that conform with local preferences as to the choice of proportions used. Daily, the women decorate the ground in front of the houses with *alponas*, complex patterns of rice powder, as an offering to Laxshmi, the Goddess of Wealth, and other deities.[23]

Of the systems for identifying the most auspicious sites for building and for the location of the parts of the dwelling, the most complex is the Chinese form of geomancy, *Feng-Shui* (Wind-Water). It was developed as a consistent theory in the tenth century AD, when different forms of geomancy were brought together in a complicated multi-plate and subdivided site compass. The Chinese binary principle of Yang (male) and Yin (female) pervades all concepts of the universe. Nevertheless they are not equal for this would imply

Alponas, patterns freely drawn in rice powder by the housewife as an offering to the gods, on the front step and in the roadway before her house. Mysore, India.

opposition; Yang is dominant in the ideal state. Astrology is closely linked with Feng-Shui—the constellations, the Chinese Zodiac, the calendar of days and months, the Four Seasons, the Five Elements, the Ten Heavenly Stems, the Twelve Earthly Branches, and the Trigrams and Hexagrams of the *I Ching*, the 'Book of Changes', all have Yang and Yin attributes which interact, wax, and wane. Important in the practice of Feng-Shui is the conducting of *Ch'i*, the Vital Breath, to the dwelling, and the avoidance of *Sha* or Noxious Vapours. Ch'i follows rivers and meandering routes and straight lines are abhorrent for they permit the entry of the 'secret arrows' of demons. Ch'i emanates from the Dragon Kings whose lairs are in the mountains. Mountains are Yang, and are also the abodes of the Gods; the complementary undulating hills are associated with the Tigers and are Yin; an ideal site is where the 'White Tiger of the East' and the 'Blue Dragon of the West' are symbolically united.

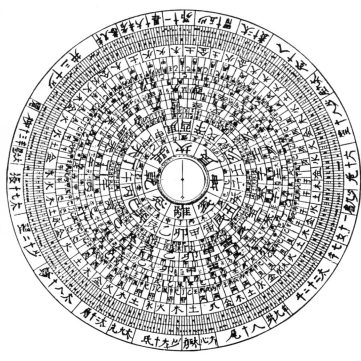

The Feng-Shui compass bearing astrological signs on a number of 'plates'. These are aligned to correspond with natural features, to determine the most propitious location for building.

With the Feng-Shui compass, on whose many plates astrological signs are inscribed, the Hsien-Sheng, or Feng-Shui master, ascertains the strength or weakness of Ch'i flow, the Dragon's pulse, the influence of Heaven, and the 'health' of the Earth. Geomancy is used both for the dwellings of the living and those of the dead, for the contentment of the ancestors in their tombs will cause them to be well-disposed to the living.

Baffling in its complexity to all but a master, Feng-Shui in application is often extremely practical, informed by centuries of accumulated wisdom. A desirable dwelling site is south facing, protected from the north, on well-drained and sloping land, served by gently flowing water, and accommodating breezes. When there is no rising ground behind the house to the north, the Hsien-Sheng may recommend the planting of a screen of trees. One is advised not to build over buried wells or dead trees, and to locate

toilets with pig-sties on the south-east corner above the slope. Windows, door openings, and furniture, not to mention trees and garden features should be positioned so that the Ch'i, the flow of the life force and of air, is neither permitted to stagnate nor so ventilated that the breezes disperse it. Bedrooms should not connect or be located over empty spaces and principal rooms should face south. Obviously, not all conditions can be met, especially in the location of houses of the poor. Propitiatory offerings and auspicious colours may be used to counter adverse forces and mirrors placed to deflect 'secret arrows'. To retain a Hsien-Sheng may be beyond the resources of many families, but popular manuals, illustrated with cartoon-like drawings and in virtual comic-strip form are available which give good advice in the context of Feng-Shui symbolism.[24]

A related system, similar in some aspects and very different in others has long been in use in Japan. *Hogaku* (Direction-Angle) is an orientation method also based on the use of the compass and linked with astrology. Directions are associated with *Go gyo* the five elements, and with the Zodiac; together they are employed in determining house orientation, or *Kaso*. The Yin/Yang principles, known as *Inyo* (*In* female, *Yo* male) also apply and the birth elements of the owner, the shape of the site, the location of the house centre are all considerations related to the positive and negative, beneficent and malignant forces which influence the precise determination of the form and situation of the house. Generally, Hogaku is site-focused, while Feng-Shui places greater emphasis on the environment.[25]

Each of the basic twenty-four divisions of the compass offered certain axioms which advised on dwelling form and plan. So, a Shinto shrine or a gate situated at the inpropitious north-east would bring misfortune, but a hillock, which acted as a screen, would be lucky. Correspondingly, a pond to the south-west could mean intemperance of the household head, a lavatory sited there would bring constant disease but a garden or trees planted would be benign. But a Shinto shrine to the north-west would bring divine protection, while a storeroom would be

The layout of a Japanese farmstead including dwelling, barns, stores, shrine, and tree planting, is determined by the principles of *Hogaku,* the 'Direction-Angle' orientation system. Near Kyoto.

beneficial because prosperity flows north-west along this axis. However, a number of the Hogaku rules could conflict with good practice—if a lavatory was sited in the most propitious position (approximately north-west by north) with a hill-slope rising to the north, then a well sited to the west of the building in a position which could bring domestic peace would nevertheless be prone to seepage from it. Perhaps because of a growing awareness of such problems some details of Hogaku have declined in use, but its broad principles are still observed in rural districts and an expert in the system is capable of weighing up the relative merits of different locations to the satisfaction of house-builders.[26]

While the cosmological meaning of the *dwelling* is

our concern here it is very frequently situated in a village or town that may have its own expanding spheres of meaning, in which the mosque, church, shrine or temple is the spiritual focus. Bali, one of the many islands of Indonesia, is a mere 80 miles in length. With the only Hindu people in a predominantly Muslim nation, it is famous for the beauty of its landscape, its people, their music, dancing, and ceremonials. But much is screened from the eyes of the casual visitor. Straight and blank brick walls edge the *karang*, the houseyard or compound, with a narrow entrance on the seaward side beyond which a screen wall effectively hides the domestic life within. A Balinese dwelling comprises a number of buildings with a karang. Its form is laid down in the *lontar*, the palm-leaf book of rules which determines the size, proportions, different kinds of construction and spatial relationships which, as we may expect, reflect

Member of the *sastria* caste presenting offerings at the *sanggah,* or household shrine for the festival of Galungan, held every 210 days, when the ancestral spirits return to the houses of their descendants. Ubud, Bali.

cosmological concepts; it also specifies the appropriate ceremonies that have to be periodically performed. A houseyard will consist of the *meten,* a simple windowless building with woven palm leaf walls, which is the sleeping place for parents, small children, and adolescent girls, and where valuable articles are kept, a kitchen shelter, a rice store, and an open-sided thatched pavilion which is the main covered living space, the site for specific rituals, and the sleeping place of the boys and young men.[27] But the most important structure is the *sanggah,* the family temple-shrine, situated on the highest point and facing the east and the sacred volcano, Gunung Agung. A karang will generally be a part of a cluster of houseyards or *dadia* occupied by members of the same clan or kinship group. One of these is the 'origin' compound, and will have the principal ancestral temple of the related families.[28]

Within the private domain of their dwellings they may feel secure and intimate with their family, but Balinese villagers are intricately bound into the structure of their communities in complex ways, that involve the recognition of status and, within their class, manifold time-consuming duties and responsibilities. Each household must be represented by both a man and a woman (usually the wife) on the *banjar* (hamlet) council, which establishes rules of behaviour and ritual observances and determines the location of new dwellings. Each banjar has mutual aid groups and a *sabak,* or irrigation society, which maintains the provision of water for the rice terraces.

Many other groups, clubs and societies exist and a Balinese commoner may be a participating member of a dozen of them. All are ultimately linked through the temple system, to which every Balinese owes allegiance.[29] It is estimated that there are some 20,000 temples, one for every hundred of the population (not to mention 300,000 household—and innumerable wayside—shrines). All the temples require ceremonials and duties including ritual cock-fights, the music of the *gamelan* orchestras of tuned gongs, and the beautiful and elegantly costumed stylized dancing of the girl-child temple dancers, whose every finger or eye movement, let alone pose and step, has symbolic significance.[30]

Many of the symbolic aspects of the buildings discussed here are reinforced through myths and legends which encapsulate the values of the societies concerned. They are mysteries, encoded in culturally determined symbols, which are only read through the acquisition of knowledge which is frequently inaccessible to all but the privileged élite: to shamans, medicine men, or priests. At successive stages in life some of the veils over these mysteries are unfolded with hallucinogen-induced visions and dreams, through the traumas of circumcision and initiation to manhood. Such 'rites of passage' may be followed by others in successive phases of life until the elders with their accumulated age and wisdom pass on their understanding to succeeding generations. But they remain symbols that help to explain the inexplicable, their meanings still implicit rather than explicit; the dwelling as living space is still a model of the cosmos though its connotations are more profound than is ever made visible through shape, form, or sometimes, decoration.

9.

DECORATED DWELLINGS

To western European eyes, some forms of indigenous building are of great beauty, well-regarded for their evidence of a highly developed design sense, or for their refined craftsmanship and attention to detail. Architects in particular admire the 'vernacular' for its demonstration of the fundamental organization of form and space in satisfying the demands of function. No traditional dwelling has been more attractive to architects, and indeed, to tourists, than the 'cubic' whitewashed houses of the Greek islands. Since they were endorsed by Le Corbusier they have been admired for the purity of their 'primary forms'.[1]

AN ISLAND AESTHETIC

Sugar white against the indigo sea, Paroikia on the western bay of Paros is almost a cliché of the Cycladic island township. In classical times it was the source of Parian marble and was attractive to invaders, and from 1537 to the Greek War of Independence (1830) it was under Turkish domination. A Venetian fortress, itself built from the ruins of an Hellenic temple, once dominated the town; now it is almost completely obliterated by the white, flat-roofed dwellings that set a consistent scale to the community, contrasted only by the massive, but drastically restored, warm-hued walls of the celebrated church of Ekatodapiliani. The village houses are generally of two storeys, built of the characteristic grey-green schist of the islands. Cypress limbs span the room spaces over which at roof level, layers of seaweed and beaten earth provide an insulating, weather-resistant surface.[2] At street level there are stores for fishing tackle, stables for donkeys, and at intervals, recesses for wells or fountains and stone hobs at the side to take waiting

A street in Paroikia. Dwellings sometimes have rooms on both sides of a lane, with steep external stairs to upper rooms. Stores, stables, and kitchen areas are situated beneath the stairs. A can of whitewash stands by the wall. Paros, Greece.

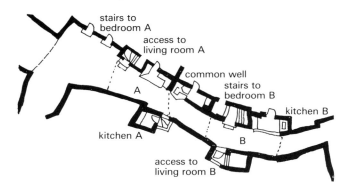

Plan of a street in Paroikia, showing rooms on opposite sides and access to upper house levels. Paros, Greece. (*After Gindroz*)

Labels in plan: stairs to bedroom A; access to living room A; common well; stairs to bedroom B; kitchen B; A; kitchen A; B; access to living room B

The irregularities of Paros houses reflect the inheritance system and the successive stages in which the houses have been built. Access routes are often steep.

pitchers. Steep flights of steps lead to upper rooms between the white walls of the narrow streets, the doors, window-frames and balconies painted in blue and sea-green.

Paroikia houses are packed together and though openings occasionally reveal small, basil-scented courtyards there is little room for expansion; dwellings span the streets in unconventional ways; a living room may be on one side of the street, a kitchen recess further along on the opposite side, bedrooms at upper levels on one side or the other. This has led to unusual spatial organization as bare, simply furnished rooms encroach on to the street. Huge stone paving slabs are edged in white, marked out territorially by agreement, appropriating the lane as living space where domestic chores may be undertaken with conversations carried on with unseen occupants of rooms nearby. Sometimes a cul-de-sac is sealed off by a low wall to mark its identity as an extension of the dwelling.[3] Though it has both suffered and gained from being a tourist centre Paroikia is still a fishing port out of season, with a small public square where the old men sit and drink ouzo, a quay where nets are repaired, and small churches and wells within the town which also act as social centres.

On the fringes, smallholdings creep up the dry hillsides. With the death of a household head the division of the patrimony may be by lots drawn among the sons; some may choose to enlarge their part of the dwelling or build on inherited land, others may decide otherwise; the factors that influence the 'interplay of forms' so admired for their audacity by architects may often be far removed from customary

design considerations, though the specialist stone masons and joiners employed to construct new houses and alter old ones bring the concept of 'anonymous building' into question. As in so many other communities, dwelling on Paros is linked inextricably with its social systems. Its beauty is undeniable, and the thick layers of lime-wash applied almost daily where walls or even paths are soiled is evidence of the islanders' awareness of it. But this, like the blue-green paintwork is an Islamic inheritance, its origins forgotten, its use by custom long absorbed by a devout Greek Orthodox community.[4] For the western modernist architect the simple, flat-roofed, lime-washed, Cycladic vernacular displays great formal unity, a reflection of the values of his own aesthetic.

Uncomfortable to accept though it may be, the fact is that the regard that we, from an industrialized culture, might have for their quality and the aesthetic pleasure we might derive from the dwellings of other cultures, may well be irrelevant. It may even be positively harmful for, by being attracted to the buildings that are formally beautiful according to our current culturally bound and transitory criteria, we can easily reject those that do not measure up to the standards we have devised. Arguments for preservation can be easily made and justified on grounds of rarity, beauty, craftsmanship or historical importance. But such arguments have their opposite, which imply that the commonplace, the simply constructed, unornamented, unremarkable dwellings without immediate aesthetic appeal are, if not expendable, at least not worthy of attention. Dwellings of a particular type may be similar to each other not merely because they are built by the same people but because they embody the collective values of a specific community.

ENRICHED GABLES

Surprisingly little research has been undertaken on the aesthetic of non-literate societies. A vast literature on tribal, peasant and folk art exists, but it is almost always described and analysed essentially in western terms and evaluated by western criteria. Even less attention has been given to the values of such societies in relation to their architecture. Some complexes of cultures share a predilection for using the building as a vehicle for visual embellishment, though this is far more characteristic of say, south-east Asia than it is of South America. Many societies in Indonesia have richly decorated, finely worked, and extravagantly formed dwellings. The Bataks of North Sumatra who number about half a million are divided in tribal groups whose territory is on a relatively high plateau (4,000 feet, 1,200 m) overlooked by volcanoes; fresh water and abundant fishing in Lake Toba contributing to its favourable conditions. Most populous are the Toba Bataks to the south of the lake, a formerly warlike people who used their captives as slave labour.

Strongly hierarchical, the typical Batak *huta* (village) had an aristocractic clan who were direct

Houses of the Toba Batak at Tomok, on Samosir Island in Lake Toba. Older houses are thatched and decorated; the foreground of the new house is more simply treated. Sumatra.

descendants of the founder and his family, and their indentured serfs. Local wars have destroyed many villages and houses, which are often situated on hilltops or are partially protected by swamps and ramparts on which bamboo thickets were grown for further protection. Within the thicket the huta comprises two rows of buildings facing the *halaman*, or village plaza, which is always oriented east-west. On the north side, facing south are the houses or *rumahs*, and opposite them the *sopo* rice barns which in recent years have frequently been adapted as houses. Deep

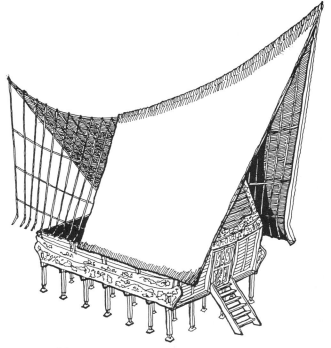

Diagram of the construction of the Toba Batak house. Front gable panels may be carved and painted.

The gable end of an old Batak house, with carved details including boraspati lizards, mythical creatures and heraldic motifs. Once richly painted the decoration has faded.

projecting pointed roofs swing over the gable fronts of the dwellings giving shade for the men repairing nets and women weaving cloths in the halaman.

Massively constructed, the Toba Batak house has a saddle-back roof and curving eaves which convey an impression of lightness. A variety of hardwoods was available and felled, after appropriate offerings, for various parts of a new building. Selected posts were placed in order of quality which reflected the hierarchy of spaces within the house. Shorter posts secured with pin-and-hole fixings helped support the floor which rested on longitudinal beams, some over 30 feet (10 m) in length, and equally substantial cross members.[5] Planked panels were fixed over the external gable end which comprised three levels, including a stair and balcony; other panels were attached to the sides of the house. These panels took the decorations,

which, in the best examples were finely carved with spiral and foliated volute patterns, and painted in black, red, and white. Female breasts and the *boraspati*, a local lizard, were also carved on the facade panels, possibly as fertility symbols.

At the sides of the house the panels were not carved but were painted. No decorations were to be found at the back of the house, where the kitchens and domestic spaces were situated and, unlike the facade which was paid meticulous attention, were carelessly maintained. The interiors of the houses today are often soiled and poorly kept, the latrines mere holes in the floor and the lighting levels low. Batak houses are meant to be seen and admired from the halaman, the hierarchies within the village expressed in the scale of the houses, the quality of the workmanship, even in restrictions on the decoration of surfaces, imposed by the village heads.[6]

Throughout south-east Asia and Melanesia, including New Guinea, related dwelling types are to be

Row of Toradja houses in the village of Palawa. Many gables are richly decorated in red, white, and black. The central *tongkonan* or ancestral house, has tiers of horns from sacrificial buffaloes. Near Rantepao, South Sulawesi.

found built on piles, with saddle-back roofs and projecting ridges, often protecting decorated gables. Many have crossed poles at the leading edges, which are sometimes decorated with foliated forms, animal heads, or buffalo horns, and variants may be traced in cultures as far apart as northern Thailand and southwest Sulawesi. Sulawesi (Celebes) is the home of many peoples including the Sa'dan Toradja, whose houses with immense roofs appear like opposing rows of giant birds that have just alighted in the forest.

Within the gables the panels and window openings are embellished with a variety of patterns, some relating to basketry, others suggesting derivations from interlaced leather and woven fabrics. Some decorations are highly abstracted but the motif of the sacred buffalo symbolized by its horns is recurrent, and powerfully emphasized by the tiers of the horns of sacrificial buffaloes mounted on the house-posts of the *tongkonan* ancestral dwelling.

Houses are ranged hierarchically opposite their rice barns, the internal spaces shared between a number of related families. However, for much of the year the *lipu*, or 'mother village' is occupied principally by the

Toradja house under construction, showing the elaborate scaffolding and complex structure necessary to build the characteristic sway-back roof. Lemo, Tanatorajah, Sulawesi.

elderly and the very young; older children and active adults sleep close to their crops in simple field shelters. Ceremonials and funerals are always conducted within the lipu, which is regarded with respect. Smiths and others, the noise of whose work might alarm the guardian spirits, are obliged to stay outside the village except, of course, when a house is being built.[7] It has been argued that the ingenious buildings, with their boat forms, curving timbers, and sail-like roofs are echoes of ancient maritime traditions, which in some cultures is reflected in their terminology.[8] But it has also been shown that there are close correlations between the technologies and forms of pile houses with oversailing gables that link, through chains of diffusion, to ancient traditions in mainland Asia.

Comparative studies have revealed remarkable linkages of design motifs between cultures far apart: the four-spiral pattern, the bull's head, a figure standing between bull's horns to be found on Toradja houses is also to be seen on dwellings of the Ao Naga in Assam two thousand miles to the north-west. The characteristic roof-types are depicted on the bronze drums of the Dongson culture, an archaic civilization of Indo-China, which appears to have been the fulcrum for the dispersal of cultural traits that survive in Indonesia. Even more remarkable perhaps, is that they also relate to late Bronze Age designs of Caucasian origin.[9]

Ritual and ceremonial play a great part in the perpetuation of ancient beliefs and with the symbols associated with them. They do not always remain the same, nor do the symbols stay constant; 'symbolic drift', the shifting of the meaning of symbols with culture change or diffusion is a common phenomenon. What we are seeing is the overlay of many principles; decorative elements, the influence of animist beliefs, the adoption of Hindu and later religious symbolism, the application of rule systems, the persistence of patterns derived from weaving or plaiting, the association of colours and shapes, the use of schemata based on anthropomorphic, zoomorphic, and phylomorphic shapes derived from human, animal, and plant life. Together they constitute for each society a form of visual language of decorative and structual elements.

Each dwelling conforms with the design 'language' of the people, but, like the individual who uses his personal 'speech' to express ideas that can be shared by others within his community, the choice and combinations may differ occasionally.[10] New ones may be acquired and assumed by a society, to contribute to the language, but the persistence of a specific range within the rule system of a tradition acts as a bond within a larger community, that expresses its values, lineages, hierarchies, history, and faith. The fact that correspondences between the Toradja and the Batak are shared by many other south-east Asian peoples is evidence of a 'meta-language' of design which, like the Finno-Hungarian and Indo-European linguistic complexes embraces the languages of many societies, each helping to reinforce the common identity of those who share it.

LIGHT AND SHADE

In many cultures it is the aggregation of dwellings within the village rather than the single units of houses that matter. This is the case with Paros, where the individual dwellings are hardly separable from the totality, and it applies too, with many other clustered villages, among them several in the Hindu Kush mountains of north-east Afghanistan. Nuristan, the 'Country of Light' is a remote region enclosed by massive mountains which is penetrated with difficulty. Its inhabitants, formerly called the Kafirs (or unbelievers), are an Aryan people who were converted to Islam by the Pushtans only at the close of the nineteenth century; much of their former polytheistic religion still remains in their beliefs. There are innumerable villages in the valleys, each with between fifty and a couple of hundred dwellings which are packed closely together, terraced against the mountain sides, with flat roofs that serve as social spaces. Often, several houses are built simultaneously and they remain virtually inseparable.

Characteristically, a Nuristan house will have a ground floor where goats or cattle are kept, and an upper floor, the *ama* or main living space, with private rooms dug into the hillside at the rear. The base of the house is usually of stone, the superstructure of squared horizontal timbers, crossed at the corners and with the dividing walls of rooms projecting to the outside, the spaces between the timbers being packed with rock and earth. In an unstable region subject to earthquakes, the house is made more secure but flexible by the use of vertical posts which are 'threaded' through the crossed timbers at the corners.[11] Entry to the house is by a notched ladder which leads to the living area; the cattle byres below have an access to the mountain meadows. The smoky interior is ventilated from above by a hole made of crossed timbers in a roof structure somewhat similar to that of many Navajo hogans.

In the strict hierarchy of the Nuristanis, the cattle men are the aristocracy; below them are the skilled craftsmen, the *bari*, and the unskilled *sewala* whose houses must be sited literally below them on the

Houses in the Bashgal valley are stacked against the mountainside, the roofs of one house serving as the access to another. Houses at upper levels indicate higher rank. Nuristan, Afghanistan.

mountains. The craftsmen are paid in cattle or kind for their work, which includes the fine carving of shutters and panels at the *ama* level on the better houses. Inside, the supporting columns, which are notched into the main beams, may also be richly carved but though the Ñuristani wood carvers take pride in their workmanship they are forbidden to decorate their own buildings and can display their skills only on the houses of the wealthier cattlemen. Basket weave, braid and probably carpet patterns predominate in the decorative motifs, with spirals,

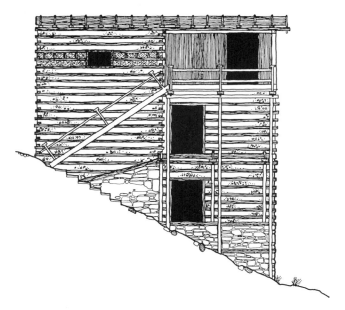

Side elevation of a Nuristani mountain house, with external decoration indicating status. (*After Hallet, Samizay*)

Detail of a joint in a Nuristani house. Vertical members are threaded at the corners to stabilize the structure. The internal columns are carved and tapered to the base.

frets, and geometric rosettes being common.[12] In some parts of the region a verandah, supported by long forest poles projects from the ama, providing the roof to a haystore. The acme of decorative carving skills is to be found in the *kantor kot*, or a house with an enclosed verandah having internal pillars carved in relief with human faces and ram and goat heads. Before Islamization these were the houses of priests but today they may function as clan houses. Clans and lineages expect the growing male members to support their kinsmen both economically and institutionally, but being of low caste the craftsmen are largely exempt from the competitive nature of the village, with its frequent disputes and emphasis on status, which their own workmanship in the service of higher class families helps to emphasize.

Some of the pillars of the kantor kot are reminiscent of the carved columns of Persopolis, (*c.* 485 BC) and certain of the motifs, though restricted schematically, relate to archaic forms of which many are still in use in Balkan peasant art and craftwork today. The apparent sources in textiles and rope work, and the ubiquitous spirals may be the echoes of a former nomadic culture; many Nuristani men still practise seasonal transhumance with their flocks. Although the carving is done with an adze and is usually comparatively shallow, the pillars of the kantar kot are deeply carved, suggesting more skilled and laborious workmanship was reserved for religious purposes.[13]

While it is not a rule, it is frequently the case that decorative treatments are richest in temples, mosques and churches. Decoration is employed as an indication of respect, or of personal or group sacrifice, as supplication, or to appease the gods. Deep carvings cast sculptural shadows that enhance the forms employed, and these can be enriched with semi-precious stones and inlays that shine lustrously in flickering candle-light, adding to the atmosphere of mystery and reverence. Palaces and houses of the aristocracy, the gentry, or the ruling classes may also be lavishly decorated. Clan and cult houses of noble clans and founding lineages may be elaborately carved and painted with symbols. In some societies such élites are closely associated with religious authority and the kind and quality of decorative embellishment is used to reinforce the relationship. Art is the handmaiden of both hierarchy and divine authority. On the dwellings of the common people decoration may often be used, but sparingly and discreetly, their membership of the society being asserted through design, but relative status can be inferred from its comparative simplicity.

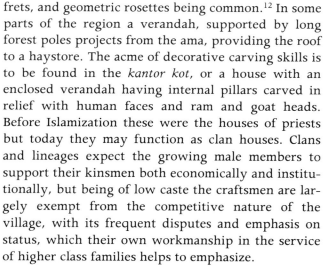

Where ornamentation and decoration may be found is conditioned by many factors, not least the materials employed in building. Some woods like palm trunks cannot be carved, other timbers are better carved on the length than on their ends, though the projecting ends of joists will often be sculptured in facial or animal likenesses. Carving of timbers used in building can reduce the weight of the components—but it can also weaken them; the same may be said of stone, which may be too hard, like granite, or too granular in texture like some sandstones to lend itself to the edge tool; others may be smooth and dense like marble or alabaster and can promote fine and detailed workmanship. Often the material itself suggests decorative treatments in grain or vein. Reeds and grass when stained in different colours and woven into mats and small panels, create patterned and textured surfaces. With the use of modular elements such as coursed stone and brickwork, or interlocking faience and tiles, complex patterns may be devised. Clay may be moulded and plaster worked in relief, such treatments being particularly suited to large planes and surfaces—walls, floors, and with greater difficulty but maximized effect, ceilings. Structural elements may be picked out in relief. Though there are exceptions, the entrance, portal, and the door itself are frequently singled out for special attention, emphasizing as they do the transition from outside to inside, from public to private realm. This is the case with the dwellings of many Hausa whose decorative motifs are sometimes incised, but in their more striking and traditional examples are modelled in relief.

An agglomerate of peoples who were gradually welded into one state, the Hausa have had a history of a thousand years. Their territory extended from the Ayr mountains of the southern Sahara to what is now central Nigeria, and though they were defeated in the Fulani *jihad*, or Holy War, of 1807 and fell again to the British under Lord Lugard a century later, they still remain one of the most powerful of African peoples. Hausa is one of the most extensively spoken African languages with some 15 million speakers. Rural Hausa live in *gida*, or farm compounds, and dis-

House of *harijans* or 'untouchables'. The mud wall has been decorated with the 'Tree of Life' motif, by marking the wet mud with sticks and impressing a pebble into the surface. Ajmer.

persed settlements of earth-wall huts, either circular or square in plan, the former with thatched conical roofs. Until the nineteenth century the rural Hausa remained animists, even though Islam had reached Hausaland in the late fourteenth century AD and the town dwellers had been converted by the teaching of travelling merchants, pilgrims and clerics.[14] For the Hausa were largely an urban people; their *birni*, or walled townships, enclosed fields which could support them in times of siege. Gradually gaining in power, such cities as Katsina, Kano, and Zaria became important trading and manufacturing centres. Trade contacts were established with other Sudanic emirates and sultanates. Today, there are strong formal links in the architecture of such towns as Zinder and Agades in Niger and those previously mentioned. A feudal system with ruling aristocratic families was expressed in the palaces of the emirs who owed allegiance to the Caliphate of Sokoto, and in the wards within the cities where the lower-class families, who followed specific trades, such as leatherwork, textile dying, or butchery, lived.

Hausa compounds. In the nearest, the entrance chamber or *zaure*, and the internal spaces of the *cikin gida* can be clearly seen. The majority of house fronts are simply decorated with white edging. Kano, Northern Nigeria.

Hausa dwellings are constructed of *tabala*, pear-shaped lumps of cured lateritic clay mixed with straw, which are laid in rows, base down, to produce thick walls, *azara*. Lengths of the fan palm, which is resistant to white termites, are used for reinforcement and to shape internal arches to support roof domes. Roofs are also constructed from lengths of palm to form a tight mesh over which raffia palm mats and earth can be laid. Traditionally, the huts were circular in plan, and a double-cylinder of linked units was a unique feature of Hausa architecture. Under the influence of Islamic architecture from the north and west, square dwelling units became increasingly popular, replacing circular ones when these eventually collapsed. Generally the Hausa compound is surrounded by a wall and has an entrance unit, the *zaure*, which leads to the *shagafa*, the hut where guests may be received. Beyond this is the household head's sleeping hut and the heart of the compound,

the *cikin gida*, where the wives and children live.[15]

Great buildings in the Hausa cities, such as the Friday Mosque at Zaria or the Kano palace, were richly decorated within, wall, panels, and ribbed arched ceilings being both sculptured in relief and elaborately painted in abstract loops, whorls, chevrons, and bosses, every inch of the surface of the reception rooms being treated in this way. Such decorative interiors are known to have existed in the early nineteenth century and may have derived, it has been suggested, from the nomadic tradition of tent hangings.[16] But it seems certain that the characteristic external house decorations of Hausa cities developed in this century, when attitudes to *azziki*, or the gaining of prosperity and respect, which had hitherto required restraint and propriety, were relaxed. Displays of success as merchants and traders appear to have been condoned, and by the 1930s many houses elaborately decorated in the *zanen gida* fashion were to be seen in such cities as Kano and Zaria. Over the mud walls the finishing mud plaster was moulded into the desired shapes by hand, and coated with a water-resistant layer of a local cement made from mud, dung and *laso*—mixed animal hair and dye-pit residues. The pattern was scribed with the fingers and the unwanted areas scooped away so that the scribed figure stood in relief against the background. It was finished with a local cement and whitewashed or painted in earth colours, or sometimes with commercial paints.

With a restricted budget a householder might have the doorway decorated; patterns around the windows would follow, but if he was wealthy enough for £15 (1950s prices) he could have the entire facade decorated. The motifs employed appear to have been pre-Islamic in some instances, but the *dagi*, the 'Northern' or 'Endless Knot', which is possibly of Roman origin, was widely used, as was the volute. Some of the patterns relate to those on the *riga*, the asymetrically embroidered Hausa robe. Others appear to be derived from leather horse trappings. By the 1940s a few representational motifs began to appear: swords, saddlebags, rifles, clocks, bicycles, and motor-cars that reflected the owner's prosperity; even the trains and aeroplanes in which he may have travelled, were used in later designs. A less expensive 'sgraffito' (incised) technique developed with the use of 'land-crete' and soil-cement blocks, patterns being scratched on their outside faces; sgraffito patterns also became popular for an overall treatment, while geometric designs became popular in the 1960s. Not only merchants but successful *karuwa*, the city's prostitutes, decorated their houses with zanen gida; it became a symbol of success and status, though by the 1970s such displays of immodesty were becoming less popular.[17]

Decoration on dwellings as an indication of relative status is by no means uncommon, but the distinction between the houses of the urban merchants of Kano and those of the farmers of rural Hausaland is marked. In Yemen the distinction is not as clear: the houses of rural farmers may be somewhat lower, and perhaps, less richly decorated but there is a continuity of form and treatment that indicates the basic unity of the tradition. In a largely dry and mountainous country, agriculture is dependent on the management of water resources. The *wadis* that bisect the midland and

Plastered and unplastered wall surfaces. The doorway has typical chevrons, volutes, and diamond motifs. The characteristic *zanko* or finials are possibly animist in origin, representing the fertility symbols of horns or hare's ears. Kano.

A high relief mud motif possibly abstracted from the *dagi* or 'endless knot', gives emphasis to a small window opening. Hausa, Northern Nigeria.

Derived from rural tower houses, the decorated buildings of San'a are built of stone and earth. Friezes and string courses have brick chevrons. Over the windows of the top storey *mafraj* are coloured glass *takhrim,* or lunettes. North Yemen.

highland regions are fertile, and skilful conservation techniques that include cisterns and conduits, canals and extensive terraces, have supported large populations for millennia. Beyond the highlands where mountain ridges run north with peaks rising to 10,000 feet (3,000 m) is the semi-desert eastern plateau. Apart from the coastal strip all regions have tall houses, approximately square in plan, which derived from the surveillance towers built to guard crops and villages from the raids of warring tribes. In the midlands they are mainly built of stone, but in the eastern highlands and the plateau, mud or fired bricks are common, and in some areas a combination of lower levels in stone and upper storeys of mud or brick is frequent.[18]

Usually dominated by the houses of the Sheikhs, villages cluster on the hilltops in the highlands, and many towns are scattered through the eastern plateau. With such a dispersal there are numerous variants but most tower houses conform to a consistent type usually of three or four storeys, but in the cities sometimes reaching seven. At the ground floor the entrance space also serves as a store with stalls for sheep and goats and, in rural areas, a stable. The floor above is the main living area, the *divan*, where the family weddings and festivals are held, and visitors received. Above are the private levels, with rooms for women and children, and the dark smoke-blackened kitchen. Finest of the rooms is the *mafraj*, on the top floor where the household head and male relatives smoke the water pipe and chew *gat*. Niches are set in the walls for domestic objects throughout the house, carpets and rugs are spread over the stone or packed-earth floors, and low mattresses surround the rooms for seating. The walls are white with gypsum plaster, which also is moulded over the irregular ceiling joists, and decorative panels of carved alabaster may be found in the less humble home. Above the shuttered windows, the fanlights may be in a mosaic of coloured glass which tints the interior, and at night, illuminated from within, enriches the street.[19]

Much of the rich decoration to be found on the exterior of Yemen houses derives from the materials that are used and the form and functions of elements in the buildings. Both stonework and fired brick are used decoratively. Blocks of stone are dressed only on the facing surface, sometimes with diamond designs; within the wall the rough shapes are locked into

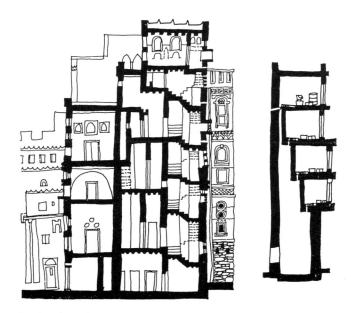

Section through a Yemen house. The lower levels of the building are of stone, upper levels of brick. Also shown is a section through the system of *garderobes* and latrine shafts. (*After Lewcock*)

Decorative open brickwork edges a roof terrace. Below, the *mafraj* windows are defined with gypsum plaster. San'a, North Yemen.

the decorative lunette plastered into the stone arch.

Many elements give additional decorative relief, among them the *shubaq*, a projecting box of stone or wood, pierced to promote air circulation which permits women to see into the street without being seen. Porous jars are kept in them as cooling devices, for drinking water, and to humidify the air within. In most Yemen tower houses the upper storeys are more elaborately decorated, and the windows are largest for the mafraj. In some areas the windows are surrounded with relief panels scribed with designs; many of the patterns relate closely to those on rugs and fabrics, though sometimes Koranic inscriptions are cut into the plasterwork. Elsewhere the walls are painted with elaborated decorations which, in the plateau city of San'a, sometimes threaten to smother the forms in exuberant gingerbread and confectionary patterns. Ostentatious, if arresting, these are the houses of the wealthy; they contrast with the restraint of the white parapets and ochre hues of the northern mud city of Sa'dah or the inventive, but controlled and modest decoration on the dwellings of the farming villages and rural towns.[20]

rubble masonry and mortar with lime and mud. Friezes and string courses marking the floor levels are customary, often with a zig-zag, or alternating chevron pattern of bricks or stone, dividing the walls of multi-storeyed houses in decorative bands. Generally the doorway is emphasized and may have a suppressed or flattened arch, with a stilted arch rising above it; the pierced lunette between ventilates and dimly illuminates the interior. On the exterior the coupling of shuttered windows with thin alabaster lunettes or *takhrim* above, is expressed by unifying frames of whitewash and plaster in low relief. The glowing shapes and multi-coloured glass of the takhrim are made by laying gypsum plaster on a board and cutting out the design before it sets. Pieces of coloured glass are held in position with wet plaster and

CHANGING MOTIFS

Buildings then, are decorated for many reasons: to appease dangerous spirits and to praise the beneficent ones, and to ensure prosperity or progeny; or they are decorated for reasons of status, and the expression of power or wealth. The motifs employed are sometimes of great antiquity like the suns and swastikas that have a history of thousands of years, or the spirals, volutes, and lozenges that have been distributed across the earth's surface by the movement of peoples. Methods of building and techniques of assembly, materials that are used and the tools employed in shaping them, have all had their influence on the forms of decoration: woven, lashed, carved, chiselled, or moulded, sometimes conservative in imitation of a former technology, sometimes innovative with the introduction of a novel one. But whatever the source, the purpose, the materials, or the skills involved, decorated dwellings assert the

Structural details such as wood ceiling joists and the supporting post and brackets have been defined by painting. Plaster work over the earth wall is modelled in low relief. Imerghan, South Morocco.

unity of the community, the values, the fundamental beliefs, and the visual language that its members share.

Nevertheless it is evident in former chapters that while some peoples have traditions of aesthetic enrichment of their dwellings, many others have placed their creative effort in dress, textiles, pottery, metalware, or other artefacts. Why, in differing societies, there is a partiality for some types and contexts for artistic activity and not for others is by no means clear, though time, utility, and relative wealth play their part. Wealth that is, not as personal acquisition—though this, as we have seen, is significant in the production of decorated buildings in many societies—but collective wealth that provides sufficient time and resources to make art possible.

Peoples that formerly lived in relative abundance, like the Haida and Kwakiutl of the Canadian Pacific north-west, or the Maoris of New Zealand, developed complex societies with elaborate rituals and creative arts which included massively-sculptured houseposts and bravura painting. Notable for their scale, technology, and construction, their dwellings are not discussed here because they were already in decline a century ago and have long since disappeared.[21] With their failing fortunes they eventually found themselves to be underprivileged minorities within larger societies from whose economy and values they were not independent. Recently, through the reconstruction of their community houses, they have attempted to salvage some of their architectural tradition. A number of the peoples who have been discussed here—the Toba Bataks, for example, have cultures threatened by similar forces, and their splendid decorative buildings are waning rapidly as population pressures are forcing large numbers to move to eastern Sumatra or to settle in the cities. Nevertheless, even if their architecture has suffered in quality, urbanized Toba Bataks in Medan have strengthened their kinship ties and formed clan associations that still perform appropriate rites for the construction of the city dwelling.[22]

An aesthetic which conforms with the collective values and formal languages of a particular society does not necessarily allow much room for personal taste or visual ideas. Individualism and the freedom of expression encouraged in western art (but *discouraged* on western domestic dwellings) has only a limited place. But it is not entirely absent, and some peoples have evolved forms of decoration which accord with the aesthetic norms of their group yet permit greater freedom for personal creativity. Such is the case with the Transvaal Ndbele whose *rondavel* form of dwelling has been replaced, under urban influence, by a rectangular unit. In common with other peoples of southern Africa, among them the Sotho, the Pedi of the Transvaal, and the Tswana of Botswana, the Ndebele have retained the *lapa* (cf. Tswana lolwapa), or courtyard, with an emphasized entrance placed as a reception apron before the dwelling huts. Divided by a wall, it has a rear cooking place and a front area which is used as an open living reception space, surrounded by stepped seating platforms designed to get the benefit of summer shade and winter sun. Usually the entrance is emphasized by moulded clay piers or by raising the level of the wall, ziggurat fashion, in a succession of steps. Both the front of the house and the outside walls of the lapa are painted in strong colours which contrast with the more sober grey and white chevron patterns of the lapa interior and the brown or grey walls of the less important sides. Slaked lime is used for the groundwork of white and a mixture of clay and soot is prepared for the strong bands of black which delineate bold designs on the vertical surfaces. Earths provide the basic palette of red-brown and ochre, with Rickett's Blue, a strong pigment used for heigh-

tening the whiteness of domestic laundry, mixed with chalk whiting or used neat.[23] A powerful symmetry is evident in the patterns which, in earlier examples, derived from the shapes of woven textiles. Like many southern African peoples the Ndebele and the related M'Pogga are noted for their inventive and colourful beadwork, bracelets, armbands, collars, headbands, and aprons. Stepped patterns produced by the careful stringing of rows of coloured beads on grass 'threads' were enlarged on the wall surfaces. Having no effective binder some of the colours were fugitive and they deteriorated on exposure to seasonal rains.

As the maintenance of a clean and decorative lapa was regarded as a virtue among the Ndebele, the women who do the painting restore them annually, generally in early spring or in anticipation of a wedding festival. In the process new designs were intermittently introduced, with motifs drawn from a variety of sources which, by the 1950s, were increasingly reflecting the influence of Pretoria. Letters from automobile licence plates enjoyed a brief fashion, but the most persistent themes were based on urban Victorian architecture. Domes and cupolas, towers and gateways, seen on the Indian mosque and the Town Hall in Pretoria which displayed a marked centrality, proved popular.[24]

Inside, the houses were normally simply furnished, but by the late 1970s imitation full-size dressers, fitted with drawer knobs, displays of plates and other china, even paper doilys based on the kitchens of white homes where some of the women had worked, were homogeneously moulded in clay and brightly painted. Some measure of social aspiration may be read into the changing motifs, but the Ndebele women appear to have drawn inspiration from white sources while retaining their ethnic identity through the cohesion of traditional lapa decoration passed from mother to daughters, and the ground rules of white field, black outlines, clear colours, and pervasive symmetry which form the constituents of the Ndebele visual language.[25]

Near to Pretoria the Ndebele settlements were engulfed by the expansion of the city, like the beautiful 'Speelman's Place', whose inhabitants were in the

Ndebele decoration. Strong abstract motifs, probably derived from blanket patterns and architectural details. The women are making typical beadwork. Near Pretoria.

mid-1950s resettled in Native Trust lands. Many Ndebele became, in the parlance of the time and the region, 'detribalized', absorbed into the city, adopting western economy. Thirty years later the rural Ndebele of the fragmented settlements of Bophuthatswana still maintain the traditional painted lapas but there is little room, time or inclination for pride in decoration in the ever-expanding shanty settlements of Kwandebele outside Pretoria. As for Kano and San'a, in the mid-1960s Kano had a population of 300,000; in twenty years it had quadrupled. The growth of San'a was even more marked. With the cessation of the Civil War in 1969 it expanded rapidly and doubled its size every four years, embracing distant villages in modern urban sprawl. Neither old city has survived this growth unscarred but they are substantially intact; beyond the spacious, but often climatically and culturally unsuitable concrete houses of the wealthy, within their walled and steel-gated compounds, are the mud houses and hastily-erected huts of new migrants. They are experiencing on a comparatively small scale the kinds of urban expansion and pressure that are changing the shape of the world's cities and that are creating new problems in the rural areas as they become depopulated.[26]

10.

VILLAGE, TOWN, AND CITY

From the floor of a valley edged by red sandstone *mesas*, or table-lands, in the desert regions of western New Mexico rises a rock with perpendicular cliffs almost 400 feet high. On it is situated, like an outcrop, the Amer-Indian *pueblo* (village) of Acoma. Pueblos are scattered along the Rio Grande valley in the central part of the state, and as far west as the Hopi settlements of the Arizona desert; Acoma, the 'Sky City', is poised between them. Occupied for a thousand years, it is rivalled only by the Hopi pueblo of Oraibi for the honour of being the oldest continually-inhabited settlement in the United States. Its breath-taking defensive site was breached in 1598 by a Spanish punitive expedition which massacred 800 inhabitants and mutilated hundreds more. Much of the town was destroyed but the survivors rebuilt it, and apart from the massive twin-towered adobe Mission church of San Estevan, built by forced Indian labour, it is probably little changed from its appearance eight centuries ago.[1]

THE 'SKY CITY' VILLAGE

As dry farmers of the south-western desert, pueblo peoples skilfully cultivate many varieties of corn, squashes, and other staples. In their belief system, successful cultivation directly corresponds to the precise observance of a cycle of dances and other rituals related to the agricultural year. Essential to this cycle are the sacred and exclusive *kivas*, or ceremonial (frequently underground) chambers, where fertility rituals take place and from which emerge the *kachinas*, the beneficent deities who are impersonated by dancers. Many archeological sites have revealed similar kivas which link these customs to Amer-

Indian rituals of pre-historic times.[2] Acoma pottery of a curvilinear, and sometimes figurative, design is amongst the finest of the pueblos', but all other aesthetic activity goes into the making of costumes and kachina masks for the ceremonial dances that are closed to Anglos (white-Americans) and even to other Amer-Indians.

Acoma rock on plan, showing the access routes and trails, water cisterns, and south facing terraces of dwellings and kivas. (*After Yellott*)

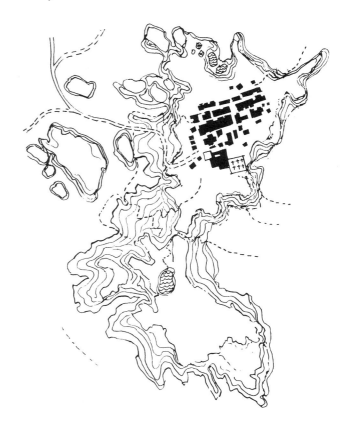

Mesa (tableland) with the Amer-Indian pueblo of Acoma to the left. Desert scrub and dried-up water-courses in the foreground. New Mexico.

Three-storeyed row houses, Acoma. Access to most houses is by ladder, but the tall double ladder is for entry to a *kiva*. The nearest and furthest dwellings have been recently 'improved' with modern windows.

It is possible to ascend the mesa by the narrow clefts with ancient hewn foot-, and hand-holds, which are still in use when water has to be obtained from the mesa-top pool, though there is now an easier main trail to the top. Acoma houses are ranged on long terraces with dividing walls between the dwellings, which are stepped back to upper storeys at the rear of each block. Traditionally, the houses were built of mesa stone bonded with a cement of sagebrush ash mixed with earth and water. As there was no timber to hand, pine logs had to be obtained from a considerable distance and manhandled up the trails. The roof timbers projected from the walls, not only to secure a better purchase but also because the logs were never cut: when re-used they might be required to span a wider void. At one time the only access was by ladder to the roof of the front storey, where a trapdoor led to the interior. The six kivas are still entered solely by this means, the notched symbols on the ladders distinguishing them from outside. Under Anglo influence perhaps, a few windows were incorporated in some of the walls, made from sheets of mica; some dwellings now have glazed windows and

doors off the street, the latter having been inserted recently. Inside, the furniture is limited; there are one or two tables and chairs, but spaces are hardly differentiated in their functions and heavy furniture is rare.

For some of the year many of the inhabitants move to the valley settlements of Acomita or McCarty's a dozen miles to the north, close to the river and fertile land. In these satellite villages 'modern' furniture and utensils are meagre, but common. But though they house much of the population, Acoma remains the ceremonial centre, the spiritual and physical home to which all return. Theirs is a conservative society which is under the theocratic rule of the *cacique*, his war-chiefs and governor, and they adhere to the customs, values, and beliefs of their clans and associations. Change comes very slowly to Acoma, though for the past century the Keresan-speaking inhabitants have bought their clothes, tools and utensils at the trading post. They send their children to school at Acomita, own a few pick-up trucks and warily accept the visits of strangers.[3]

Of course, Acoma is a small community—there are perhaps 2,500 'people of the White Rock' on a reservation of a quarter of a million acres. Their lands are large enough to support them; their modest expansion in McCarty's and Acomita has absorbed such natural growth in their population as has occurred. But not without problems. Some men were employed by the Anaconda Copper Mining Company at the Jackpile uranium mine in the 1950s until they were laid off in 1962. Soon after, the Indian Unemployment Survey of the House Committee on Interior and Insular Affairs reported that unemployment among potential wage-earners at Acoma was 89.6 per cent. Its people shared the statistics of other Indian nations in cases of pneumonia, hepatitis, and dysentry many times higher than that of the American population as a whole: today, wooden privies are still perched over clefts in the Acoma rock.[4]

Yet Acoma remains on its mesa-top with its culture remarkably intact and its terraces of houses substantially unchanged. This could be because of its introverted nature or because of its relative isolation, some

The Mission church of San Estevan at Acoma. Between the church and the foreground house, private privies balance on the cliff edge.

fifty miles west of Albuquerque, though it is not far from the railroad and the pueblo of Laguna. No one joins Acoma; even the Rio Grande valley pueblos that are Keresan-speaking have difficulty in understanding the speech of its people. There are few texts about Acoma; less is known of its people than of the more distant yet more persistently-studied Hopi. It is the epitome of the closed society, a cultural island but one that is by no means divorced from the influence of what is arguably the most powerful industrialized and wealthy nation of the world. The Mission has done its work, though it is a moot point whether the people have been converted to Catholicism or have assimilated its teachings into their belief system. While Acoma has been self-sufficient for centuries, Anglo contact, especially since the late nineteenth century has been persistent and continual, with effects on the spiritual, educational, and material welfare of the pueblo. In spite of this, urban life does not seem to have attracted its inhabitants—which is not the case with village dwellers everywhere.

Increasingly, urban centres exert their fascination for villages that are not as self-sustaining as Acoma; there are strong inducements to move to the towns. And millions of people are doing so.

MARKET TOWN

For the villager who is attracted to it, the town contrasts with the village by the duplication of services and resources that are to be found within it and the greater measure of choice that it affords: instead of one baker possibly half a dozen bakers, a selection of butchers, meeting perhaps the special needs of religious groups, several merchants of textiles and clothes, tailors, shoemakers and seamstresses. In the village, the potter or the basket-maker may satisfy local demand, but in the town there will be metal bowls and plastic vessels imported from the city. Feed and seed merchants, makers of implements and repairers of tools, smiths and the garage workers that have succeeded them offer services; packed foods and other goods from the central city are on display and available for purchase. For the peasant farmer there are opportunities to purchase new livestock and to sell his own; the process of bargaining and haggling may be long as points are compared, teeth examined,

Women gather to wash and collect water at a brick-built village well, Kathmandu valley, Nepal. The deep eaves, large upper level windows, and roof terraces are typical of rural Newar houses.

and fowl weighed at the markets, *souqs*, and fairs in hundreds of thousands of centres throughout the world.

Though the focus of the market town is basically commercial, the concentration of activities and people offers far more to a rural populace with the opportunities that it affords for the exchange of prices, stories, and gossip. The attractions of social exchange and discourse are evident in the saloons and bars, the *cantinas*, *caikanas*, and cafes of countless centres. They are frequently, one is tempted to say almost invariably, male preserves; in the traditional settlement women have gathered at the wells, fountains, and wash-houses for the daily news and in the living room, harem, or salon for domestic exchange.

This is the case with the half million Newars of the Kathmandu Valley in the kingdom of Nepal. Formerly Buddhist, they have a syncretic religion which combines Hindu elements with Buddhism: Buddha is recognized as the seventh incarnation of Vishnu. Essentially the Newars are farmers who have been blessed with rich and productive phosphatic blue clays and peat deposits, or *ko*, which were used as fertilizer. The landscape is intensively cultivated and terraced, producing two crops a year—of rice and grain. Because the population is considerable, Newar villages often have more than 2,000 residents and towns like Kirtipur more than 10,000, with densities of 500 per hectare not uncommon. Situated on a long, hilltop site, Kirtipur is lozenge-shaped within the protective mandala of many temples and stupas. With their plazas, or *chowks*, these are important social centres within the community. Narrow streets follow the contours and wind over the hilltop, linked by steep lanes and flights of steps. To the southern edge of the town is the Kasi market, another, the recent Nayaa market, is disengaged from the town to the east but is close to the University.[5]

Clustered in *tols* or enclaves, the density of the houses is relieved by the traditional custom of maintaining a *kheba*, or kitchen garden, close to the household which provides staples and also, if necessary, room for further building. Whether they are in the villages or the towns Newar houses are similar, being

Mwane Tol, Kirtipur. Guardian lions overlook a row of old houses. The main living floor is beneath the eaves; the kitchen area is in the roof. A stone podium extends in front of the nearest house; others have ground floor extensions. Nepal.

generally constructed on three or four floors, to conserve land and to permit extended families to live in close proximity. In Kirtipur they are some 20 feet (6 m) deep with a spine wall, and are frequently built in rows though they retain their symmetrical facades. Often the rear is extended around a small courtyard to make an enclosed dwelling complex shared by the *fukee*, a household often of several families comprising members of the same caste and clan and acknowledging one head.

Built on deep and solid foundations of stone, the main facade is of fired brick but for the internal cross and spine walls sun-dried, unfired bricks are used. As they are affected by rising damp, the ground floors are used as byres or, when opened up and benefiting from better ventilation, as shops. Steep, open-tread stairs, each step dedicated to a god, rise tightly at one side and can be closed off at the landings with heavy doors. The *matan*, or first floor, is used for sleeping and storage, its windows fitted with carved lattices to repel malignant spirits. Above is the *chota*, the main living floor, which has columns instead of the spine wall, giving considerable space. Well-illuminated with large windows which give good cross-ventilation and through which the *good* spirits can pass, it is where weaving and household craft activities take place. In the loft, nearest to the gods, are the kitchen and the household shrine. This area, which is restricted to the fukee, sometimes has a secluded roof terrace of sacred significance open to the sky. Roof tiles, bedded on sterile clay, sweep upwards to the ridge.[6]

A new house is built on the advice of an astrologer-priest who consults the *Vastu-vidya* for guidance on siting, the timing of construction, and the necessary

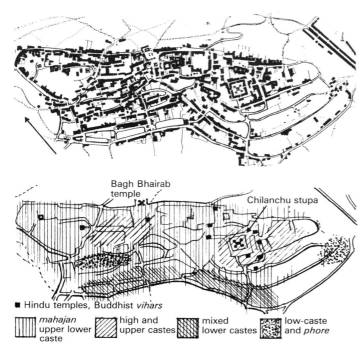

Map of Kirtipur, Nepal, showing the protective 'mandala' of temples and the residential areas of specific castes. The 'untouchable' *phore* live in a settlement on the periphery. (*Developed from Davies et al.*)

Section through a typical Newar house row. Lower floors have a spine wall, upper floors are open and cross-ventilated. The kitchen is nearest the roof.

sacrifices that will ensure the health, wealth, and long life of the occupants, provided they maintain their ritual *puja*. Each day commences with the women taking offerings to the nearest temple or shrine of Ganesh, the protector of their *tol*. Household gods are also worshipped, with appropriate offerings and burning of incense.[7] Acoma and Kirtipur, each in its own way, represent as village and town many of the aspects of dwelling and living, custom and community which I have discussed in previous chapters. Each too, has its problems.

In Kirtipur, all residents of the town are subject to the strict rules of the caste system. People in the same tol are generally of the same caste, though in Kirtipur the *kahajan*, the farmers of the upper low caste, predominate and are dispersed through the town. Other clean castes live in specific tols but the unclean castes and particularly, the untouchable *phore*, the sweepers, live in a sector of thatched earth dwellings outside the town limits. It is their job to collect the manure and sweep the streets, for Kirtipur has almost no sanitation apart from a few toilets owned by Brahmins, and the streets and alleyways are used for defecation. Side 'latrine alleys' become extremely unpleasant and it is not surprising to find that dysentry, worms, and other diseases are rife among the children who play in them. The poor conditions are exacerbated by the fact that the town's 10,000 inhabitants have to depend for their water-supply on a score of unreliable stand-pipes which are prone to breaks and pollution. Some phore work for specific wealthy families and do nothing to keep the latrine alleys clean, while others attempt to escape their 'untouchable' outcaste status by seeking other kinds of work.[8]

Under increasing pressures on land and resources, particularly those caused by the appropriation of a third of its lands by the University, many people have migrated from Kirtipur (and other towns) to the big cities of Bhaktapur, Patan, and Kathmandu—the smallest of these, Bhaktapur, has grown from an estimated 36,000 in 1977 to more than 100,000 in less than a decade. This qualifies it for city recognition in United Nations statistical terms which rate as a city a place with above 100,000 people. But cities are not merely defined by numbers—some English cities (Ely or Truro, for instance) have only a few thousand population; the city is identified more by the kind of government, social structure, occupational differentiation, and the kind and quality of life experienced within it, than by its size.[9] Size anyway, is relative: a 'great' city in the distant past when national populations were a tenth of their present numbers, was correspondingly smaller in size, though it supported a large population.

MEDIEVAL CITIES

With their high densities of both inhabitants and their dwellings, 'pre-industrial cities' (in Sjoberg's terms) depend for their existence on many factors, from a constant supply of fresh water and food to the maintenance of trade and communication routes for the transport of essentials that the city cannot provide, and to the technology for the transformation of raw materials into products. These necessitate the protection of territory, property, supplies, and life and they have implications which are reflected in the relative values of commodities, a system of laws and the means for enforcing them, the authority to impose them, and the consequent stratification of society.[10]

We might consider Provins, a French city—or today perhaps a 'town'—in the Department of Seine-et-Marne on the eastern edge of the Brie Plateau. A promontory overlooks a well-wooded valley through which flow the Durteint and the Voulzie, tributaries of the Seine. In Carolingian times a fortress was established on the bluff, the origins of the Ville Haute (Upper Town) of Provins (probably Celtic, *pro, win*: high, between). But in AD 996 the remains of Saint Ayoul were miraculously recovered in the chestnut groves of the marshy ground below, and soon after a church and monastery were built and dedicated to the Saint in a new Ville Basse. Provins was chosen by the rulers of Champagne for their capital, and its situation on the trade route from Italy to the Low Countries brought Italian commercial systems, including banking. With the great commercial fairs initiated in the

Though densely packed with houses, Bhaktapur is a city with a predominately rural Newar population. Fields are close by and many dwellings have the traditional *kheba* or kitchen garden.

The ancient French city of Provins, looking from the 'Ville Basse' to the 'Ville Haute', which is dominated by the medieval *donjon*, or fortress tower, and the church of Saint Quiriace.

eleventh century Provins became the third city in France, exceeded only by Rouen and Paris.

Local industries developed, among them textiles, leather-tanning, dyeing, and pottery, including the making of roofing tiles. Famous for its vineyards, and its red roses which were made into preserves, the city was also an important manufacturing base, evident in the massive thirteenth century cellars and warehouses in much of the city. They were constructed when Count Thibault IV built the great rampart walls, embracing an area large enough to contain several farms which could sustain the city under seige. The church of Saint Quiriace and other major ecclesiastical buildings date from this time. Provins enjoyed its fame for a brief period but a royal marriage brought it into the Kingdom of France, and losing its independence, it was heavily taxed by the Crown. Plague and pillage, flood and famine, sacking by the British and again during the Religious Wars, were valiantly succeeded by periods of regeneration.[11] After further pillaging during the French Revolution Provins recovered somewhat in the nineteenth century with the reinstatement of its markets. But the transfer of

Map of Provins, France. The 'Ville Haute' lies to the west; below is the 'Ville Basse' centred on L'Eglise Saint Ayoul. Rue Courloison gives access from the north.

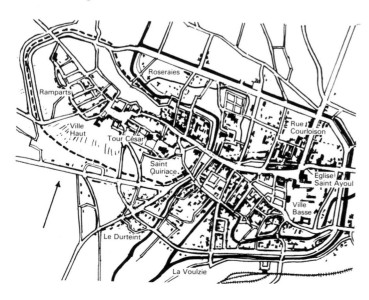

the Department capital to Melun and the bypassing of the city altogether by the railway between Paris and Basle, effectively terminated its function as a major entrepôt.

In more than its ramparts, its underground labyrinth of tunnels, and the 'Fosse rivière' along its moat, Provins retains the evidence of its medieval past. Many houses are of a very early date, and even one medieval shop still stands. Beyond narrow frontages, houses with narrow courtyards and wooden balconies extend back from the road, often with an extension or rear house with huge fireplaces built for rent to visiting merchants and pilgrims coming to the church of Saint Ayoul. Houses on the Ville Haute are entirely of stone, but those in the Ville Basse may be timber-framed at first-floor level under fine, massively built timber-trussed and tiled roofs. Modernization in the eighteenth and nineteenth centuries involved symmetrical re-fenestration, the use of stucco render, and plaster details which often hide the medieval building behind. Throughout the Ville Basse the rivers provided movement of offal, faeces, dyes from tanning; wash-houses and one or two *garderobes* (or long-drop latrines) still stand as witness to the conditions of living in the medieval city which persisted until a century ago.[12]

A desire for privacy, common in French towns, is taken to considerable lengths in Provins, houses of all types present blank walls or heavily shuttered windows to the street and have uninhabited rooms on the ground floor; the effect is to emphasize the public and private dichotomy and make corridors of the streets. This introverted nature of the house, which is almost obsessional in Provins, may reflect its vulnerability in the past. In consequence, even the wealthier houses may be in poor condition externally, though immaculate and well-furnished inside. While few people are in dire poverty, some of the elderly live in poor circumstances, without adequate water supply or drainage.

A transverse section across the city would reveal a familiar profile of high and prestigious buildings near the centre, with tall merchant houses (now often with shops beneath them), the *gendarmerie*, water-powered

Rue Courloison runs across the town of Provins. Behind the houses fronting on the road are smaller buildings originally let to pilgrims. Farm plots within the city wall, beyond.

grain mills, and warehouses nearby. The level drops away from the centre with three-, two- and some single-storeyed buildings stretching to the town limits.[13] The profile rises a little with the suburban houses of the middle-class and on the valley slopes beyond the line of the town walls rise the ungainly slabs of Champbenoist, a recent housing project, providing few amenities for the workers in local industries who reside there.

Ceramics is still an important industry—and preserves are still made from rose petals. But Provins has seen both fame and decline, the growth of craft industries and their redundancy. Today it survives as a bustling provincial town supporting a considerable military base in the Ville Basse, and as a ghost town in the conserved Ville Haute, still largely surrounded by its ancient ramparts. With a population in 1980 of around 13,000 it is smaller now than it was in medieval times, but the townspeople's concern about the prospect of accommodating 400 new inhabitants anticipated with the building of a nuclear plant at Nogent-sur-Seine nearby, partly occasioned the field study on which this account is based.[14] Accepting its backwater provincial status has been difficult for its inhabitants, but it has avoided the pressures of population growth and gross unemployment that have afflicted bigger and dominant cities. In spite of its small size its long history encapsulates much of the past of many European traditional towns and cities— the pilgrimage site and the rise of secular power groups, prosperous trade and harsh exploitation, dependence on effective communications and subordination to the rising power centre of the capital.

It has been argued by Paul Wheatley that if the origins of urban morphology are traced in such primary regions as Eygpt, the Indus Valley, the North China plain, or Mesoamerica among others, one finds that the settlements are dominated not by market or defensive system but ultimately by a 'ceremonial complex'.[15] Here the key word is 'dominated', since to some degree they will *all* be present in any coherent and permanent settlement, irrespective of scale.

Acknowledged by many European travellers from the seventeenth to the twentieth century as being one of the most beautiful and cultivated cities in the world, Isfahan, 'the place of horses' is situated on the relatively arid central Iranian plateau. There a fertile plain is fed by a river, the Zayendeh-Rud, which flows for some two hundred miles before dispersing

Bazaar shops cluster around the eleventh-century mosque, the Masjid-i-Jame at Isfahan. The mosque faces internally and there is no facade.

in salt marshes. Midway between the Caspian Sea and the Gulf, and on the trans-middle-Eastern route which brought goods from China to the Mediterranean ports of the Roman Empire it attracted early settlements. Over a thousand years the bazaars and caravanserais were clustered in a dozen villages and towns which gained strength from their strategic importance. In the tenth century AD the Buyyids brought them together in a circling wall, and established a city which had as its focus the great Masjid-i-Jame mosque and, nearby, the shrine of Harun-i-Vilayet.[16]

During the ensuing centuries a network of covered bazaar routes was woven, tying the scattered serais, *timches* (display arcades), the mosques and *madressehs* (theological schools) into the urban fabric. The requirement that the *kibla* wall of a mosque should face Mecca was the generator of much of the urban form. Apart from having its own workshops and serais, which were served by caravan routes that were kept distinct from the pedestrian lanes, each guild of craftsmen worshipped at its own local mosque, and bathed at the *hammam*, the public baths.

Its strategic position made Isfahan an irresistible prize for successive dynasties and conquering armies,

and the catalogue of wars, massacres and destruction makes distressing reading. But in the late sixteenth century the Safavid Shah Abbas defeated the Turks and the Uzbeks and made Isfahan his capital, instituting in 1597 a programme of building and development that continued for thirty years. With his planner Sheikh Behai he shifted the centre of the city outside its former limits to a polo ground which he made into a new *maidan*, still one of the largest public spaces in the world. Beside it a Timurid gatehouse became the entrance to his palace gardens; opposite he built a mosque to the memory of his father-in-law Sheikh Lutfullah and at one end of the maidan a mosque to himself, the Masjid-i-Shah, both remarkable for their beauty and skilful, eccentric orientation. To bring merchants to the new city he threw two bridges across the Zayendeh-Rud and built a boulevard, the Chahar-Bagh, lined with gardens, fountains, and *jubs* or watercourses, which brought fresh water through the city. At the far end of the maidan the Kaiserieh gate denoted the entrance to a new Bazaar-i-Shah, formally planned but ingeniously linked with the meandering route of the old bazaar.[17]

These were the greatest years of Isfahan's history, when literature, poetry, learning, scholarship, religious thought, judicial systems, architecture, and the visual arts flourished alongside its commercial activity. Some 1,600 caravanserais and 300 hammams were in use besides numerous mosques and madressehs and the network of routes and lanes which made the Isfahan bazaar the largest in the world. Between them were the houses of the merchants, with great garden courts, *talars* (loggias), and winter rooms, and separate smaller secluded *anderun*, the courts for the women, and blood or marriage kin.[18] In the remaining spaces the houses of the artisans were ingeniously sited, with small rooms and stores taking up the irregularities so that the courtyards, though small, could be square with a central pool and tree. Though many of the merchant houses are in disrepair today, the artisan dwellings are still in use. Approached by twisting narrow lanes between the high blank walls, an unobtrusive doorway opens on to a small reception chamber from which access to the entertaining area

Houses take up the spaces in the oldest part of Isfahan, the site of the Maidan-i-Qadim. Roofs are used for drying dyed wools; a standpipe serves the community of guild members and their families.

for male non-relatives may be gained. Beyond, a modest dwelling may have a kitchen, latrine, several personal rooms, and a joint family room opening on a single court. Service lanes facilitate the evacuation of the latrines.

Lanes that were built to take camel trains and donkeys cannot take vehicles; when a major serai burned down in the 1970s there was no access for a fire tender.[19] Under the late Shah's programme of modernization the city suffered draconian measures which introduced modern thoroughfares that sliced across its grain and severed the link between the Masjid-i-Jame and the bazaar, violating rather than complementing its organic structure. The city has continued to attract newcomers, of whom many were domiciled in old serais of the bazaar area that had lost their former function. Others were joined by their families and moved to the slowly expanding low-rise suburbs.

In spite of its turbulent history, Isfahan has weathered the tempest of its past, maintaining the essence of the city as a complex of communication systems

Interior courtyard of a small house in the Isfahan Bazaar. The angled entrance to the street is to the right of the arch; a woman prepares food before the entrance to the guest and reception room. In the court a tree and garden pool help to keep the courtyard cool.

through which are channelled the exchange of concepts, creativity, and commerce on which it thrives, and within the pattern of its culture enhances the quality of life of its inhabitants.[20]

URBAN CRISIS

Much time and paper has been spent on defining the city. Louis Wirth attempted a sociological definition, concluding that it was distinguished by the great size of the population aggregate, its high density, and the heterogeneity of its population. He noted the greater secularization of the community and the growth of voluntary organizations through which the urbanite acquires status and satisfaction, and he commented upon the segmented social roles of the urban population. He believed that contacts within the city were impersonal and transitory and that competition and formal control had been substituted for the bonds of kinship and neighbourliness that exist within the 'folk' community. Wirth's theories were based on a western concept of the city and some of his conclusions were challenged by William Bascom when, in 1955, he compared them with the urbanization patterns of the Yoruba in Nigeria.[21]

Before the 'Scramble for Africa' and its partition at the close of the nineteenth century into colonies of the European Imperial countries, the continent south of the Sahara had very few cities. Most African peoples lived in villages, or sometimes within somewhat larger settlements from which the chiefs ruled their peoples and territories. But there were some, as we have seen, in the savannah regions, and there were significant early exceptions even in the forest areas such as the Ashanti capital of Kumasi. The Yoruba, one of the most influential people in Africa, who occupy a large territory of Western Nigeria, were inclined to form towns and cities under the direct authority of a ruling élite claiming descent from a common ancestor or king. As they were largely an agricultural people, this necessitated frequent contact with the farmlands even when residing in cities, so the reasons why the Yoruba favoured town-dwellings are not altogether clear; some urban geographers contend that they were not essentially *urban* because of their rural dependency and nature, viewing the Yoruba towns including Ibadan as large agglomerates of villages.[22]

Historically the largest indigenous city in Africa, Ibadan is well situated in hilly and once wooded country at a confluence of rivers. Its site was formerly occupied by the Egba who, in a war between the Yoruba factions, were defeated in 1829 and the hill made a base for the armies of the Ife, Ijebu, and Oyo. In the ensuing struggle for supremacy the Oyo and Yoruba emerged as victors and Ibadan came to dominate the other Oyo settlements. As families clustered around the military leaders the city assumed over a few generations a complex, but bewilderingly unplanned, character.[23]

Yoruba compounds are usually square in plan, surrounded by a continuous and walled enclosure of rooms with an internal loggia, under a thatched, or later sheet iron, roof. Rooms opened on to the central courtyard where kitchens and community activities and craft industries were conducted. Typically a man might have more than one wife, each of whom would have her own room while he would occupy another. Several families shared a compound, which might have as few as a couple of dozen inhabitants or, in some large examples, even a few hundred. In the

A large traditional Yoruba compound providing accommodation for over a score of families. Under pressure of population growth such compounds were divided and built over.

traditional compound therefore, children grew up in a highly social environment, though often a dirty one. The lack of latrines, or the money to pay for night soil to be removed, the deteriorating conditions of drainage channels, laterite earth courtyards, and lanes, all made for difficult living conditions in the rainy seasons as the population increased.[24]

In part, the population grew by natural increase for large families are common even among the educated urban élite. But the craft industries and the markets also attracted numbers of people from other Yoruba villages and towns and from further afield. Ibos took administrative posts, Hausa secured their position as intermediaries in trade, living in the *sabon gari* or *zongo* areas, the divisions of the city to the north-west where non-indigenous people lived (even so, today 95 per cent of the city is Yoruba, and largely Ibadan-born), contributing to Ibadan's high population densities. The attractions of the growing cash economy, combined with the greater social freedom of the city continued to attract migrants. Ibadan had an estimated population of 70,000 in 1856 which had grown to 200,000 by the end of the century.

With European colonization the railroad came to Ibadan shifting the city's focus from the markets as its business and administrative districts developed close to the station on land leased by the Council of Chiefs. Land is owned by the descent groups and the settler who wishes to build must seek permission and a lease. Few traditional compounds remained intact by the late 1960s; most had been built over or replaced by later housing in which rows of narrow rooms flank a corridor or covered hall, which performs some of the functions of the earlier open courtyard; at the rear a small courtyard may contain a kitchen, a bathing space, and a pit latrine. Even so, at least a third of the houses do not have these facilities and more than half do not even have electricity.[25] By 1963 the population had grown to 600,000 and it had topped a million by the end of the decade. To a great extent Ibadan's expansion depended on crafts and services. Its business and its industrial sector grew in importance, though relatively few people are employed in the city's small number of machine-powered industries,

The old city of Ibadan. Single-storeyed buildings give way to larger, axial houses divided into several apartments. Western Region, Nigeria.

which include tobacco, plastics, and soft-drinks bottling factories.

Unemployment in Ibadan is a serious problem, and the majority of the self-employed males live by petty trading which demands small capital but also produces little profit. There are two periodic 8-day markets, and many daily and night markets with complex channels of distribution. The role of women in market trading is vital; spare cash after basic needs are met may be invested in the *esusu*, the traditional Yoruba savings associations, which help finance building on a cyclic basis.

Half of the city's dwellings and the majority within the walled town, are in a seriously deteriorated condition. Though there is some planning legislation it is applied to the newer, middle-class residential

Towns and cities offer opportunities for sale of produce and commodities. Yoruba markets reflect the needs of both rural and urban people and are mainly organized by the women. Western Nigeria.

areas; more than three-quarters of the population live in slum conditions.[26] Yet the life of the residents is not uncongenial. Bascom found that kinship bonds were strong, and that the instability and social fragmentation that Wirth identified with the city, did not apply. Though size and density were certainly manifest, the Yoruba city was homogenous rather than heterogeneous, and more recent studies by Schwerdtfeger confirm Bascom's view. This is not to minimize Ibadan's physical problems which are shared by many of the world's expanding cities and which are in some, vastly inflated.

Calcutta for example, defies description: every definition of the city is to be found within it, every characteristic is present in its vast size, high densities, heterogeneous population, diversified structure, social stratifications and sheer numbers of people. It has fine administrative buildings and museums, large public spaces, light and heavy industry, and many citizens with considerable wealth. It also has for hundreds of thousands of people probably the worst living conditions in the world: the teeming population of slum dwellers and squatters whose numbers increase by literally hundreds every day. 'Hooghly-side', the metropolis of greater Calcutta which spreads west and north along the Hooghly river for 40 miles (65 km), provides a tenth of India's total industry and mining, and employment for a million workers—a third in Calcutta itself. Power for the large jute industry and numerous engineering works comes from the hydro-electric plants on the Damodar River and from the coal and gas-fuelled power stations of Duragapur that were built to serve the iron and steel works. India is the tenth industrial nation in the world, with its greatest concentration of industry in the north-east. 'Growth corridors' along the railroads and canals mark the expansion of the cities and the linking of the centre in an increasingly vast conurbation, between which are the farms and villages of West Bengal.[27]

Of the Calcutta Urban Agglomeration's population of nine million, well over four million (of whom more than half are migrants) are in the Metropolitan Howrah-Calcutta twin cities area. Since its role as administrative centre for the British East India Company began and, until 1912, as the capital of India, Calcutta has always attracted large numbers from rural areas. Lying in the swamp-lands at the head of the Ganges Delta its physical location is scarcely healthy. But the sacred river gave trading access to the Indian hinterland, from which many migrants came. Rural West Bengal remains under-developed; there are still caste-ridden villages with strictly-applied rules of ritual purity and pollution. Land-owners, including the Brahmans and other high caste households within thirty miles of Howrah and Calcutta, may have educated members who work daily in the city, commuting by the unbelievably over-crowded trains. *Muchis* and *Santals* at the bottom of the caste structure, often landless and desperately poor, work as sharecroppers and day-labourers in their villages. Frequently, work is only obtainable for four or five months in the year and starvation threatens most of West Bengal's eleven million.[28]

Thousands of young men leave for the city where their lives may be less constrained by stifling

Painted dwellings of the Transvaal Ndebele. The designs relate to
textile patterns and architecture seen in the city. Near
Johannesburg, South Africa.

High walls, broken only by a few doorways, screen houses from the lanes by which camels brought goods to Isfahan's bazaar. The dome and minarets of the Masjid-i-Shah rise beyond. Iran.

Opposite Verandah in the courtyard of a Newar house, Bhaktapur, Nepal. Living rooms are at higher levels.

In the all-purpose houseyard of a Yoruba compound a woman paints *adire* cloth with patterns in starch. Dyed with indigo, it will be sold in the market. Nigeria.

A *harijan,* or outcaste family, by their squatter dwelling made of poles and rags. East Calcutta.

A *gecekondu* of illegally-built dwellings on an Ankara hill-slope.
Many are built on unstable ground. Once they are officially
recognized, services are installed.

New roads, paths and drainage channels serve Jakarta's
squatters. Under the Kampung Improvement Programme,
standpipes, communal sanitation, health clinics and schools have
been provided, benefiting over a million people. Java, Indonesia.

Incremental building, with rooms and floors added to the
dwelling as family size requires and funds permit it. Near
Iraklion, Crete.

Above Squatter housing on the banks of the Calcutta canal. Rural techniques of building have been used. Most of the squatters are outcaste *harijans* who collect large quantities of dung to sell as fuel.

Right Houses in a West Bengal village, with the typical deep verandah, earth plinth and high thatched roof. A small shrine stands in the yard.

traditions and where they may gain some pittance from the spin-offs of industry and commerce. Land reforms in 1955 limited holdings to 25 acres and a homestead but in the small, fragmented farms there are too many people living on too little, and unproductive, land. Many of Calcutta's immigrants are therefore seasonal, returning to the farms when work is available, especially for harvest. More migrants are male than female—employees in the jute mills live with fellow males from the same village leaving their wives and children behind. This results in a serious

Squatter houses, East Calcutta. Waste cloth and jute wrappings are used as roof cladding. In the foreground are stacks of cardboard boxes used for serving food on the railway, being made under contract.

imbalance in the urban population: 700 women to 1,000 men.

Calcutta has attracted large numbers of people from the neighbouring states of Orissa, Uttar Pradesh and Bihar—rural poverty in Bihar state is even more serious than in West Bengal. Nearly 60 per cent of the rural population of some 20 million live in poverty; half of the poor own less than 4 per cent of the land. Even before Calcutta ceased to be the capital its population was already more than half from other states.[29]

Following the partition of India, between four and six million refugees poured into India between 1940 and 1956 from East Pakistan, a quarter of them settling in Calcutta. Five million more refugees arrived as a result of the Civil War with similar impact upon Calcutta's population, and still another massive influx followed the 1977 flood disasters in Bangladesh.

How have these vast numbers been assimilatd by the city, and in what kinds of dwelling do they live? Hundreds of thousands live in *bustees*, or registered slums, which are on land owned by landlords but with houses built by the *Thika* tenants. Thika tenants build two or three houses, to occupy one and rent out the others to refugees. Such bustees have been eligible for slum improvement. Unregistered refugee colonies also sprang up, sometimes with larger plots and perhaps some access to services such as a standpipe or public latrine. Immense numbers of people live in squatter settlements, illegally built and with no direct access to services whatever. These squatter dwellings, built of sticks and mud, covered in jute wrappings, cardboard or waste materials held down with old tyres usually enclosing a single space, stand in the filth of excreta and mud; squalid in the heat, unimaginably unpleasant in the monsoons. Every vacant lot is filled, huts line the railroads, perch on the edge of the Calcutta canal, and sprawl in a limitless, heaving sea of grey-brown detritus beyond the station at Howrah.

But the dwellers of the squatter settlements are not the most disadvantaged of the residents of Calcutta; half a million people, perhaps more, live without a dwelling of any kind; the pavement dwellers of the city who sleep on the steps of shops, in the station precincts, on rooftops, on traffic islands, on the sidewalks. With no cover but a cloth in which to wrap themselves at night, whole families live and somehow raise their children. Squatters and pavement dwellers have set up enterprises selling matches or pencils, cleaning shoes, or, with bathroom scales, weighing passers-by. Others live by scavenging, turning over piles of refuse and waste for recycling materials or, if they are near water, as *dhobis*, or washermen. Many collect dung from the old cattle turned loose in the streets, to make and sell dung-cakes for fuel as they had in their villages, while in numerous squatter houses—of which at least one in ten is a workshop—families work on contract, making the cups for railroad *chai* (tea) from playing cards, and paper bags from magazines or computer print-outs.[30]

With little or no sanitation, and with water tanks that are used for washing, drinking, washing clothes, and even excretion, disease is rife. An infrastructure appropriate for two million people now has to support a population of more than four times that. Yet the squatter settlements and the bustees provide a foothold for the low-caste or *harijan* migrant and the conditions of living are often little worse than in his village. The city offers opportunities for making some kind of living, however marginal, even of establishing a small business. The Thika tenant system encourages small-scale enterprise, as Colin Rosser has argued, while the bustees afford basic living accommodation close to places of work. Faced with the reality that the bustees will not be replaced this century (the city managed to build only 9,000 replacement housing units over a fifteen-year period), ambitious Bustee Improvement Schemes were initiated. Between 1971 and 1979 over 1.5 million slum dwellers benefited from better sewerage and services. But the communities were not involved in the decision-making and subsequent maintenance has been poor. Meanwhile, even more migrants flock to the improved locations.[31]

If conditions of homelessness appear in sharpest relief in Calcutta the problems of Bombay are no less massive, nor the housing any better. In countries throughout the developing world, and increasingly, on the doorsteps of Europe, squatter camps and illegal settlements have developed around the cities. In a rapidly urbanizing world the dwellings of the new migrants, as much as those of the underprivileged rural poor and the problems of the homeless, present an unprecedented challenge.

An improved *bustee* in East Calcutta. Electricity, a fitful water supply, and some sewerage disposal have been introduced. Roofs have been tiled, brick will replace woven mat walls, and the road is being stabilized.

11.

HOUSING THE HOMELESS

Few readers, I know, are likely to have seen an Eskimo iglu. But I opened this discussion with the snow-house because, as a stereotype, it was familiar in illustrations, and because in its authentic form it clearly demonstrated how resources, technology, climate, environment, settlement patterns, lifestyle, values, and meanings all play their part in shaping a dwelling type appropriate to a particular culture. However, I did not tell the whole story: dramatic changes have come to the Arctic in the past thirty years. In many ways, Inuit culture has been altered: rifle, *skidoo* (motorized sledge), and frame house have replaced harpoon, husky team, and snow-block iglu. The hunters of the white desert have been invaded by hunters of black oil. Eskimos have been drawn into an economy based on national and commercial interests rather than their own. The north is still under-developed and for many Eskimos neither adequate job opportunities in modern technology nor an appropriate development of their own indigenous culture has evolved.[1]

Dwellings illustrate the situation. As the skidoos enabled hunters to depart and return in a day or two, the skills in building iglus died; as the industries were established and framed houses were imported, Eskimos adopted the new house types. They have brought with them many problems. Houses built on permafrost lose their heat rapidly through the floor; interiors are cold, yet the permafrost melts beneath them and causes subsidence. Houses can be built on gravel plinths or on timber piles—but the timber has also to be brought in. Eskimos need to heat their houses and this means the consumption of kerosene, inevitably expensive. Frame houses for the lowest economic sector cost twice as much as they do in southern

Canada or in the United States; hunting seldom meets the additional living costs and over half the Eskimo population is on welfare.

Unable to purchase frame houses many build their own from packing cases, tar-paper and material jettisoned by the construction and oil companies. But there is little servicing for many of their communities, and seldom any system for the treatment of wastes, which cannot be disposed of in the permafrost. Inuit found the 'modern' houses extremely uncomfortable, running with condensation. In Alaska some were covered completely with sods to provide insulation so that they appeared like awkward versions of the traditional house; others are lined with cardboard and floored with linoleum. Sitting on the floor when eating or preparing skins is still preferred, but it is very cold. In the 1960s prefabricated 'Eskimo Units' were sent to settlements like Sugluk on the Hudson Bay, but though they were subsidized no Eskimo families could pay the $1,000 expected of them. With chemical toilets, but with no water supply they were inconvenient; larger houses costing eight times as much were later available but few Inuit were able to pay the rent, so when they can Eskimo families still prefer to use traditional tents in the summer months.

In rather patronizing attempts to please the Eskimos some buildings—including a cathedral—have been constructed of concrete in iglu form. Perhaps it is not surprising that some 25,000 Canadian Inuit are seeking to establish their own self-governing homeland, *Nunavut* (Our Land) beyond the tree-line in the North-West Territories. Or that, in preparation, night-school classes are held at Igloolik in skinning seals and building snow-houses.[2]

Similar accounts describing the abandonment of

Frame cabins and makeshift extensions in a snow-bound Eskimo settlement at Kotzebue, Alaska.

traditional lifeways could be written about many other peoples, including some, such as the Bushmen and Tuareg, discussed in this book. Dwelling types that evolved over millennia are disappearing fast. In many cases alternative housing has been provided but it has often been a poor match to requirements. Australian aborigines, for instance, are widely dispersed but though there are local tribal differences in the construction and form of their simple windbreaks and shelters, they all serve the function of rudimentary protection from the weather and the intense heat of the sun. Even at times of the year when physical shelter for such protection is not strictly necessary, aborigines build a dwelling; most of their daily activities occur outside the structure but within the dwelling place.[3] However, as the environmental psychologist Joseph Reser has shown, the provision of permanent houses has been successful neither in meeting aborigine social and cultural needs nor in bringing the improvement in health that modern sanitation and facilities might ensure.

There are many reasons why the housing fails. Tribes-people are accustomed to a different relationship between internal and external space than that of

Prefabricated trailer homes are poorly insulated and houses are heated by kerosene stoves. To the right a 'skidoo' is being serviced for winter travel. Rankin Inlet, Hudson Bay.

a conventional house; they also experience a disconcerting loss of 'environmental control' which comes with being unable to relocate or alter the dwelling to suit specific social or climatic circumstances, as they had been accustomed to do. An inability to cope with

Although the Australian aboriginal dwellings suit their life-way, their apparent material impoverishment induces resettlement programmes. Blyth River, Arnhem Land Reserve.

the technical devices, such as electrical equipment when it fails, let alone the lack of money to pay for their servicing, causes problems. Standards of domestic cleanliness that a modern house demands are unrelated to the customs of those who use the bush for household chores and personal hygiene. Similarly, traditional methods of cooking and eating cannot be followed. To live in a western styled house requires the fragmentation of personal spaces and getting accustomed to the lifeways of whites; to adopt them involves a loss of identity. Many aborigines are seeking to return to their homelands, their own values and their traditional dwellings.[4]

DISASTER HOUSING

Providing standardized units that do not take into consideration cultural mores is seldom wholly successful, though people who are deprived of a home may readily accept any form of shelter. This is evident even in the terrifying circumstances of a natural disaster, as we have already noted, when hundreds, thousands, even hundreds of thousands of people may lose their dwellings, if not their lives. In such circumstances the provision of shelter is a major priority. While it is hard to draw direct correlations between disasters and time of year, heavy seasonal

flooding or the onset of winter mean that disaster victims have to be protected swiftly. Tents, of course, are the most immediate form of shelter provision that can be despatched and raised quickly, but they offer poor insulation from the climate, especially for non-nomadic peoples unaccustomed to the specialized way of life that tents demand.

A number of emergency shelters have been professionally designed and commercially produced. They would seem to be the right answer, meeting the need for a swift provision of high levels of protection in difficult circumstances. But the production of the units contributes to the economy of the donor society and seldom helps the economy of the stricken one: like many forms of 'aid' they have to be paid for, and the beneficiaries are frequently in the affluent West. They usually have high unit costs, and coupled with the expenditure on transport cost more per square metre than fully-serviced permanent housing. 500 polyurethane 'igloos' designed by the West German Bayer Corporation and developed with the Red Cross were donated following the Nicaraguan earthquake of 1972. Fabricated by spraying, each took two hours to make, but the numbers, the technical skills and equipment involved, and logistical problems such as obtaining the necessary approvals to build them, meant that it was *five months* before they were ready for occupation. Though they were free, only 30 per cent were occupied—partly because the victims of the earthquake had already built their own dwellings in that time, and partly because they were culturally unsuitable.[5]

Bayer domes had been used previously following the Gediz earthquake in Kütahya province, Turkey, in 1970 when the inhabitants of the township of Akçaalan were rehoused in them. The delay was shorter, but it still took two months. Later, when the permanent apartment-styled housing was built the peasants were glad to use the domes as stores, chicken houses, or stables—all necessary amenities which the flats did not provide. They were not the only form of donor-housing; two-storeyed hexagonal prefabricated units encircled with reinforcing hoops were given by the Austrian Government. Bizarre in the

Post-earthquake housing of sprayed polyurethane supplied by Bayer and the West German Red Cross. Only one in three of the 'igloos' were occupied. Masaya, near Managua, Nicaragua.

context of the Gediz peasant environment they were greatly disliked and remain uninhabited.[6]

Nevertheless the main response to the earthquake was the provision by the Government of permanent housing to accommodate the estimated seventy thousand homeless. Over 1,000 people had been killed, 15,000 houses destroyed or heavily damaged, 2 towns and over 300 villages affected. The supply of housing units was undertaken speedily—one new village was completed within two months and all were finished in twenty. The house type was a single-storey compact design of four rooms, built either by contractors to standard plans, or prefabricated; the village layouts were drawn up to ensure swift communications and safety in the event of another earthquake. Yet, a

dozen years later, whole villages stood empty, while in others the prefabricated houses had been heavily adapted and extended, or used as stores.

As the research project on the long-term cultural implications of this policy in which I was involved for some years revealed, the reasons were complex. In some cases where the houses were unoccupied they had been sited where there was no water, or were placed too far from the farming land. But for the most part they were simply inappropriate to the lifeways of the people of Kütahya province (whose dwellings we have already seen in chapter 7). The 'disaster housing' was designed for occupation by nuclear families, but the peasant families were of the extended type—living in the prefabricated dwellings either meant overcrowding to accommodate the family, or the break-up of the family system.[7] Similarly the lack of a *salon* and reception space meant that there was no transitional

Twelve years after they were built, houses provided by the State for earthquake homeless remain unoccupied. Kerenköy, Kütahya Province, Turkey.

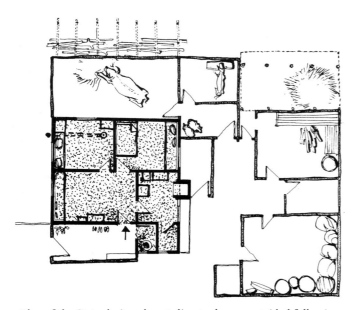

Plan of the State-designed post-disaster house provided following the 1970 Gediz (Turkey) earthquake. Extensions were built by the occupants to make the houses functionally and culturally acceptable.

zone in which to receive guests or visitors; most families built an extension to the entrance for this purpose. There were more intimate problems, such as the exposure to view of the toilet in a society which placed great emphasis on privacy, and screen walls were generally added on. Though they were adapted to make them more convenient to live in, like other adaptations and extensions, including the adding of outbuildings that the peasant farmers required, the additions made the house more vulnerable in the event of another earthquake. The peasants would have preferred to have had the money or the materials to repair their old houses or to build new ones. It would have been cheaper and culturally more effective; in these communities all people have building skills adequate for the purposes.[8]

SETTLING IN THE CITY

'Homeless' is not necessarily intended to imply 'without a home' but rather, 'without a dwelling'. Just how many people in the world are truly homeless in this sense is unknown; the International Year of Shelter for the Homeless organizers estimate 100 million but the number may well be several times this. As for the people who live in inadequate or substandard housing this runs into many hundreds— even thousands—of millions depending upon the criteria used to define minimal standards. Though inadequate housing in these terms is to be found in rural areas throughout the so-called 'Third World', conditions are most extreme in the expanding cities.

Why do the cities grow at such rates? In the first place, their growth is not solely due to immigration, for they would grow anyway, by 'natural increase'. Although family size tends to drop in the industrially and technologically developed world, where infant mortality rates are high large families are the norm. More children may mean more mouths to feed, but they also mean more potential earnings for the family and an insurance against old age. Even where health standards have improved to the point that fewer children die in infancy, the habit of having large families, and the approval given to the bearing of many sons persists, contributing to the growth in population. Lack of knowledge of methods of contraception, or access to them, and perhaps more important, religious and social inhibitions against them, are contributory factors, while in some societies polygamy further accounts for the drive to increase, flourish, and multiply.[9]

Enclosed entrance, chimney, further rooms, stables, and
out-buildings, added to a post-earthquake house to make it
acceptable. New Muhipler, Kütahya Province, Turkey.

Peasants coming to the city bring village values
with them which may persist in the new communities
for a long time; large families, customary in rural
areas, seldom diminish when peasants settle in the
city. Why then, do they migrate? Obviously some
reasons are specific to each migrant family but there
are others that can be generalized. Significant among
these are what have been termed the 'push' factors—
the thrust from the rural areas caused by the local
pressures that threaten their survival. Technological
innovations on the farms have meant that tractors
have increasingly replaced horses and oxen, machines
have replaced manual labour. Mechanization has been
paralleled by the 'Green Revolution' of the 1960s and
the nurturing of high yield crops, while the increased
use of pesticides and artificial fertilizers has meant

that production has often been improved by the eli-
mination of inhibitors; increased yields may mean
that more people can be fed—but with less dependence on large numbers of people to do the work. But
there are other, contrary push factors; the green revolution has not always been a success and production
has sometimes been reduced. The famine of Ethiopia
and the Sahel, caused by a decade of drought and the
advancing deserts created by overcultivation, have
also forced peasants and farmers to migrate to the
cities.[10]

Compared with the pressures of underemployment,
exploitation, and landlessness in rural areas the
attractions of the city are magnetic. Cities mean jobs
which, if the immigrant is lucky, has the appropriate
skills, or is prepared to accept minimal wages and
conditions of work, may mean steady employment in
a factory or industry. But if, which is more likely,
there are no such jobs the resourceful immigrant still

The city generates trade and promotes services which provide employment for the poor, Chandni Chowk, Delhi.

may find work. Cities encourage industries, and industries engaged in the production of a commodity need raw materials, packaging, despatch, and much else; the 'multiplier effect' is such that the presence of one industry generates others in an expanding spiral of supplies and services. At the bottom of the heap perhaps, but *somewhere*, there are jobs that the newly arrived can obtain if not within the 'formal sector' of officially recognized, endorsed, and taxed enterprises then in the 'informal sector' of unofficial, casual, spin-off endeavours. We have noted a few in Calcutta. They may range from the preparation and vending of food and tea, the cutting of hair or the polishing of shoes, which require little capital investment and which abound in the city, to the salvaging, stripping, re-cycling or collecting and re-selling of waste pro-

ducts from the factories. Such activities are 'marginal' and they do not constitute full employment. But they can, and sometimes do, grow into small businesses and recognizing this, some aid organizations have assisted them. So the 'pull' factors, which attract migrants and which also include the entertainments, the chance encounters, the freedom and, if desired, the anonymity of the city, are considerable.

It takes nerve to migrate, courage to chance a new life with no assured job and no dwelling. In their various ways the poor have surmounted these problems, often exploiting the specific circumstances of a particular urban context. Of course they are heavily circumscribed by limited opportunities, lack of access to power, the unavailability of land, and the cost of transport. The poor must live in the forsaken areas, the exhausted and depressed ghettos of the old quarters, or they must occupy, usually illegally, the marginal spaces on the fringes of the city.[11]

Part of the coastal settlement of Tondo, Manila, where 1½ million people live. Close-packed squatter houses are clad in corrugated iron sheeting. Philippines.

This new state of urban living does not mean that all migrant settlements are reduced to a single state of poverty and uniformity. In some settlements dwellings are largely constructed of *bidons*—cut and flattened oil drums: they make large, standard units which can be nailed to wooden framing to provide a relatively impervious cladding material, as they are in the aptly termed *bidonvilles* of Morocco. Kerosene cans are also employed in this way, producing a smaller modular unit, which can be overlapped like shingles and used also for roofing. But in some settlements, sheet corrugated iron is ubiquitous, as it is in Tondo, Manila; in others, traditional materials may be used for roofing such as Roman tiles, and walls of stone and adobe—as they are in Istanbul, or pole and mud, as they are in the Mathare Valley, Nairobi.

In 1930 Nairobi had a pre-war population of around 36,000 but it trebled in size during World War II. A modern city with a sprawling railway depot, a commercial and central business district, national and local government buildings, a large shopping centre and manufacturing industries which employ more than 40 per cent of all industrial workers in Kenya, it obviously attracted migrants. With Independence they flowed in from rural areas, and by 1970 its population was half a million; many built homes in squatter settlements including those in the Mathare Valley, where the Mathare river runs to the north-east from the city, in a broad declivity overlooked by the Mathari Mental Hospital.

A chain of illegal villages with a total population of 3,000 in 1965, grew to 20,000 by 1969 and trebled two years later. More than half of the settlers were, and are Kikuyu, though only in the outlying villages of the Valley do they still use the rural type of Kikuyu

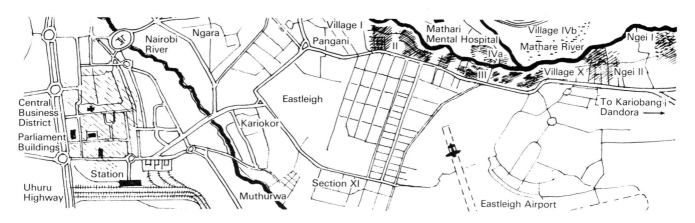

Map of the Mathare Valley showing the relationship of the squatter settlements to the central city of Nairobi. The Dandora housing project lies still further to the east.

dwelling, with its strong cylindrical walls of cedar posts and thatched roof. Close to the city the 'Swahili' type of house, influenced by those of the coastal peoples with rectangular plan, pitched roof and wattle and daub walls, has replaced it. Some dwellings were of the four-room plan with a central corridor, which permitted incomes to be made from the letting of rooms; some had rows of rooms under a single roof of corrugated iron, flattened cans or, sometimes, thatch. Small shops opened off many of the dwellings, and most had guard dogs, chickens, even rabbits sharing the living space.[12] Exceptionally high densities, comparable with those in Bogotà or Alexandria were reached by the early 1970s, with over 1,300 persons to the residential hectare (1 hectare = approx. 2.5 acres).

A common reaction of city councils to growing squatter settlements is to destroy them, and this had been the fate of Kaburini village built near the city cemetery, which was burned down by City Council *askaris*.[13] They are generally perceived as a menace to health and morality. But the bulldozing of squatter settlements on the excuse that they are 'breeding grounds for vice and crime', 'insanitary, degrading', 'unsightly' (and visible to tourists), and all the other familiar epithets, is no solution to the problems of the expanding cities.

Mathare was popular because it was only five miles from the city centre, and condoned perhaps, because it was out of sight. Many people survived largely on the illicit distilling and selling of *pombe* beer, most had some form of employment. The National Christian Council of Kenya (NCCK) took an interest in them, helped the settlers build a school and started minor cottage industries. The settlements flourished because they were socially very well organized. Leaders and village committees were supported by the KANU, the Kenya African National Union party, and even elected their own Member of Parliament. Many attempts were made by the community to obtain safe water, but though the villagers brought their own pipes to within a yard of the city supply, for years the city authorities refused to make a connection with an illegal settlement. At last, in 1969, the connection was made and a modest water tax was imposed by the settlers themselves which helped pay for the village police force of KANU Youth Wingers.

Unable to obtain City Council and Central Government recognition which would lead to better facilities and a proper infrastructure, many squatters formed themselves into co-operatives (or small share-holding companies) and purchased Mathare land on which to build 'company housing'. As they were unable to meet the Council's required standards of services most commenced without planning controls and provided varying degrees of services, building with pole structures clad with timber planking and finished with waste engine-oil—a deterrent to termites.[14]

Squatter homes and enterprises in the Mathare Valley. In the main street (foreground) an 'hotel' and 'bathroom' can be seen. Nairobi, Kenya.

Like millions of 'homeless' people in other parts of the industrially developing world, these squatters demonstrate that they seek a stake in the city, that they are resourceful, they can organize themselves, that they are interested in the future of their communities, and that they can and will build their own dwellings even when land, resources, and services are minimal.

SITES AND SERVICES

Not the least of the problems is defining what constitutes acceptable minimum standards for housing and what defines the 'slum environment', for what is culturally appropriate in one context may be inadmissible in another. There are many conditions which specialists consider. Among them is population density, which frequently reaches 1,000 persons per hectare but which in Bangkok or Karachi may be double this. Inadequacy in housing provision is also often related to the number of habitable rooms used by a family, the number of persons per room occupied or the number of square metres of occupiable space per person; but 'net' densities based on spaces within the *building* are different from 'gross' densities of *land* occupied. Another factor is the definition of the materials used in building construction, many local authorities and financing bodies considering that dwellings are inadequate if they are not constructed of 'durable materials'. The problem is that definition of what is non-durable depends on perceptions that are highly subjective, often relating to the culture and conditions of the observer rather than the observed.[15]

Perhaps the most consistent measure of inadequacy in housing relates to the provision of basic services.

Low-cost housing projects the world over have the same dreary
features. Brave attempts have been made to plant gardens in this
housing scheme. Costa Rica.

But, if the installation of electricity, a domestic water
supply, efficient sanitation and disposal of waste are
considered to be necessary in the definition of the
acceptable minimum, perhaps two-thirds of the
world's housing does not meet it. A World Health
Organization survey in 1970 revealed that over half
the urban population of the *developed* countries did
not have connections to a water supply and in the
developing countries the situation is far more serious.
The WHO reported in 1975 that, excluding China, 85
per cent of the rural populations in less-developed
countries (or 'developing countries') had no organized
system of human waste disposal, and estimated that
over three-quarters of the combined urban and rural
population, nearly 1,200 million, lacked adequate
sanitation. Yet even in 1977, the World Bank's projected estimates for the provision of safe water to the
developing world was in the region of $60 billion and
for adequate sanitation systems as much as $200 bil-
lion. The implications for the health and life-
expectancy of thousands of millions of people are
incalculable.[16]

Even where there is agreement in housing densities, occupancy rates, building materials admissible,
and services required, there are serious problems
when rehousing projects are planned. These are
related to the cost and availability of land, the price of
building materials, the methods of funding projects,
issues of self-help or contracted labour, controls and
restrictions, methods of servicing, supply of essential
services and maintenance, and much else.

Is there any alternative to the slow, costly, and
seldom wholly successful process of total rehousing,
with its regimented rows of insufficient dwellings
which do not even keep pace with growing population? One alternative is to provide land and essential
services on which the homeless may build their own
dwellings. Such 'Sites and Services' (S&S) schemes
were officially supported by the World Bank in 1972.
Successful projects had been in operation for a
number of years, especially in Lima, Peru, where the
work and advocacy of the anthropologist William
Mangin, and architect John Turner, profoundly
changed attitudes to the self-built *barriadas*.[17] Kenya
had experimented with S&S projects even in the
1950s and several were initiated in Nairobi in the
1970s. Largest was the Dandora Community Project,

A Sites and Services scheme. Some plots have been scarcely begun, others are partially constructed. A few are near completion with two or more floors. Benavides, Lima, Peru.

which was aimed at the lowest-income sector of the community, those earning between K. Sh. 280 (about £10, or $25 at 1975 rates) and K. Sh. 650 *per month*, of which a quarter was paid back on monthly charges for the sites and services. Several options were available but typically, a residential plot of 100 m² to 160 m² would have a 'wet core' (toilet and shower) with water and sewerage connections, access to roads, collection of refuse, and street lighting. A number of demonstration houses showing how they could be built to incorporate the service facilities were constructed. Primary schools, two health centres and two community centres, a sports complex, and a market were planned. 26,000 households applied for the 6,000 sites; they were required to have lived for two years in Nairobi, but to own no plot or property, to pay a deposit of K. Sh. 400 within two months, and to pay the fees for services connections. What happened to the 20,000 who did not get an allocation is not recorded.

Construction of Phase 1 of the Dandora Project—1,000 serviced plots—began in November 1976. Technical advisers were on hand to instruct families

Serviced 'wet' cores (toilet and shower) on to which houses could be built to suit the owner's needs and funds. Dandora Project, Phase II, Nairobi, Kenya.

in necessary building skills and to help organize building groups. Within 18 months all households had completed at least two rooms, living in the kitchen or a temporary shelter until they were ready for occupation. Many houses were substantially built in stone or cement block—durable materials acceptable to the City Council. Phase 2 was completed late in 1982, with the benefit of lessons learned from the problems that had arisen in Phase 1.[18]

Of course there were difficulties—not least one of time: the planning stage alone, from the first World Bank survey in 1970, took six years. There were many management problems and misunderstandings arising from poor communications; there was no community participation in site planning and there was no community development programme. Meanwhile, inevitably, the Mathare Valley and other squatter settlements continued to grow, even though new self-build projects were planned and commenced.[19]

S&S schemes potentially make it possible for households to build the dwellings they want, largely in the form most appropriate to their cultural requirements, with proper servicing and often, community facilities. In practice, some schemes are too rigidly controlled by the site layout, servicing systems, plot size, and regulations exercised by the local government for the

potential to be fully realized. Community involvement in the planning stage is often minimal and the means to facilitate community development without restrictions given little consideration. S&S schemes range in kind from a minimally 'pegged-out' lot with shared standpipes and sanitation, to the core unit, and the core unit with additional kitchen or living space, such as at Dandora, to shell or 'envelope' dwellings serviced and roofed but capable of subdivision or extension. Again, the type of service may differ according to the locality; earth closets in some, water-borne systems of sanitation in others, on-site or off-site treatment of human and household wastes, garbage collection, separation and disposal. Other considerations include the nature and surfacing of pedestrian access, the degree of need for vehicular transport now or in the future, access to public transit systems. And there are the physical conditions relating to the nature and stability of the site, soils, gradient, proneness to inundation or seismic activity, and much more.[20]

Because of these complex issues most S&S projects require extensive feasibility studies which, apart from assessing the need and the proposed site and their implications, have to consider the financing of the undertaking: how much can local government provide or borrow, how much can be expected in repayments from householders, at which rate of interest and over how long (8.5 per cent over 20-30 years in the case of Dandora)? And there is a key question which even S&S projects do not resolve: what happens to those who are truly homeless and jobless—those too poor even to be eligible? An alternative policy which partially meets this problem is Settlement Upgrading (SU).

UPGRADING—RIGHT AND LEFT

One model of settlement upgrading is offered by the Kampung Improvement Programme (KIP) in Jakarta, Java (Indonesia), initiated in 1969 when a survey revealed that in a city of 4.5 million people over 65 per cent had no toilets, 80 per cent no electricity and

90 per cent no water connections. *Kampungs* are villages, but the kampungs of Jakarta are urban settlements largely situated on swampy land prone to serious flooding and occupied by low-income families. Less than a quarter of the houses have solid floors and walls; the majority have bamboo walls and roofs, with floors of earth. In the first phase 87 kampungs involving over a million people were connected with water supply, tube wells being drilled where possible. A system of drainage canals to mitigate the flooding followed the improved roads and the concrete paths serving individual houses. Communal sanitation and a system of garbage disposal were also introduced. A second phase, for which a World Bank Loan was obtained, commenced in 1974. More ambitious, it also provided community facilities, with schools and health clinics being built employing local labour. One of the merits of the system was that *all* benefited by the Programme, and not merely the relatively more affluent.

While the KIP projects were not concerned with housing, it was found that, with security and the upgrading of their settlements, families gradually improved their dwellings. No taxes have been exacted from the residents, who are, however, expected to make voluntary contributions to maintenance and garbage disposal. However, the Programme has been criticized for what some see as its low-level provision, and for its 'top-down' policy and limited community involvement—any discussion on decisions was left to the *camat* and *lurah*, or local leaders, to organize.[21] Nevertheless, the impact of the KIP on the kampungs is impressive and its methods of settlement upgrading are now applied to 200 cities in Indonesia; meanwhile, attracted perhaps by the KIP commitment, the population of Jakarta has grown to 7 million.

Jakarta's Kampung Improvement Programme arose from political pressure; politics was also significant in the improvement of the illegal settlements of Ankara. When Kemal Ataturk chose the ancient hilltop township for the capital of his new Republic of Turkey in 1923, it was to be a planned city with an anticipated eventual population of 300,000: this figure doubled

Guntur Kampung, Jakarta, before improvement. The low-lying settlement was without drainage or made-up paths, sanitation or water supply. Java, Indonesia.

Concrete footpath and drainage channels, Guntur Kampung, after improvement. Roads were brought within 100 metres of all houses; communal sanitation facilities and standpipes were provided.

by the late 1950s. Marshall Aid, post-war industrial development and underemployment in the rural areas brought immigrants from Anatolia, who settled on the hilly, empty public lands around the centre. *Gecekondus*—literally 'built overnight'—mushroomed on the

Houses in a *gecekondu* (illegal settlement) Ankara. An early house in village style, foreground, has an established orchard. Others are in different stages of completion. Ankara, Turkey.

slopes. New migrants hastily erected and occupied temporary shacks and invoked in their defence a law of 1924 which decreed that a court order was necessary before an inhabited house could be destroyed. By 1967 100,000 gecekondu dwellings surrounded the capital, the settlers already representing over 60 per cent of the population. Once established, their houses were solidly built with Anatolian village house forms, networks of lanes winding between the mud and stone-walled houses.

The settlements were organized on the village principles of *malhalles* with elected *muhtars*, or village leaders who represented community interests; problems such as the necessary adjustments to sites with the introduction of roads, or trade-offs for the provision of schools were negotiated through this system. The traditional village customs of *emece*, or collective voluntary labour, also flourished, ensuring that houses reached a far higher standard than that in most illegal self-build settlements. Some parliamentary delegates recognized their merits and as early as 1958 laws were passed giving authority for the upgrading of the gecekondus and for the sale of land at cost to co-operatives who wished to build. Then in 1966 the Gecekondu Act led to the provision of an infrastructure and services, the removal of dangerously-sited settlements but the rehousing of those displaced, and a number of measures to facilitate fully-serviced new building. As sites were legalized and settlements upgraded, householders altered and improved their homes replacing components through the *ardiyes*, the depots where bricks, tiles, window frames, etc, were for sale and recycled.[22]

By the 1970s land was running out and speculative developers were buying sites from early settlers. Eventually, the growth of the gecekondus, so imaginatively supported in earlier years, was officially

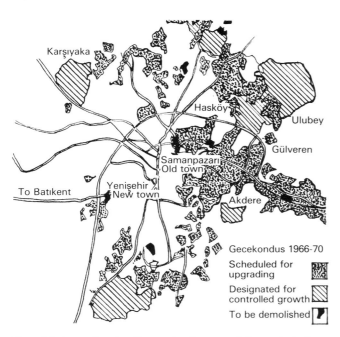

Map of Ankara, showing the *gecekondus* around the central city at the time of the 1966 Act and areas scheduled for gecekondu development.

An *ardiye* or *gecekondu* builder's yard, where materials are recycled and available for purchase. Note doors under shelter, centre. Ankara.

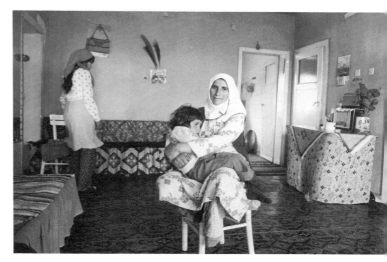

Interior of a recent *gecekondu* house. Details are urban and the doors come from the *ardiye*. The space use is traditional and rural. Ankara.

halted, but a large housing project, Batikent (West City) planned to accommodate 300,000 people was commenced in 1981, which initially included self-help projects, with loans from the Social Insurance Agency for housing co-operatives.[23]

Like all illegal settlements, Ankara is special in certain respects. But there are some overriding issues that are generally applicable and of these, from the settler's point of view, security of tenure and title to the land are probably the most important; the guarantee of security encourages sound building in durable materials and permanent residence. Nevertheless these are concepts new in many parts of the world. Traditional views of land ownership may present considerable problems, which cannot be overcome—any more than can the application of housing standards—by rigid adherence to European systems.

There are several criticisms that have been made of Sites and Services and Settlement Upgrading schemes; that they accept the status quo and tend to consolidate it, that they exploit the labour of the homeless and encourage government to abrogate some of its responsibility to ensure that all people are properly housed. It can be argued, justifiably I believe, that the problems of expanding cities, homelessness and poverty are due to the inequalities of land ownership,

Kaluderica, a 'wild' settlement outside Belgrade. The houses, many unfinished, follow the lines of peasant farm plots. Serbia. Yugoslavia.

Reinforced concrete framed, semi-detached housing units in Kaluderica. Some houses and low-rise apartment blocks have been built from books of plans.

the exploitation of the poor by the very rich and the control of industry and manipulation of markets by multinational corporations; that in essence, the problems of the city arise fundamentally from problems of western-styled capitalism.[24]

Far less information is available on the housing demand in the centrally-planned economies of the socialist countries, but it would appear that urbanization, even with direction of labour and strict controls on housing supply and demand, is still a problem.[25]

Since 1956 Yugoslavia has been a decentralized Federation of Socialist Republics of which Serbia is the largest. The capital, Belgrade, with a population of 1.5 million, expanded with migrants from rural villages seeking work in its factories. Theoretically all are entitled to housing but, though Belgrade is notable for its extensive, often well-designed high-rise housing estates, the supply does not meet the demand. Workers may apply for a dwelling unit from local government but the waiting lists are interminable. Alternatively they may obtain it from the firm with which they work, if this provides accommodation. In some instances the latter is of good quality; in others wooden barracks or dormitory conditions in a grim *radnička kolonija* (worker's colony) will have to suffice. Many people live in poor circumstances though the houses are dispersed throughout the city rather than concentrated in specific areas. In these conditions some families have chosen to build their own houses on the fringes of the city.[26]

Divija gradnja are illegally-built houses which are clustered in a number of settlements around Belgrade. Kaluderica is one, a growing self-built settlement of some 20,000 people centred on a small village. Peasants who are finding it difficult to make a living from agricultural products only, have been selling off strips of land for housing, their own single-storeyed vernacular dwellings still standing among the new brick buildings. Because of this building developments occur in somewhat haphazard fashion, following the strip patterns and old bridle paths across the hilly terrain.

Many of the immigrants come from east or south Serbia bringing with them considerable building skills, which are evident in the high quality of the houses. Slowly rising as time and money permit, the houses are largely in an unfinished state, the families often keeping animals on the ground level, living on the first floors and building upper storeys when they can afford to, or when the family size demands it. These co-operative ventures are, for most families, the most significant aspects of their lives. Attempts to demolish the illegal dwellings soon ceased, but the community still depends primarily on the services, including transport and electricity, provided for the original village. New houses are piped for water and sewage disposal, but there are no connections; wells, septic tanks and latrines have been built while they wait for the expected connections to be made.[27] Already Belgrade, like Ankara, has come to accept its illegal housing and now intends to upgrade the settlement with appropriate services. And also, like Ankara and thousands of other communities in countries where rapid urbanization is occurring, part of the problem is to be found in the decline of the rural economy.

For the problems of the cities are also the problems of the rural areas; the realization that the world's cities are growing by at least 50 million people a year inevitably draws attention to the urban catastrophies confronting us in the future. Rural development is probably less considered than is the urban crisis and insufficient attention is given to the half of the world's population that will *not* be urbanized by the end of the century. Here, no less than in the city, land reform is urgent. Every aspect of the housing problem inevitably has its economic and its political dimensions, which are obviously beyond the scope of the present book.[28] In their enormity the rights, the needs and the contributions of the individual household or the small community within the larger urban or national plans, may be subordinated if not overlooked.

DWELLINGS, DESIGNERS, AND DEVELOPMENT

In a sense, the homeless who have been solving their housing predicament by building their own dwellings have carried on the vernacular tradition of using available resources, even though those accessible to the poor in the city are usually limited to the waste of the affluent. Eventually they have been able to

improve them. Long-established settlements that have been provided with services have become indistinguishable from the customary low-income housing of the city. This is not to say that they are necessarily well-designed, or make the best use of sites and resources. Is there then, a place for the architect to share his training, knowledge, and experience to the benefit of the least affluent sectors of the community?

One important indicator was the building in 1945 of New Gourna on the Nile opposite Thebes by the Egyptian architect Hassan Fathy. Using Nubian builders from Aswan (whose remarkable mud vaults have already been described), he designed new houses constructed of mud bricks, incorporating such traditional devices as the malqaf (Egyptian windscoop) and methods of cooling by evaporation jars. Working closely with the villagers from Old Gourna who were to be relocated, he developed a modern community architecture based on indigenous means. A remarkable achievement in many ways, not least because of his painstaking documentation of the technical performance of materials and techniques, and meticulous costing of the project, it was, nevertheless, a failure. From an outbreak of cholera to official obstruction, the project was hampered throughout. Hassan Fathy's architectural lessons were not willingly learned in Egypt.

At the time when Fathy was building New Gourna, Laurie Baker, an English architect who was personally inspired by Mahatma Gandhi, moved to India. Eventually he settled in Kerala where he revived traditional techniques and, in the face of the opposition of conventional contractors, developed his own work force. Though the Public Works Department and engineers were implacably opposed to his work, Baker designed and built a storm-resistant fishing village and a number of low-cost housing projects. Then the State Government sought his advice and his influence became widespread.[29]

While Hassan Fathy and Laurie Baker challenged the accepted role of the architect they still practised as designers. From their example it seems obvious that architects should be able to produce a higher level of design for communities as a whole. In 1969,

Traditional system of room cooling by evaporation. Air is drawn through the ventilator past water jars. Designed by architect Hassan Fathy. New Gourna, Egypt.

Low-cost storm-proof houses by Laurie Baker for a fishing village, employing traditional *jali* open brickwork for cooling and glare-free light. Units cost only £108 (1975 prices). Poonthura, India.

under the auspices of the United Nations and the Government of Peru, a housing competition, the Proyecto Experimental de Vivienda (PREVI) was initiated with some of the world's most esteemed architects and theorists, among them Aldo van Eyck, James Stirling and Christopher Alexander, invited to participate. Five winning schemes were built, but fifteen years later the houses had been heavily adapted and altered: patios were covered over to make additional spaces, walls and barriers raised, gables built over flat roofs. Moreover, none of the proposals would have aided the poor; all would have been too expensive, even if mass production had been employed.

Five years later an international competition was held for the design of 500 dwelling units for Dagat-Dagatan, an area of Manila scheduled for the rehousing of 17,000 squatters (the city had a total population of 4.5 million at the time). 500 architectural firms submitted, many proposing standardized grid plans of mathematical beauty but little understanding of the nature of the need, others endeavouring to encourage community participation. Many competitors appreciated the importance of tenure and of generating jobs. But the winning design by New Zealander Ian Athfield was not carried out.[30]

Since then, confidence in the architect's capacity to cope from a distance with the design problems of large-scale, low-cost settlements has been much reduced; an architect who functions as an 'enabler' and who works in an advisory capacity with the members of a community is believed to be more effective. Ensuring safe methods of construction and appropriate systems of servicing, assisting with the transfer of information and technology, acting as intermediary and advocate between settlers and authorities, he would seem to be a special breed of professional. Yet there are a number of architects and firms who function in this manner, helping builders to use and develop their skills, and to make the best use of vernacular techniques and indigenous materials. Design teams like the Development Workshop, which has undertaken community projects in many parts of the Middle East and Africa, have acknowledged their debt to Hassan Fathy's inspiration, and have considerably advanced the use of available skills and materials, particularly in rural areas.

Aided Self Help (ASH) projects in various parts of the world have made effective use of local materials and indigenous techniques, improved by experimental methods. In Sri Lanka, ASH became official housing policy for the construction of 36,000 low-cost houses in some 300 projects during the five years of Prime Minister Premadasa's '100,000 House Programme', 1977-1982. With the transfer of information and technology gained in such projects it is possible to share successes, guard against failures and anticipate future developments.[31]

Constant problems confront those working in the field, which relate to specific climate or environmental conditions, or the nature of particular resources. Woods, for example, are attacked by termites, eaten by insects, rot, or decay: timber structures attract rodents, birds and parasites which contribute to disease, while much timber is consumed as fuel. This nevertheless most valuable of renewable building material is not being adequately replaced by plantations and reforestation.

To aid the process of 'information transfer' Technical Notes on, for instance, the use of indigenous materials for roofs or walls, or methods of installing non-water borne sanitary facilities are published by the United Nations Centre for Housing and Settlements at Nairobi, the Building Research Establishment in England, and research centres in a number of other countries. Experiments are conducted in making 'semi-permanent' materials like mud and brick more durable—such as 'land-crete', using 1:12 mixture of cement and laterite soils; 'asfadobe', combining asphalt with earth and adobe blocks; using waste engine oil as an emulsifyer and binding agent in earth bricks; or compressing earth blocks with manually-operated equipment, like the Cinva-Ram invented by a Colombian, Raul Ramirez. But the trade-off between costs of labour-intensive hand production, manually-operated machines and powered cement block-making machines which may greatly improve output, but which require fuel to run and

Experimental low-cost brick houses, of unfired clay mixed with waste engine oil. After two years' exposure there were no signs of deterioration. Near Khartoum, Sudan.

are liable to breakdown, needs to be carefully evaluated.[32]

Part of the means of reducing the cost of buildings is to eliminate the amount of imported materials— steel, concrete, glass—employed. Sometimes the imported material *is* more effective in the long-term because it may reduce time and money spent on maintenance—corrugated iron roofs for instance. The unsightliness of the rusting material is widely deplored, but as its widespread use in Australia, with diverse details to cope with climatic problems, indicates, it can be employed with the simplicity and efficiency of traditional materials.

In spite of the information resources based on the outcome of research such advice on 'intermediate' or 'appropriate' technologies may still reach only a small percentage of those involved in housing. To a great extent the solutions to immediate housing needs are met by national governments and local authorities, engineers and builders whose attitudes and values have been shaped in western moulds. Whatever their political shade their commitment to high technologies for prestigious buildings seems universal. As for the shelter of the homeless, housing of replicated kinds is customary. Standardized in plan and structure, multiplied and arranged in geometric settlements for ease

Simple standard corrugated iron sheeting details on a small outback house. New South Wales, Australia.

of service runs and drawing-board formalism, such bureaucratized, centralized mass-housing solutions are not designed to be responsive either to the cultural patterns of established traditions or to emerging aspirations. They neither utilize local skills nor make intelligent use of received knowledge. Instead, family and individual spatial allocations are drawn from rule-books and standard designs, rather than from the analysis, let alone understanding, of physical, psychological, and social needs. The problem is largely one of prejudice; hostility to the use of 'bush' or 'backward' methods, antipathy to certain materials and techniques, and fears of being 'held back' from modernizing.

As we have seen, in the processes of building, in the organization of space, the subtleties of detail, even in the disposition of domestic articles and the patterns of daily use, the dwelling is expressive of the values of its occupiers. These need to be articulated and accommodated in the building of new dwellings or the adaptation and upgrading of traditional ones. Unfortunately, the research publications and technical data that support the architect/enabler are not paralleled by similar support as a result of anthropological field work. Consequently, Government

agencies, local authorities, contractors, technical advisors, engineers, architects and planners, frequently plan communities and design housing on pragmatic data with little or no knowledge of indigenous dwelling types and patterns.

Even so, it is too easy to lay the blame on authorities, architects or anthropologists for our ignorance of mankind's housing and our lack of concern over homelessness. Our own lack of interest manifests itself in the failure to meet the needs of the large numbers of people in the United Kingdom or the hundreds of thousands, especially among ethnic minorities, who live in substandard housing in the United States. At least in the USA it is still possible, within limitations, to purchase a plot and build one's own dwelling: the restrictions in Britain are so limiting that any of the housing solutions such as Sites and Services schemes advocated, and successfully applied in other parts of the world, would not be permitted, even though they could go a long way to solving our own housing problems.

IN CONCLUSION

The twentieth century has witnessed technological advances in architecture unimaginable in the past. But it has also seen the eclipse of countless cultures, the loss of the accumulated wisdom of generations in innumerable societies, the destruction or decay of man's dwelling types: the end of building traditions and the need to resort to the meanest shelters by millions of people is not a record of which our times should be proud.

As I have endeavoured to show in this book through many examples from across the world, the dwellings of mankind represent the complex interaction of many aspects of culture essential to specific societies. In this, organization of settlements and their relationship to territory and site, social structure, economy, markets, and communications are of basic importance. Dwelling types are influenced by resources available, and the skills and technologies employed in obtaining, making, and building with them, which in turn affect occupational patterns.

Through generations means have been evolved of adjusting to extremes of environment by modifying climate within the building while accommodating particular living patterns. Community structure and family type make demands upon spatial relationships, while the cycles of the day, the seasons, the working year, and of life itself profoundly affect internal and external space use.

Societies and individuals attach significance to their dwellings which relate to their value systems, ranging from personal identification to the cosmic symbolism of the house, its location, and orientation. Sometimes wholly implicit, they may be expressed visually through built form, in detail and craftsmanship or in both sacred and secular decoration, which reflect beliefs, hierarchy, status, and aspirations.

Though the larger settlement forms of town and city embrace these in complex ways, only in the post World War II years have escalating population growth, mass migration to the cities, and the decay of urban living under extremes of economic and spatial pressures obscured many of these cultural values and blunted perception of them.

The International Year (surely it should have been a *Decade*?) of Shelter for the Homeless was intended to heighten the awareness and stimulate response to the plight of millions of people. The physical needs must be met, but where the scale of the problems confronting them invites or necessitates assistance, this should not be at the expense of cultural needs. Humane and appropriate housing will only be achieved when Dwelling as artefact is again possible for every culture through the fully realized potential of Dwelling as process.

Dwelling as artefact and process: a peasant family lays the foundation for a new home near the city. Ankara, Turkey.

NOTES

Dates for Field Notes are given below. Full details of the texts cited can be found in the Bibliography.

Introduction

1. Oliver, *Shelter and Society*
2. Typical alternative terms used by the authors of subsequent books include Guidoni, *Primitive Architecture*; Schoenauer, *Contemporary Indigenous Housing*; Brunskill, *Illustrated Handbook of Vernacular Architecture*; Feduchi, *Spanish Folk Architecture*; Viaro, Ziegler, *Architectures Traditionelles dans le Monde*
3. Examples include Kahn, ed., *Shelter*; Davis, *Shelter after Disaster*; Talib, *Shelter in Saudi Arabia*; Frescura, *Rural Shelter in Southern Africa*
4. United Nations Housing Division
5. Hoebel, *The Cheyennes*, 2
6. United Nations Centre for Human Settlements (Habitat)

Chapter 1

1. Spink, Moodie, *Eskimo Maps* gives many examples
2. Brown, Page, 'Chronic Exposure to Cold'
3. Pearson, 'The Family'
4. Balikci, *Netsilik Eskimo*, 61-3
5. Boas, *Central Eskimo*, 131-9, 141-2
6. Briggs, *Never in Anger*, 76-7, 31-6, 153
7. Nelson, *Hunters*, 174-7
8. Oswalt, *Alaskan Eskimos*, 95, 110-12
9. Birkett-Smith, *Eskimos*, 127-30
10. Marshall, *Sharing, Talking and Giving*, 231-49
11. Yellen, 'Settlement Patterns', 49-65
12. Lee, *The !Kung San*, 273-7
13. Spencer, *Nomads in Alliance*, 18-25
14. Grum, *Migration among the Rendille*, 1-11
15. Faegre, *Tents* is a general study
16. Ekvall, *Fields on the Hoof*, 61-4
17. Feilberg, *La Tente Noire* is the definitive work on the 'black tent' culture
18. Barth, *Nomads of South Persia*, 8-16, 43-7
19. Nicolaisen, *Pastoral Tuareg*, 350-91, gives a full typology of all Tuareg dwellings
20. Rodd, *People of the Veil*, 83-95, 241-53

Chapter 2

1. Worth, *Dartmoor*, 99-132, 403-18
2. Minter, 'Medieval Village, Dartmoor', 284-7
3. Jones, 'Devonshire Farmhouses', 35-75
4. Oliver, *English Cottages*, 19-21; Oliver, Field Notes, 1974
5. Havinden, Wilkinson, 'Farming', 157-65, 174-81
6. Moore, *Rights of Common*, 10-12, 64-6, 156-9
7. Netting, *Balancing on an Alp*, 36-42
8. Netting, op. cit., 107-8, 171-3, 217
9. Johnston, *Fulani Empire*, 17-26
10. Beguin, et al., *L'Habitat au Cameroun*, 56-64
11. Dumont, *Rural Economy*, 83-6
12. David, 'Fulani Compound', 11-131; Prussin, *Hatumere*, 215-16
13. Grove, *Africa South*, 2-161
14. Staszewski cited in Clarke, *Population Geography*, 18; Beaujeu-Garnier, *Geography of Population*, 45-6
15. Haggett, *Geography: A Modern Synthesis*, 4
16. Huntington, *Mainsprings of Civilization* takes an environmental determinist position, which is indirectly rebutted by Rapoport, 'Cultural Determinants', 7-35
17. Allan, 'Settlement Patterns', 211
18. Heinrick Von Thünen's theory of land utilization (1926) is discussed by many geographers. See Chisholm, *Rural Settlement*, 20-41
19. Walter Christaller's 'Central Place' theory is developed in many works, e.g., Everson, Fitzgerald, *Settlement Patterns*, 102-8
20. Chagnon, *Yanomamö*, 39-44
21. *Report of the Committee of Land Utilization in Rural Areas*, 1942, cited by Sharp, *Anatomy of Village*, 3; Chisholm, *Rural Settlement*, 59
22. Some terms for types of settlement summarized here are as commonly used by planning theorists; I have used others where I have felt necessary
23. Oliver, Field Notes, 1960, 1972, 1980
24. Oliver, Field Notes, 1981
25. Prussin, *Architecture in Ghana*, 51-65; Fortes, *Web of Kinship*; Oliver, Field Notes, 1964
26. Oliver, Field Notes, 1964
27. Russell, Stowell, 'Ksar Tinezouline'; Mitchell, 'Tinezouline in 1968'; Ichter, 'Les "Ksour" du Tafilalt', 35-51
28. Oliver, Field Notes, 1964; McLeod, *Asante*, 20-40
29. Oliver, Field Notes, 1981

Chapter 3

1. Blazejewicz, *Arquitectura Tradicional*, 265-71
2. Oliver, Field Notes, 1975
3. Allen, *Stone Shelters*, 77-130
4. Oliver, Field Notes, 1969
5. Cain, et al., *Indigenous Building*
6. Fathy, *Architecture for the Poor*, 8-11, 122-3
7. Peristiany, *Social Institutions*, 154-8, 170

8. Orchardson, *The Kipsigis*, 83-8
9. Andersen, *African Traditional Architecture*, 89-96
10. Oliver, 'Vernacular Know-How'
11. Oliver, Field Notes, 1977
12. Leis, *Enculturation*, 54, 71, 97; Read, *Children*, 76-8
13. Cohn, 'Changing Status', 53-7; Gough, 'Tanjore Village', 36-52; Gutschow, Kölver, *Ordered Space Concepts*, 55-8
14. Barnett, *Being Palauan*, 35-6, 41-3
15. Godard, *Art of Iran*, 312, 325-7; Oliver, Field Notes, 1973

Chapter 4

1. Oliver, Field Notes, 1972
2. Jessen, 'Las Viviendas Trogloditicas', 137-57
3. Oliver, 'Cones of Cappadocia', 98-9; Ozkan, Onur, 'Another Pattern: Cappadocia', 95-106; Makal, *Village in Anatolia*
4. Myrdal, *Chinese Village*, 50-4
5. Oliver, Field Notes, 1958, 1970; Walton, 'Megalithic Building', 106-22
6. Fernandes, *Arquitectura Popular*, 219-35
7. See for example Feduchi, *Spanish Folk Architecture*, 19-25, 37-94, 231-58
8. Hommel, *China at Work*, 273-7
9. Spence, Cook, *Building Materials*, 35-47; McHenry, *Adobe Buildings*, 47-58; Oliver, 'Earth as a Building Material', 31-8; Agarwal, *Mud, Mud . . . .*
10. Oliver, Field Notes, 1964; Bourdier, *African Spaces*, 160-3
11. Oliver, *Shelter in Africa*, 18, 20; Beguin et al., *L'Habitat au Cameroun*, 33-40; Gardi, *Indigenous African Architecture*, 91-3
12. Hommel, *op. cit.*, 293-6; Williams-Ellis, *Cottage Building*, 57-103
13. Oliver, Field Notes, 1975; Barnes, *Sod House*, 57-70
14. Aljundi, *L'Architecture Traditionelle*, 34-49
15. Oliver, Field Notes, 1973; Cain et al., *Indigenous Building*, 38-9
16. Sinha, *Housing Growth in India*, 48-51; Robson, *Self-Help Housing*, 40-1
17. Oliver, Field Notes, 1977, 1986; Spence, Cook, *op. cit.*, 71
18. Many types are described in Bakirer, 'Brickbonds', 143-81
19. Oliver, Field Notes, 1957, 1966, 1970; Guedes, *Technological Change*, 243

Chapter 5

1. The properties of woods are discussed in detail in Tiemann, *Wood Technology*
2. Economist Intelligence Unit, *World Economic Atlas*, 40-1
3. Dicken, *Economic Geography*, 100-37
4. Kennedy, *Field Notes of Vaitupu*, 265-84
5. Oliver, Field Notes, 1982; Redfield, *Chan Kom*, 33-5
6. Oliver, Field Notes, 1981; Hansen, ed., *Architecture in Wood* 153-180; Suzuki, ed., *Maisons de Bois*, 110-130
7. Findrik, *Prilozi Poznavanju Organizacije Stambenog*
8. Oliver, Field Notes, 1985
9. Oliver, Field Notes, various 1959-1983; Hartley, *Made in England*, 23-8

10. US Department of Agriculture, *Bamboo*, 12
11. Janssen, ed., *Bamboo*
12. Ritzenthaler, *Cameroon Village*, 95-8
13. Beguin et al., *L'Habitat au Cameroun*, 66-89; Gardi, *Indigenous African Architecture*, 35-42
14. Spence, Cook, *Building Materials*, 114-15
15. Thesiger, *Marsh Arabs*, 164 et seq.; Maxwell, *A Reed Shaken*, 178 et seq.; Thesiger, 'Marsh Dwellers', 204-39
16. Oliver, Field Notes, 1958, 1986
17. Biermann, 'Indlu', 96-105; Walton, 'Peasant Architecture', 30-9
18. Knuffel, *Bantu Grass Hut*, 15-46

Chapter 6

1. Ron, 'Climatological Aspects', 111-21
2. Givoni, *Man, Climate and Architecture* gives details of biophysical aspects of climate, 19-67
3. Saini, *Building Environment* suggests 31 °C (88 °F) as the lower figure, 22-3
4. Olgyay, *Design with Climate* gives dry-bulb and wet-bulb readings and bioclimatic charts, 14-31; Lippsmeier, *Building in the Tropics*, 57-9
5. Biernoff, 'Traditional Structures', 161-7
6. Kukreja, *Tropical Architecture*, 14
7. Trewartha, *The Earth's Problem Climates* gives the basis for the classification of climate zones. See also Snead, *World Atlas of Geomorphic Features*
8. Lippsmeier, op. cit., 19-21; Kukreja, op. cit., 5; Konya, *Design Primer for Hot Climates*, 17
9. Oliver, Field Notes, 1967; Norris, 'Cave Habitations', 82-5
10. Rimsha, 'City Building', 55; Prasad, *The Haveli*, 2-11
11. Al-Rawaf, *Traditional Courtyard Houses*, 7-10, 16-35
12. Fethi, Roaf, 'Traditional House', 41-52
13. Al-Azzawi, 'Oriental Houses', 91-102; Warren, Fethi, *Houses in Baghdad*, 42-113
14. Talib, *Shelter in Saudi Arabia*, 52-4; Danby, 'Building Design', 117; Etherton, 'Algerian Oases', 187
15. Khan, *Jeddah Old Houses*, 12-19; Elawa, *Housing Design*, 68-71
16. Roaf, 'Wind-Catchers', 57-72; Lewcock, Freeth, *Architecture in Kuwait*, 40-2
17. Konya, op. cit., advises on appropriate trees for planting in arid climates, 57, 114-16
18. Oliver, Field Notes, 1959, 1962, 1983, 1986; Kukreja, op. cit., 121-2
19. Danby, 'Design of Buildings', 63-6
20. Cuny, *Disasters and Development*, 29-39
21. Davis, *Shelter after Disaster*, 19-23, 104-17
22. Extensive coverage of case studies is given in May, ed., *Earthen Building*
23. UNDRO, *Shelter after Disaster*, 65-73
24. Davis, op. cit., 10-15; Davis, 'Guatemala', 16-41
25. Oliver, 'Context of Earthen Housing', 167-89

Chapter 7

1. Le Corbusier, *New Architecture*, 215-45
2. Oliver, Davis, Bentley, *Dunroamin*
3. Ravuvu, *Fijian Way of Life*, 14-24; Hocart, *Northern Fiji*, 285-7. The term *mbure* refers to any building; *vale* refers to the dwelling.
4. R. M. W. Dixon, Field Notes. I am indebted to Professor Dixon for his account of house-building in Waitabu, Taveuni
5. Schapera, *The Tswana*, 26, 39-40
6. Schapera, *Married Life*, 94-9, 100-2
7. Larsson, *Traditional Tswana Housing*, 51-60, 72, 88 *et seq.*
8. Oliver, Field Notes, 1978; Evans, 'Ulster Farmhouse', 27-31
9. Danachair, 'Three House Types', 22-6; McCourt, 'Outshot House-type', 27-34
10. Gailey, 'Kitchen Furniture', 18-31
11. Evans, *Irish Folkways*, 59-71; Glassie, *Passing the Time*, 327-98
12. Aljoofre, 'Early Malay Dwellings', 6-13; Hilton, 'Basic Malay House', 132-55; Stewart, Voon, 'Adaptation and Change', 31-9
13. Ali, *Malay Peasant Society*, 44-51, 191-3
14. Endicott, *Malay Magic*, 133
15. Oliver, Field Notes, 1982-5; Oliver, 'Resettlement Housing'
16. For comparable communities see Magnarella, *Tradition and Change*; Stirling, *Turkish Village*
17. Whittier, 'The Kenyah', 92-108; Miles, 'The Ngadju Longhouse', 45-57
18. Wright, Morrison, Wong, *Ibans of Borneo*, 28-58 *et seq.*; Dickson, *Sarawak*, 98-101
19. Freeman, *Report on the Iban*, 114-25
20. Aspects of gender and the use of space are illustrated in Ardener, ed., *Women and Space*. See also, Friedl, *Women and Men*
21. For examples see Herskovits, *Economic Anthropology*, 67-108, 124-79
22. For examples see Stephens, *Cross-Cultural Perspective*; Queen, Habenstein, Adams, *The Family*
23. Fox, *Kinship and Marriage*; Murdock, *Social Structure*

Chapter 8

1. Dennis, *Hopi Child*, 115-60; Whorf, 'Hopi Architecture', 199-206
2. Kluckhohn, Leighton, *The Navajo*, 87-91, 109-11; Kluckhohn, Hill, Kluckhohn, *Navajo Material Culture*, 402-4
3. Oliver, Field Notes, 1972; Oliver, 'Navajo Hogan'; Jett, Spencer, *Navajo Architecture* gives a full typology
4. Curtis, *The Indian's Book*, 356-8, 382-8, 533. For a full description see Wyman, *Blessingway*; Pinxten, *Anthropology of Space*, 9-11, 36
5. Gill, *Songs of Life*, 6-21; Oliver, 'Form and Symbol'
6. Forde, *Habitat, Economy, Society*, 251-328
7. Hallett, Samizay, *Architecture of Afghanistan*, 35-51

8. Guidoni, *Primitive Architecture*, 72-376 (From Micheli, 1964; no other details given); Faegre, *Tents*, 91-3
9. Tserendulam, 'In Praise of Life in a Ger'; Oliver, 'Anthropology of Shelter', 9-15
10. For early examples see Lethaby, *Architecture, Nature, Magic*; for brief notes on many cross-cultural examples see Lord Raglan, *Temple and the House*
11. Oliver, 'Introduction' in *Shelter, Sign and Symbol*, 7-37
12. Lebeuf, *L'Habitation des Fali*, 457-559. Source works on the Dogon include Griaule, *Conversations with Ogotemmêli*; Griaule, Dieterlen, *Le Rénard Pâle*; Parin, Morgenthaler, Parin-Matthey, *Les Blancs Pensent Trop*; Spini, *Togu Na*. Dogon examples have been cited in Duly, 36-44; Guidoni, 267-96; Rapoport, 50; Gardi, 105-15; Lagopoulos, 207-10; Morgenthaler, 149-51; Van Eyck, 188, among others.
13. Griaule, Dieterlen, 'The Dogon', 83-96
14. For examples see Needham, ed., *Right and Left*; see also Tuan, *Topophilia*, 16-26
15. Bourdieu, 'The Berber House', 99-110
16. Bourdieu, *Theory of Practice*, 90-1, 143-58
17. Griaule, Dieterlen, op. cit., 97-9
18. Discussed in detail in Hugh-Jones, *Palm and Pleiades*
19. Hugh-Jones, *Milk River*, 40-53, 238-74
20. Dahl, 'House in Madagascar', 181-7; see also Ruud, *Malagasay Customs*
21. Rowland, *Art and Architecture of India*, 164-7; for a full study see Acharya, *Manasara*; Pieper, 'Three Cities of Nepal', 55-64, 69
22. Sanskrit manuals from South India are discussed by Dagens in *Ajitagama and the Rauravagama*
23. Windass in 'ARTIC in Andhra Pradesh', 103-4
24. Skinner, *Manual of Feng-Shui*; for Chinese geomancy in Malaysia, see Lip, 'Malaysia's Architectural Heritage', 26-8
25. Gale 'Orientation', 38-50
26. Beardsley, Hall, Ward, *Village Japan*, 79-81
27. Geertz, *Kinship in Bali*, 49-52
28. Ramseyer, *Art of Bali*, 129-34
29. For detailed analysis of Balinese social structure see Geertz, *Pedlars and Princes*; Lansing, *Three Worlds of Bali*
30. Bandem, de Boer, *Balinese Dance in Transition*

Chapter 9

1. Oliver, 'Introduction', *Shelter and Society*, 30-3
2. Clarke, Radford, *Cyclades*, 30-3
3. Oliver, Field Notes, 1962
4. Oliver, 'Primary Forms', *Shelter in Greece*, 11-15
5. Sargeant, 'House Form in Sumatra', 27-32; Sargeant, *Traditional Buildings: Batak Toba*, 5-9
6. de Boer, 'Het Toba Bataksche Huis', 31-41
7. Domenig, *Primitiven Dachbau*, 45-61, 94-175; Sumintardja, 'Poso-Toraja', 45-50
8. Sherwin, 'Batak to Minangkabau', 38-42; Lewcock, Brans, 'The Boat as Symbol', 107-16

9. Heine-Geldern, 'Tribal Art Styles', 165-221; Coedes, *Making of South-east Asia*, 17-19

10. Barthes, *Elements of Semiology*; for discussions of architecture as language see Broadbent, Bunt, Jencks, *Sign, Symbol and Architecture*

11. Biddulph, *Tribes of the Hindu Koosh*; Edelberg, 'Nuristani House'

12. Hallet, Samizay, *Architecture of Afghanistan*, 75-9, 86-101; 'Nuristan's Cliff-hangers', 65-72

13. Edelberg, 'Architecture of Nuristan'; Edelberg, Jones, *Nuristan*

14. Trimingham, *Islam in West Africa*, 198-207; Hill, *Rural Hausa*, 10-15, 213, 215-23; Richards, 'Village Life', 1419-1450

15. Schwerdtfeger, 'Housing in Zaria', 58-71; Schwerdtfeger, *Housing in African Cities*, 28-62; Moughtin, 'Settlements of the Hausa'

16. Leary, 'Palace in Kano', 11-17; Prussin, 'Fulani-Hausa Architecture', 8-19; Prussin, *Hatumere*, 220-4

17. Kirk-Green, *Decorated Houses*; Salmonu, 'Decorated Houses in Zaria', 14-17; Moughtin, *Hausa Architecture*, 125-47

18. Lewcock, 'Towns in Arabia', 4-19

19. Costa, Vicario, *Yemen*, 13-26, 165-215; Varanda, *Building in Yemen*, 78-131

20. Serjeant, Lewcock, *San'a*, Chapter 2; Kirkman, ed., *City of San'a*, 47-65

21. Boas, *Kwakiutl Ethnography*, 29-35; Buck, *Coming of the Maori*, 113-35

22. Cunningham, *Post-War Migrations*; Bruner, 'Role of Kinship', 122-34

23. Murdock, *Africa: Its Peoples*, 380-4; Meiring, 'The Amandebele', 26-35; Spence, Biermann, 'M'Pogga', 35-40

24. Walton, 'Southern Bantu Vernacular'; Frescura, 'Rural Indigenous Architecture', 26-269

25. d'Alpoim Guedes: personal communication, September 1979; Frescura, *Rural Shelter*, 165-70

26. Moughtin, op. cit., 68-73; Varanda, op. cit., 264-7

Chapter 10

1. Terrell, *Pueblos, Spaniards*, 199-216

2. Longacre, *Pueblo Societies*, 29-37, 43-6

3. Oliver, Field Notes, 1982; Eggan, *Western Pueblos*, 223-52

4. Steiner, *New Indians*, 197-200

5. Oliver, Field Notes, 1986

6. Korn, *Kathmandu Valley*, 18-23; Blair, *4 Villages*, 55-67; Jacobsen, 'Landsby i Nepal', 83-114

7. MacFadyen et al., 'City is Mandala', 307-9

8. Davies et al., *Kirtipur*, 41-68

9. For a discussion of relative size of towns and cities see Morrill, *Spatial Organization*, 155-74

10. Sjoberg, *Preindustrial City*, 80-142, 182-254

11. Bourquelot, *Provins*

12. Oliver, Field Notes, 1980

13. Opher et al., *La Ville Basse*

14. Oliver, Samuels, eds., *Action Pilote*, 1980

15. Wheatley, *Four Quarters*, 225

16. Golombek, 'Pre-Safavid Isfahan', 18-44; Oliver, 'Organic Growth: Isfahan'

17. Blunt, *Isfahan*, 51-84; Ardelan, Bakhtiar, *The Sense of Unity*, 96-127

18. Khatib-Chahidi, 'Shi'ite Iran', 133-4

19. Bakhtiar et al., 'Bazaar at Isfahan'; Gaube, Wirth, *Der Bazar von Isfahan*

20. Oliver, 'Binarism', 121-46; Cantacuzino, Browne, 'Isfahan', 253-319

21. Wirth, 'Urbanism', 1-24; Bascom, 'Urbanization', 446-54

22. Krapf-Askari, *Yoruba Towns*, 154-64; Lloyd, 'The Yoruba', 107-23

23. Mabogunje, 'Morphology of Ibadan'; for detailed discussion see Lloyd et al., *City of Ibadan*

24. Callaway, 'Spatial Domains', 168-86

25. Mabogunje, *Urbanization in Nigeria*, 186-237; Schwerdtfeger, *African Cities*, 101-81; Adedeji, 'Ibadan', 55-69

26. Hodder, Ukwu, *Markets in West Africa*, 94-109; Gugler, Flanagan, *Change in West Africa*, 140-1, 167-9

27. Johnson, *India*, 159-61, 170-3, 194-200; Oliver, Field Notes, 1986

28. Sarma, 'West Bengal', 180-201; Basu, *Bengal Peasant*, 5-84; Oliver, Field Notes, 1986

29. Connell et al., *Migration*, 2, 161; Nayyar, 'Rural Bihar'·

30. Mukherjee, Menefee Singh, 'Urban Poor, Calcutta', 135-63; Oliver, Field Notes, 1986

31. Dwyer, *People and Housing*, 209-23; Rosser, 'Calcutta Experience', 126-31; Shah, 'People's Participation', 201-3

Chapter 11

1. Tussing et al., *Alaska Pipeline*, 19-26; Riches, 'Ungava Eskimos'; Jenness, 'Economic Situation', 99-119

2. Van Stone, *Point Hope*, 65-72; Graburn, *Eskimos Without Igloos*, 162-6; Ellsworth-Jones, 'Nunavut', 11

3. Rapoport, 'Definitions of Place', 38-51; Stoll et al., 'Housing', 146-7

4. Reser, 'Values in Bark', 27-35; Reser, 'Matter of Control', 65-96

5. UNDRO, *Shelter After Disaster*, 26-34; Davis, *Shelter After Disaster*, 50-2

6. Ozkan, 'Roam Home' 279-80; Oliver, Field Notes, 1983, 1984

7. Oliver, Aysan, *Cultural Aspects*

8. Oliver, 'Acceptability of Resettlement'

9. For example, Wilsher, Righter, *Exploding Cities*, 30-41

10. Butler, Crooke, *Urbanization*, 18-33, 48-51

11. Roberts, *Cities of Peasants*, 88-107

12. Etherton, *Mathare Valley*, 9-37

13. Hake, *African Metropolis*, 113-46

14. Oliver, Field Notes, 1977; Etherton op. cit., 43-56; Hake op. cit., 147-70

15. UNCHS Habitat, *Survey of Slum Settlements*, 134-8; UNCHS Habitat, *Building Materials*, 17
16. Pacey, *Sanitation*, 48-9
17. Goerthert, 'Sites and Services', 28-31; Mangin, Turner, 'Benavides', 127-36; Turner, *Freedom to Build*; Turner, *Housing by People*
18. Chana, 'Dandora', 17-36
19. Oliver, Field Notes, 1977
20. Shankland Cox, *Third World Housing*, 12-13, 155-214
21. Sumintardja *et al.*, 'Kampung Improvement Programme', 61-74; Holod, ed., 'Kampung Improvement Programme', 212-21; Baross, 'Settlement Improvement Policies', 150-72
22. Payne, 'Gecekondus of Ankara', 71-82; Karpat, *Gecekondu*, 56-65; Danielson, Keles, *Politics of Urbanization*, 62-80
23. Payne, 'Critique of Gecekondus', 117-39; Oliver, Field Notes, 1983, 1984, 1986; Tokman, 'Ankara', 89-107
24. For discussions see Ward, *Self-Help Housing*; Skinner, Rodell, *People, Poverty, Shelter*
25. Abrams, *Housing*, 276-85; Burns, Grebler, *Housing of Nations*, 3-11; Musil, *Urbanization in Socialist Countries*
26. Simić, *Peasant Urbanites*, 44-107; Oliver, Field Notes, 1985
27. Grzan-Butina, 'Background', 4-12; Oliver, ed., *Kaluderica*
28. See for example Coates *et al.*, *Geography and Inequality*; Goldthorpe, *Sociology of Third World*; Myint, *Economics of Developing Countries*
29. Fathy, *Architecture for Foor*; Spence, 'Laurie Baker', 30-9
30. Alexander *et al.*, *Generated by Patterns*; Swan *et al.*, *Sites and Services*, 6-18; Fromm, 'Peru: Previ', 48-54; Seelig, *Self-Help Communities*
31. Cain *et al.*, *Indigenous Building*; Robson, *Aided Self-Help*
32. Examples of Technical Notes are listed in Spence, Cook, *Building Materials*, 319-27; Stewart, *Technology and Underdevelopment*, 239-73, 280-95

PHOTOGRAPHIC CREDITS

Aga Khan Architecture Award, 74*r* (Charles Little), **207**, 225*lr*, 225*t* (M. K. Noer Saijindi DKI)
American Arts AMCAS, Exeter, 14, 130
Arts Council of Great Britain, 8*lr*
Associacao Arquitectos Portugueses, 77, 78
Aysan, Yasemin, 182, 183
Bruce-Dick, Timothy, 7, 43*lr*, 104, 167, 179
CARE, 29*t* (Rudolph von Bernuth), 30*t* (Sandy Laumark), 161*l*
Cash, J. Allan, 169, 186, **201**
Crooke, Patrick, 219
Danby, Miles, 75, 116, 120, 121*l*, 121*r*, 122, 199
Davis, Ian, 97*lr*, 115*lr*, 215
Development Workshop, 64*l*, **105**, **112**, 123, 230*t*
Dickins, Douglas, 103*t*, 138, 173, 175
Dixon, Robert M. W., 129*t*
Forman, Werner, 30*lr*, 174
Grey, Rupert, 140, 157*lr*
Halliday Photographs, Sonia, 23*t* (Jane Taylor), 25*t*, **51** and **52** (Jane Taylor), 84, 118

Harding, Robert, Associates (Sassoon), 26, **50**, **55** (Hanbury-Tenison), 69*l*, 155
Hicks, David, 15*lr*, 25*lr*, 47, 82, 119, 144, **152**, 160, 161*r*, 184, 213*t*
Hutchison Library, The, 41 (Brian Moser), **146** (Moser/Taylor), 164 (Brian Moser)
Kenya Information Service, 24
Leake, Irene, **148**, 170
Leslie, Jolyon, **56**
McDermott, Deirdre, **145**
McDermott, Neil, 132
Milwaukee Public Museum 98 (Robert Ritzenthaler), 99*t* 99*lr*
Nicolaisen, Johannes, courtesy of Professor Ida Nicolaisen, University of Copenhagen, 27, 29*lr*
ODA/Oxford Polytechnic Project, 137*t*, 137*lr*, 216, 217
Oliver, Paul, title page, 8*t*, 9, 11, 13, 15*t*, 31, 33*t*, 33*lr*, 37*lr*, 39, 42, 43*t*, 43*lr*, 44, 45*t*, 45*lr*, 48, **49**, **53**, **54**, 59, 60*t*, 60*lr*, 63, 66, 67*t*, 67*lr*, 68, 69*r*, 71*t*, 71*lr*, 73*t*, 73*lr*, 74*l*, 76, 80, 81, 83*t*, 83*lr*, 85, 86*t*, 87, 91*l*, 91*r*, 92*c*, 92*lr*, 93*t*, 94, 95, 96*t*, 96*lr*, 97*t*, **106**, **107**, **108**, **109**, 111, 113, 115*t*, 124*l*, 124*r*, 125, 126, 141, 142, **150**, **151**, 154*t*, 154*lr*, 156*lr*, 171, 172, 180, 181*t*, 181*lr*, 188*t*, 188*lr*, 189, 190, 191, 193*t*, 196, 197*t*, 197*lr*, 200, **202**, **203**, **204**, **205**, **206**, **208**, 209*t*, 209*lr*, 210, 211, 216, 218, 222, 228*t*, 228*lr*, 231, 232
Opher, Philip, 58, 92*t*, 166
OXFAM, 70, 127, 215 (Ian Davis)
Patrimoine Historique et Artistique de la France (PHAF) Project, 195
Payne, Geoffrey, 221, 224, 226, 227*t*, 227*lr*, 233
Pelinski, Ramón, 213*lr*
Picton, John, 162, 163

Pitt Rivers Museum, Oxford, 90, 103*lr*, 129*lr*, 140, 156*t*
Public Archives, Canada, 17 (Harrington), 18 (Harrington), 19, 20 (Harrington)
Reser, Joseph, 117, 214
Ridgeway, Rupert, 69*lr*, **149**, 176
Smith, Graham Paul, 62*t*, 62*lr*, 110
Snailham, Richard, 157*lr*
Snaith, David, 157*t*
Spence, Robin, 230*lr*
Stewart, Graham, 133, 134, 135, **147**
Stirling, Kate, 159
Thesiger, Wilfred, originally published in *Desert, Marsh and Mountain* (Collins, 1979), 100, 101, 102, 177
Turner, John F. C., 223
Wagner, Hanspeter, 35, 36, 37*t*

DRAWINGS

The line drawings have been specially prepared for this work. Where they have been based on a specific source the word *'After'* followed by the author's name is given. Where additional material has been incorporated the words *'Developed from'* precede the name of the author. Full details will be found in the Bibliography.

Drawn by Stuart Parker: 23, 61, 65, 90, 93, 95, 104, 120, 122, 131*l*, 132, 133, 134, 139, 157, 172, 174, 178*l*, 178*r*, 182, 193*lr*.
Drawn by Paul Oliver: 12-13, 16, 21, 34, 38, 39, 46, 64, 68, 75, 76, 79, 89, 114, 130, 136, 143*l*, 143*r*, 158, 162, 163, 165, 166, 168, 187, 192*t*, 194, 198, 216, 220, 227.

BIBLIOGRAPHY

Few world-wide bibliographies on dwellings have been published. The following are useful:

Viaro, Alain, M. and Ziegler, Arlette, *Architectures Traditionelles dans le Monde: Reperages Bibliographiques*, (Paris Etablissements, Humains et Environment Socio-Cultural, UNESCO, 1984)

Wodehouse, L., *Indigenous Architecture Worldwide: A Guide to Information Sources*, (Detroit, Gale Research Company, 1980)

and for rapid urbanization:

Buick, Barbara, *Squatter Settlements in Developing Countries: a Bibliography*, (Canberra, Research School of Pacific Studies, The Australian National University, 1975)

The following Bibliography gives publishing details of all sources cited in the Notes. Many of the works listed have additional bibliographies.

Abrams, Charles, *Housing in the Modern World: Man's Struggle for Shelter in an Urbanizing World*, (London, Faber and Faber, 1966)

Acharya, P. J., *Manasara on Architecture and Sculpture*, (London, 1933-4)

Adedeji, Adebauyo, 'Ibadan', *Rural Urban Migrants and Metropolitan Development*, ed., Laquian, Aprodicio A., (Toronto, Intermet, 1971)

Agarwal, Anil, *Mud, Mud: The Potential of Earth-based Materials for Third World Housing*, (London, Earthscan, 1981)

Al-Azzawi, Subhi H., 'Oriental Houses in Iraq', *Shelter and Society*, ed., Oliver, Paul, (London, Barrie and Jenkins, 1969)

Alexander, Christopher, Hirschen, Sanford, Ishikawa, Sara, Coffin, Christie and Angel, Shlomo, *Houses Generated by Patterns,* (Berkeley, California, Center for Environmental Structure, n.d., *c.* 1970-1)

Ali, S. Husin, *Malay Peasant Society and Leadership*, (London, New York, Oxford University Press, 1975)

Aljoofre, Syed H., 'Early Malay Dwellings', unpublished thesis, (Department of Tropical Studies, Architectural Association, *c.* 1964)

Aljundi, Ghiyas, *L'Architecture Traditionelle en Syrie*, (Paris, UNESCO, Dec. 1984)

Allan, William, 'Ecology, Techniques and Settlement Patterns', *Man, Settlement and Urbanism*, Ucko, Peter J., *et al.*, (London, Duckworth, 1972)

Allen, Edward, *Stone Shelters*, (Cambridge, Mass., MIT Press, 1969)

Al-Rawaf, M. K., 'Traditional Courtyard Houses in Baghdad', unpublished thesis, (School of Architecture, University of Newcastle- upon-Tyne, 1972)

Andersen, Kaj Blegvad, *African Traditional Architecture*, (Nairobi, Oxford University Press, 1977)

Ardelan, Nader and Bakhtiar, Laleh, *The Sense of Unity*, (Chicago, London, University of Chicago Press, 1973)

Ardener, Shirley, ed., *Women and Space, Ground Rules and Social Maps*, (London, Croom Helm, 1981)

Bakhtiar, Ali, Donat, John, Maravasti R. and Oliver, Paul, 'The Bazaar at Isfahan' (unpublished manuscript, 1978)

Bakirer, Omur, 'A Study on the Use of Brickbonds in Anatolian Seljuk Architecture', *Journal of the Faculty of Architecture*, vol. 6, no. 2 (Ankara, 1980)

Balikci, Asen, *The Netsilik Eskimo*, (Garden City, New York, The Natural History Press, 1970)

Bandem, I. Made and de Boer, Fredrik Eugene, *Kaja ans Kelod: Balinese Dance in Transition*, (Oxford, New York, Oxford University Press, 1981)

Barnes, Cass G., *The Sod House*, (Lincoln, University of Nebraska Press, 1930)

Barnett, H. G., *Being a Palauan*, (New York, London, Holt, Rinehart and Winston, 1960)

Baross, P., 'Four Experiences with Settlement Improvement Policies in Asia', *People, Poverty and Shelter*, eds., Skinner, R. J. and Rodell, M. J., (London, New York, Methuen, 1983)

Barth, Fredrik, *Nomads of South Persia*, (Boston, Little, Brown and Company, 1961)

Barthes, Roland, *Elements of Semiology*, (London, Jonathan Cape, 1967; New York, Hill and Wang, 1968)

Bascom, William, 'Urbanization among the Yoruba', *The American Journal of Sociology*, vol. 60 (Chicago, University of Chicago Press, 1955)

Basu, Tara Krishna, *The Bengal Peasant from Time to Time*, (London, Asia Publishing House; Calcutta, Statistical Publishing Society, 1962)

Beardsley, Richard H., Hall, John W. and Ward, R. E., *Village Japan*, (Chicago, London, University of Chicago Press, 1959)

Beaujeu-Garnier, J., *Geography of Population*, (London, Longmans, 1966)

Beguin, Jean-Pierre, Kalt, M., Leroy, J., Louis D., Macary, J., Pelloux, P., and Peronne, H., *L'Habitat au Cameroun*, (Paris, L'Office de la Recherche Scientifique Outre-Mer, 1952)

Berg, Lasse and Berg, Lisa, *Face to Face: Fascism and Revolution in India*, (Berkeley, California, Ramparts Press, 1970)

Biddulph, John, *Tribes of the Hindu Koosh*, (Karachi, Indus Publications, 1977)

Biermann, Barrie, 'Indlu: The Domed Dwellings of the Zulu', *Shelter in Africa*, ed., Oliver, Paul, (London, Barrie and Jenkins, 1971)

Biernoff, D., 'Traditional and Contemporary Structures and Settlement in Eastern Arnham Land with Particular Reference to the Nunggubuyu', *A Black Reality*, ed., Heppell, M., (Canberra, Australian Institute of Aboriginal Studies, 1979)

Birkett-Smith, Kaj, *The Eskimos*, (London, Methuen and Co., 1959)

Blair, Katherine D., *4 Villages: Architecture in Nepal*, (Los Angeles, Craft and Folk Art Museum, 1983)

Blazejewicz, Dorota, Lund, R., Schonning, K. and Steincke, S., *Arquitectura Tradicional—Guine-Bissau*, (Stockholm, Swedish International Development Authority, 1981)

Blunt, Wilfrid, *Isfahan: Pearl of Persia*, (London, Elek Books; Toronto, The Ryerson Press, 1966)

Boas, Franz, *The Central Eskimo*, (Lincoln, University of Nebraska Press, 1964)

Boas, Franz, *Kwakiutl Ethnography*, (Chicago, London, University of Chicago Press, 1966)

Bourdier, Jean-Paul and Minh-ha, Trinh T., *African Spaces: Designs for Living in Upper Volta*, (New York, London, Africana Publishing Co., 1985)

Bourdieu, Pierre, 'The Berber House', *Rules and Meanings*, ed., Douglas, Mary, (Harmondsworth, Penguin, 1971)

Bourdieu, Pierre, *Outline of a Theory of Practice*, (London, New York, Cambridge University Press, 1977)

Bourquelot, Felix, *Histoire de Provins* (1839/40), (Marseilles, Lafitte Reprints, 1976)

Briggs, Jean, *Never in Anger*, (Cambridge, Mass., Harvard University Press, 1970)

Broadbent, Geoffrey, Bunt, R. and Jencks, C., eds., *Signs, Symbols and Architecture*, (Chichester, New York, John Wiley and Sons, 1980)

Brown, C. Malcolm and Page, John, 'The Effect of Chronic Exposure to Cold', *Journal of Applied Psychology*, (1952)

Bruner, Edward M., 'Medan: The Role of Kinship in an Indonesian City', Peasants in Cities, ed., Mangin, William, (Boston, Houghton Mifflin Co., 1970)

Brunskill, R. W., *Illustrated Handbook of Vernacular Architecture*, London, Faber and Faber, 1970)

Buck, Sir Peter, *The Coming of the Maori*, (Wellington, Whitcombe and Tombs, 1950)

Burns, Leland S. and Grebler, Leo, *The Housing of Nations*, (London, New York, The Macmillan Press, 1977)

Butler, John and Crooke, Patrick, *Probe: Urbanization*, (London, Angus and Robertson, 1973)

Cain, Allan, Afshar, F., Norton, J. and Daraie, M., *Indigenous Building and the Third World*, (Tehran, Development Workshop, 1976)

Callaway, Helen, 'Spatial Domains and Women's Mobility in Yorubaland, Nigeria', *Women and Space*, ed., Ardener, Shirley, (London, Croom Helm, 1981)

Cantacuzino, Sherban and Browne, Kenneth, 'Isfahan', *The Architectural Review*, vol. CLIX, no. 951 (London, May 1976)

Castro, D., 'Building with Bamboo', *Bamboo*, ed., Janssen, Jules J. A., (Eindhoven, University of Technology, 1974)

Chagnon, Napolean A., *Yanomamö: The Fierce People*, (New York, London, Holt, Rinehart and Winston, 1968)

Chana, T. S., 'Nairobi: Dandora and Other Projects', *Low-income Housing in the Developing World*, ed., Payne, Geoffrey K., (Chichester, New York, John Wiley and Sons, 1984)

Chisholm, Michael, *Rural Settlement and Land Use*, (London, Hutchinson, 1962)

Clark, Geoffrey and Radford, Antony, 'Cyclades: Studies of a Building Vernacular', unpublished thesis, (School of Architecture, University of Newcastle-upon-Tyne, *c.* 1974)

Clarke, John I., *Population Geography*, (Oxford, Pergamon Press, 1972)

Coates, B. E., Johnston, R. J. and Knox, P. L., *Geography and Inequality*, (Oxford, New York, Oxford University Press, 1977)

Coedes, G., *The Making of South East Asia*, (London, Routledge and Kegan Paul, 1966)

Cohn, Bernard S., 'The Changing Status of a Depressed Caste', *Village India, Studies in the Little Community*, ed., Marriott, McKim, (Chicago, University of Chicago Press, 1955)

Connell, John, Dasgupta, B., Laishley, R. and Lipton M., *Migration from Rural Areas: The Evidence from Village Studies*, (Delhi, Oxford University Press, 1976)

Costa, Paulo and Vicario, Ennio, *Yemen: Land of Builders*, (New York, Rizzoli International Publications Inc.; London, Academy, 1977)

Costello, V. F., *Urbanization in the Middle East*, (Cambridge, New York, Cambridge University Press, 1977)

Cunningham, Clarke, *The Post-war Migration of the Toba-Bataks to East Sumatra*, (New Haven, Yale University Press, 1958)

Cuny, Frederick C., *Disasters and Development*, (New York, Oxford, Oxford University Press, 1983)

Curtis, Natalie, ed., *The Indians' Book*, (New York, Harper and Brothers, 1923

Dagens, Bruno, *Architecture in the Ajitagama and the Rauravagama*, (Pondicherry, Institut Francais d'Indologie, 1984)

Dahl, Otto Chr., 'The House in Madagascar', *The House in East and South-east Asia*, eds., Isikowitz, K. G. and Sorensen, P., (Malmo, London, Curzon Press, 1982)

Danachair, Caoimhin O., 'Three House Types', *Ulster Folklife*, vol. 2 (Belfast, 1956)

Danby, Miles, 'The Design of Buildings in Hot-dry Climates and the Internal Environment', *Build International*, 6 (Applied Science Publishers, 1973)

Danby, Miles, *Buildings and the Environment*, Overseas Building Notes, no. 165 (Garston, U.K., Building Research Station, Dec. 1975)

Danby, Miles, 'Building Design in Hot, Dry Climates', *Desert Planning*, ed., Golany, Gideon, (London, Architectural Press 1982)

Danielson, Michael N. and Keles, Rusen, *The Politics of Rapid Urbanization: Government and Growth in Modern Turkey*, (New York, London, Holmes and Meier, 1985)

David, Nicholas, 'The Fulani Compound and the Archaeologist', *World Archaeology*, ed., Derek, Roe, vol. 3, no. 2 (London, Routledge and Kegan Paul, October 1971)

Davies, E. P., Davis, R. W., Flinn, W. R., Miers, C. J. P., Park, M. and Robertson, G. V. L., *Kirtipur: A Newar Community in Nepal*, Project report under the auspices of UNESCO, November 1980, (Dept. of Architecture, University of Bristol)

Davis, Ian, *Guatemala: Shelter and Housing Policy following the Earthquake, 1976*, (Oxford, The Research and Development Group, Dept. of Architecture, Oxford Polytechnic, 1976)

Davis, Ian, *Shelter After Disaster*, (Oxford, Oxford Polytechnic Press, 1978)

de Boer, D. W. N., *Het Toba Bataksche Huis*, (Batavia Weltevreden, G Rolff and Co., 1920; selective translation in *Traditional Buildings of Indonesia: Batak Toba*, Sargeant, G. T., Building Research Institute, n.d.)

Dennis, Wayne, *The Hopi Child*, (New York, John Wiley and Sons, 1965)

Denyer, Susan, *African Traditional Architecture*, (London, Heinemann, 1978)

Dicken, Samuel Newton, *Economic Geography*, (Boston, London, D. D. Heath and Co., 1955)

Dickson, M. G., *Sarawak and its People*, (Borneo Literature Bureau, 1962)

Domenig, Gaudenz, *Tektonik im Primitiven Dachbau*, (Zurich, 'Gottersitz und Menschenhaus' an der ETH Zurich, 1980)

Doumanis, Orestis B. and Oliver, Paul, eds., *Shelter in Greece*, (Athens, Architecture in Greece Press, 1974)

Downs, James F., *The Navajo*, (New York, London, Holt, Rinehart and Winston, 1972)

Duly, Colin, *The Houses of Mankind*, (London, Thames and Hudson Ltd., 1979)

Dumont, René, *Types of Rural Economy*, (London, Methuen, 1957)

Dwyer, D. J., *People and Housing in Third World Cities*, (London, New York, Longman, 1975)

Eades, J. S., *The Yoruba Today*, (Cambridge, New York, Cambridge University Press, 1980)

Economist Intelligence Unit, *Oxford Economic Atlas of the World*, (London, New York, Oxford University Press, 1965)

Edelberg, Lennart, 'The Nuristani House', *Cultures of the Hindukush*, ed., Jettmar, Karl, (Wiesbaden, Franz Steiner Verlag, 1974)

Edelberg, Lennart, 'The Traditional Architecture of Nuristan and its Preservation', *Cultures of the Hindukush*, ed., Jettmar, Karl, (Wiesbaden, Franz Steiner Verlag, 1974)

Edelberg, Lennart and Jones, Schyler, *Nuristan*, (Graz, Austria, Akademische Druck-u Verlagsastalt, 1979)

Eggan, Fred, *Social Organization of the Western Pueblos*, (Chicago, London, University of Chicago Press, 1950)

Elawa, Sami, 'Housing Design in Extreme Hot Arid Zones with Special Reference to Thermal Performance', (Sweden, Department of Building Science, University of Lund, 1981)

Ellsworth-Jones, W., 'Eskimo Hunt for a Treeless Nunavut', *The Sunday Times*, (London, 22 Dec. 1985)

Ekvall, Robert B., *Fields on the Hoof: Nexus of Tibetan Nomadic Pastoralism*, (New York, Holt, Rinehart and Winston, 1968)

Embree, John F., *A Japanese Village: Suye Mura*, (London, Kegan Paul, Trench, Trubner and Co., 1946)

Endicott, K. M., *An Analysis of Malay Magic*, (Oxford, Clarendon Press, 1970)

Etherton, David, *Mathare Valley: A Case Study of Uncontrolled Settlement in Nairobi*, (Nairobi, Housing Research and Development Unit, University of Nairobi, 1969)

Etherton, David, 'Algerian Oases', *Shelter in Africa*, ed., Oliver, Paul, (London, Barrie and Jenkins, 1971)

Evans, E. Estyn, 'The Ulster Farmhouse', *Ulster Folklife*, vol. 1 (Belfast, 1955)

Evans, E. Estyn, *Irish Folk Ways*, (London, Boston, Routledge and Kegan Paul, 1957)

Everson, J. A and FitzGerald, B. P., *Settlement Patterns*, (London, Longmans, 1969)

Faegre, Torvald, *Tents: Architecture of the Nomads*, (Garden City, New York, Anchor Press, 1979)

Fathy, Hassan, *Architecture for the Poor*, (Chicago, University of Chicago Press, 1973)

Feduchi, Luis, *Spanish Folk Architecture*, (Barcelona, Editorial Blume, 1974)

Feilberg, C. G., *La Tente Noire*, Etnografisk Roekke, II, (Copenhagen, National Museum, 1944)

Fernandes, Inacio Peres, *Arquitectura Popular Em Portugal*, (Lisboa, Edicao da Associacao dos Arquitectos Portugueses, 1980)

Fethi, Ihsan, and Roaf, Susan, 'The Traditional House in Baghdad', *The Arab House*, ed., Hyland A. D. C. (Newcastle-upon-Tyne, CARDO, 1986)

Findrik, Ranko, *Prilozi Poznavanju Organizacije Stambenog Prostora U Narodnom Graditeljstvu Sela*, (Belgrade, Univerzitet u Beogradu, Arhitektonski Fakultet, 1980)

Forde, C. Daryll, *Habitat, Economy and Society*, (London, Methuen and Co.; New York, E. P. Dutton and Co., 1934)

Fortes, M., *The Web of Kinship Amongst the Tallensi*, (London, Oxford University Press, 1949)

Fox, Robin, *Kinship and Marriage: An Anthropological Perspective*, (London, Baltimore, Penguin, 1967)

Freeman, Derek, *Report on the Iban*, (London, University of London, The Athlone Press; New York, Humanities Press Inc., 1970)

Frescura, Franco, *Rural Shelter in Southern Africa*, (Johannesburg, Raven Press, 1981)

Frescura, Franco, 'Major Developments in the Rural Indigenous Architecture of Southern Africa of the Post-Difaqane Period', unpublished thesis for D.Phil, (Johannesburg, Faculty of Architecture, University of the Witwatersrand, Nov. 1985)

Friedl, Ernestine, *Women and Men: An Anthropologist's View*, (New York, Holt, Rinehart and Winston, 1975)

Fromm, Dorit, 'Alternatives in Housing: Peru: Previ', *The Architectural Review*, vol. CLXXVIII, no. 1062 (London, August 1985)

Gailey, Alan, 'Kitchen Furniture', *Ulster Folklife*, vol. 12 (1966)

Gale, Simon J., 'Orientation', *Process Architecture*, no. 25 (Tokyo, Process Architecture Publishing Co., August 1981)

Gardi, Rene, *Indigenous African Architecture*, (London, New York, Van Nostrand Reinhold Co., 1973)

Gaube, Heinz and Wirth, Eugen, *Der Bazar von Isfahan*, (Wiesbaden, Dr. Ludwig Reichert, 1978)

Geertz, Clifford, *Pedlars and Princes*, (Chicago, London, University of Chicago, 1963)

Geertz, Hildred and Geertz, Clifford, *Kinship in Bali*, (Chicago, London, University of Chicago Press)

Gilbert, Alan and Gugler, Josef, *Cities, Poverty, and Development: Urbanization in the Third World*, (Oxford University Press, 1962)

Gill, Crispin, ed., *Dartmoor: A New Study*, (Newton Abbot, David and Charles, c. 1970)

Gill, Sam D., *Songs of Life*, (Leiden, E. J. Brill, 1979)

Givoni, B., *Man, Climate and Architecture*, (London, New York, Elsevier Publishing Co., 1969)

Glassie, Henry, *Passing the Time in Ballymenone*, (Philadelphia, University of Pennsylvania Press; Dublin, The O'Brian Press, 1982)

Godard, Andre, *The Art of Iran*, (London, George Allen and Unwin, 1965)

Goerthert, 'Sites and Services', *The Architectural Review*, vol. CLXXVIII, no. 1962 (London, August 1985)

Golany, Gideon, ed., *Housing in Arid Lands*, (London, Architectural Press, 1982)

Golany, Gideon, ed., *Desert Planning*, (London, Architectural Press, 1982)

Goldthorpe, J. E., *The Sociology of the Third World: Disparity and Development*, (Cambridge, New York, Oxford University Press, 1975)

Golombek, Lisa, 'Urban Patterns in Pre-Safavid Isfahan, *Iranian Studies*, vol. VII, nos. 1-2 (Boston, Boston College Press, 1974)

Gough, E. Kathleen, 'The Social Structure of a Tanjore Village', *Village India, Studies in the Little Community*, ed., Marriott, McKim, (Chicago, University of Chicago Press, 1955)

Graburn, Nelson H. H., *Eskimos without Igloos: Social and Economic Development in Sugluk,* (Boston, Little, Brown and Co., 1969)

Griaule, Marcel, *Conversations with Ogotemmêli*, (London, Oxford University Press for IAI, 1965)

Griaule, Marcel and Dieterlen, Germaine, 'The Dogon', *African Worlds*, ed., Forde, Daryll, (London, New York, Oxford University Press, 1954)

Griaule, Marcel and Dieterlen, Germaine, *Le Rénard Pâle*, (Paris, Institut d'Ethnologie, 1965)

Grove, A. T., *Africa South of the Sahara*, (London, Oxford University Press, 1967)

Grum, Anders, 'Migration and Settlement Patterns among the Rendille', unpublished address, (Nairobi, University of Nairobi, 1977)

Grzan-Butina, Georgia, 'Background to Kaluderica', *Kaluderica: Observations on the Wild Settlement of Kaluderica*, ed., Oliver, Paul, and Shelter and Settlements Unit, (Oxford, Dept. of Architecture, Oxford Polytechnic, April 1985)

Guedes, Pedro, ed., *The Macmillan Encyclopedia of Architecture and Technological Change*, (London, New York, The Macmillan Press, 1979)

Gugler, Josef and Flanagan, William G., *Urbanization and Social Change in West Africa*, (Cambridge, New York, Cambridge University Press, 1978)

Guidoni, Enrico, *Primitive Architecture*, (Milan, Electa Editrice, 1975; New York, Harry N. Abrams, 1978)

Gulick, John, *The Middle East: An Anthropological Perspective*, (Pacific Palisades, California, Goodyear Publishing Co., 1977)

Gutschow, Niels and Kolver, Bernhard, *Ordered Space Concepts and Functions in a Town of Nepal*, ed., Voigt, Wolfgang, Nepal Research Centre, Publications 1 (Wiesbaden, Kommissionsverlag Franz Steiner GmbH, 1975)

Haggett, Peter, *Geography: A Modern Synthesis*, (London, New York, Harper and Row, 1972)

Hake, Andrew, *African Metropolis: Nairobi's Self-Help City*, (London, Chatto and Windus for Sussex University Press, 1977)

Hallett, Stanley Ira, and Samizay Rafi, 'Nuristan's Cliff-Hangers' *Afghanistan Journal*, Jg. 2, Heft. 2 (Graz, Austria, 1975)

Hallett, Stanley Ira, and Samizay, *Traditional Architecture of Afghanistan*, (New York, London, Garland STPM Press, 1980)

Hance, William A., *Population, Migration, and Urbanization in Africa*, (New York, London, Columbia University Press, 1970)

Hansen, Hans Jurgen, ed., *Architecture in Wood*, (London, Faber and Faber, 1971)

Hardoy, Jorge E., and Satterthwaite, David, *Shelter: Need and Response*, (Chichester, New York, John Wiley and Sons, 1981)

Hartley, Dorothy, *Made In England*, (London, Eyre Methuen, 1939)

Havinden, Michael, and Wilkinson, Freda, 'Farming', *Dartmoor: A New Study*, ed., Gill, Crispin, (Newton Abbot, David and Charles, n.d. (c. 1970))

Heine-Geldern, Robert, 'Some Tribal Art Styles of South-east Asia: an Experiment in Art History', *The Many Faces of Primitive Art*, ed., Fraser, Douglas, (Englewood Cliffs, New Jersey, Prentice-Hall, Inc., 1966)

Heppell, M., ed., *A Black Reality: Aboriginal Camps and Housing in Remote Australia*, (Canberra, Australian Institute of Aboriginal Studies, 1979)

Herskovits, Melville J., *Economic Anthropology*, (New York, Alfred A. Knopf, 1952)

Hill, Polly, *Rural Hausa, a Village and a Setting*, (Cambridge, New York, Cambridge University Press, 1972)

Hilton, R. N., 'The Basic Malay House', *Journal of the Malayan Branch of the Royal Asian Society*, vol. XXIX, part 3 (1956)

Hocart, A. M., *The Northern States of Fiji*, (London, Royal Anthropological Institute, 1952)

Hodder, B. W. and Ukwu, U. I., *Markets in West Africa*, (Ibadan, Ibadan University Press, 1969)

Hoebel, E. Adamson, *The Cheyennes: Indians of the Great Plains*, (New York, London, Holt, Reinhart and Winston, 1960)

Holod, Renata, ed., 'Kampung Improvement Programme: Jakarta, Indonesia', *Architecture and Community: Building in the Islamic World Today*, (Geneva, The Aga Khan Award for Architecture; Millerton, New York, Aperture, 1983)

Hommel, Rudolf, P., *China at Work*, (New York, The John Day Company, 1937)

Hugh-Jones, Christine, *From the Milk River: Spatial and Temporal Processes in North-west Amazonia*, (London, New York, Cambridge University Press, 1979)

Hugh-Jones, Stephen, *The Palm and the Pleiades: Initiation and Cosmology in North-west Amazonia*, (Cambridge, Cambrige University Press, 1979)

Huntington, Ellsworth, *Mainsprings of Civilization*, (New York, John Wiley and Sons, 1945)

Hull, Richard W., *African Cities and Towns before the European Conquest*, (New York, W. W. Norton and Company Inc., 1976)

Hyland, A. D. C. and Al-Shahi, Ahmed, eds., *The Arab House*, Proceedings of the Colloquium at University of Newcastle-upon-Tyne, March 1984, (Centre for Architectural Research and Development Overseas, University of Newcastle-upon-Tyne, 1986)

Ichter, Jean Paul, 'Les "Ksour" du Tafilalt', *Architecture and Urbanisme, 5* (Rabat, 1967)

Izikowitz, K. G. and Sorensen, P. eds., *The House in East and South-east Asia*, (Malmo, London, Curzon Press, 1982)

Jacobsen, Werner, *Landsby i Nepal*, (Copenhagen, National Museet, reprinted from Arkitekten 5/1969)

Janssen, Jules J. A. ed., *Bamboo*, (Eindhoven, University of Technology, 1974)

Jenkins, J. Geraint, ed., *Studies in Folk Life*, (London, Routledge and Kegan Paul, 1969)

Jenness, Diamond, 'The Economic Situation of the Eskimo', *Eskimo Administration: Canada*, Technical Paper, 14 (Montreal, Arctic Institute of North America, 1964)

Jessen, O., 'Las Viviendas Trogloditicas en los Paises del Mediterraneo', *Estudios Geographicas*, (Madrid, 1955)

Jett, Stephen C. and Spencer, Virginia E., *Navajo Architecture*, (Tucson, University of Arizona Press, 1981)

Jettmar, Karl, ed., *Culture of the Hindukush*, (Wiesbaden, Franz Steiner Verlag, 1974)

Johnson, B. L. C., *India: Resources and Development*, (London, Heinemann Educational Books; New York, Barnes and Noble, 1979)

Johnston, H. A. S., *The Fulani Empire of Sokoto*, (London, Oxford University Press, 1967)

Jones, S. R., 'Devonshire Farmhouses Part III—Moorland and Non-moorland Longhouses', *Report and Transactions*, vol. 103 (Barnstaple, The Devonshire Association, 1971)

Kahn, Lloyd, ed., *Shelter*, (Bolinas, California, Shelter Publications, 1973)

Karpat, Kemal H., *The Gecekondu: Rural Migration and Urbanization*, (Cambridge, New York, Cambridge University Press, 1976)

Kennedy, Donald Gilbert, *Field Notes on the Culture of Vaitupu*, Memoirs of the Polynesian Society, vol. 9 (New Plymouth, New Zealand, 1931)

Khan, Sultan Mahmud, *Jeddah Old Houses*, (Saudi Arabia, Saudi Arabian National Centre for Science and Technology, 1981)

Khatib-Chahidi, Jane, 'Sexual Prohibitions, Shared Space and Fictive Marriages in Shi'ite Iran', *Women and Space*, ed., Ardener, Shirley (London, Croom Helm, 1981)

Kirk-Greene, Anthony, *Decorated Houses in a Northern City*, (Kaduna, Baraka Press, 1963)

Kirkham, James ed., *City of San'a'*, exhibition catalogue, Museum of Mankind, (London, World of Islam Festival Publishing Company, 1976)

Kluckhohn, Clyde, and Leighton, Dorothea, *The Navajo*, (Garden City, New York, Doubleday Anchor, 1962)

Kluckhohn, Clyde, Hill, W. W. and Kluckhohn, Lucy Wales, *Navajo Material Culture*, (Cambridge, Mass., Harvard University Press, 1971)

Knuffel, Werner E., *The Construction of the Bantu Grass Hut*, (Graz, Akademische Druck-u Verlagsanastalt, 1973)

Konya, Allan, *Design Primer for Hot Climates*, (London, The Architectural Press, 1980)

Korn, Wolfgang, *The Traditional Architecture of the Kathmandu Valley*, Bibliotheca Himalayaica, series III, vol. II (Kathmandu, Ratna Pustak Bhandar, 1979)

Krapf-Askari, Eva, *Yoruba Towns and Cities*, (Oxford, New York, Oxford University Press, 1969)

Kukreja, C. P., *Tropical Architecture*, (New Delhi, Tata McGraw-Hill Publishing Co., 1978)

Lagopoulos, Alexander-Phaedon, 'Semiological Urbanism: An Analysis of the Traditional Western Sudanese Settlement', *Shelter, Sign and Symbol* ed., Oliver, Paul, (London, Barrie and Jenkins, 1975)

Lansing, J. Stephen, *The Three Worlds of Bali*, (New York, Praeger, 1983)

Laquian, Aprodicio A., ed., *Rural Urban Migrants and Metropolitan Development, (Toronto, Intermet, 1971)*

Larsson, Anita and Larsson, Viera, *Traditional Tswana Housing*, Report, D7. (Stockholm, Swedish Council for Building Research, 1984)

Leary, Allan, 'A Decorated Palace in Kano', *Art and Archaeology Research Papers*, no. 12 (1977)

Lebeuf, Jean-Paul, *L'Habitation Des Fali*, (Paris, Librairie Hachette, 1961)

Le Corbusier, *Towards a New Architecture*, (1927), (London, The Architectural Press, 1946)

Lee, Richard Borshay, *The !Kung San: Men, Women and Work in a Foraging Society*, (Cambridge, Cambrige University Press, 1979)

Leis, Philip E., *Enculturation and Socialization in an Ijaw Village*, (New York, London, Holt, Rinehart and Winston, 1968)

Lerner, Daniel, *The Passing of Traditional Society; Modernizing the Middle East*, (New York, The Free Press; London, Collier-Macmillan, 1958)

Lethaby, W. R., *Architecture, Nature and Magic*, (London, Gerald Duckworth and Co., 1956)

Lewcock, Ronald, 'Towns and Buildings in Arabia, North Yemen', *Architectural Association Quarterly*, vol. 8, no. 1 (London, 1976)

Lewcock, Ronald and Brans, Gerard, 'The Boat as an Architectural Symbol,' ed., Oliver, Paul, *Shelter, Sign and Symbol*, (London, Barrie and Jenkins, 1975)

Lewcock, Ronald and Freeth, Zara (Introduction), *Traditional Architecture in Kuwait and the Northern Gulf*, (London, Archaeology Research Papers, 1978)

Lewis, David, ed., *Urban Structure*, (London, Elek Books, 1968)

Lip, Evelyn 'An Aspect of Malaysia's Architectural Heritage,' *Majallak Akitek*, vol. 1, 81, (March 1981)

Lippsmeier, G., *Building in the Tropics*, (Munich, Callweg Verlag, 1969)

Little, Kenneth, *Urbanization as a Social Process*, (London, Boston, Routledge and Kegan Paul, 1974)

Lloyd, P. C., Mabogunje, A. L. and Awe, B., eds., *The City of Ibadan*, (Cambridge University Press Press, 1967)

Lloyd, P. C., 'The Yoruba: An Urban People?', *Urban Anthropology*, ed., Southall, Aidan, (New York, London, Oxford University Press, 1973)

Longacre, William A. ed., *Reconstructing Prehistoric Pueblo Societies*, (Albuquerque, University Press of New Mexico Press, 1970)

Mabogunje, Akin L., *Urbanization in Nigeria*, (London, University of London Press, 1968)

Mabogunje, Akin L., 'The Morphology of Ibadan', *The City of Ibadan*, eds., Lloyd, P. C., Mabogunje, A. L., and Awe, B., Cambridge, Cambridge University Press, 1967)

MacFadyen, J. Tevere and Vogt, Jay Woodworth, 'The City is a Mandala: Bhaktapur', *Ekistics: The Problems and Science of Human Settlements*, vol. 44, no. 265 (Athens, Centre of Ekistics, Dec. 1977)

Magnarella, Paul, *Tradition and Change in a Turkish Town*, (New York, Wiley, 1974)

Makal, M., *A Village in Anatolia*, (London, Vallentine Press, 1984)

Mangin, William, ed., *Peasants in Cities*, (Boston, Houghton Mifflin Co., 1970)

Mangin, William P. and Turner, John C., 'Benavides and the Barriada Movement', *Shelter and Society*, ed., Oliver, Paul, (London, Barrie and Rockliff, 1969)

Maretzki, Thomas W. and Maretzki Hatsumi, *Taira: An Okinawan Village*, Six Cultures Series, vol. VII (New York, London, John Wiley and Sons, 1966)

Marriott, McKim, ed., *Village India: Studies in the Little Community*, (Chicago, University of Chicago Press, 1955)

Marshall, Lorna, 'Sharing, Talking and Giving: Relief of Social Tensions among 'Kung Bushmen', *Africa*, vol 31 (March, 1961)

Maxwell, Gavin, *A Reed Shaken by the Wind*, (London, New York, Longmans, Green and Co., 1957)

May, Gerald W. ed., *International Workshop on Earthen Building in Seismic Areas*, Conference Proceedings, vols. 1-3 (Albuquerque, University Press of New Mexico, 1981)

McCourt, Desmond, 'The Outshot House-type and its Distribution in County Londonderry', *Ulster Folklife*, vol. 2 (Belfast, 1956)

McHenry, P. G., 'Building Materials and Technology in Arid Lands', *Housing in Arid Lands*, ed., Golany, Gideon, (London, Architectural Press, 1980)

McLeod, M. D., *The Asante*, (London, British Museum Publications, 1981)

Mead, Margaret, *New Lives for Old*, (London, Victor Gollancz, 1956)

Meiring, A. L., 'The Amandebele of Pretoria', *SA Architectural Record*, (South Africa, April, 1955)

Miles, Douglas, 'The Ngadju Longhouse', *Oceania*, no. 35 (1965)

Minter, C., 'Medieval Village on Houndtor Down, Devon', *Medieval Archaeology*, vol. 8 (1963)

Mitchell, Clyde J., *The Yao Village: A Study in the Social Structure of a Malawian People*, (Manchester University Press (1956), 1971)

Mitchell, Maurice, 'An Attempt at Describing the Situation of Tinezouline in 1968', unpublished report, (London, Architectural Association School of Architecture, 1969)

Moore, Stuart A., *A Short History of the Rights of Common upon the Forest of Dartmoor and the Commons of Devon*, (Plymouth, The Dartmoor Preservation Association, 1890)

Morgenthaler, Fritz, 'Reflex-Modernization in Tribal Societies', *Shelter, Sign and Symbol*, ed., Oliver, Paul, (London, Barrie and Jenkins, 1975)

Morrill, Richard L., *The Spatial Organization of Society*, (Belmont, Cal., Duxbury Press, 1970)

Moughtin, J. C., *Hausa Architecture*, (London, Ethnographica, 1985)

Mukherjee, Sudhendu and Menefee Singh, Andrea, 'Hierarchical and Symbiotic Relationships among the Urban Poor: A Report on Pavement Dwellers in Calcutta', UN (Habitat), *The Residential Circumstances of the Urban Poor in Developing Countries*, (New York, Praeger, 1981)

Murdock, George Peter, *Social Structure*, (New York, The Macmillan Co., 1949)

Murdock, George Peter, *Africa; Its Peoples and Their Culture History*, (New York, London, McGraw-Hill Book Company, Inc., 1959)

Musil, Jiri, *Urbanization in Socialist Countries*, (White Plains, New York, M. E. Sharpe, Inc., 1980; London, Croom Helm, 1981)

Myint, H., *The Economics of the Developing Countries*, (London, Hutchinson and Co., 1964)

Myrdal, Jan, *Report from a Chinese Village*, (Harmondsworth, Pelican Books, 1967)

Nayyar, Rohini, 'Poverty and Inequality in Rural Bihar', World Employment Programme, *Poverty and Landlessness in Rural Asia*, (Geneva, International Labour Office, 1977)

Needham, Rodney, ed., *Right and Left: Essays on Dual Symbolic Classification*, (Chicago, London, University of Chicago Press, 1973)

Nelson, Richard K., *Hunters of the Northern Ice*, (Chicago, London, The University of Chicago Press, 1969)

Netting, Robert McC., *Balancing on an Alp*, (Cambridge, Cambridge University Press, 1981)

Nicolaisen, Johannes, *Ecology and Culture of the Pastoral Tuareg*, Etnografisk Roekke, IX, (Copenhagen, National Museum, 1963)

Norris, H., 'Cave Habitations and Granaries in Tripolitania and Tunisia', *Man*, vol. 53 (London, 1953)

Olgyay, Victor, *Design with Climate: Bioclimatic Approach to Architectural Regionalism*, (Princeton, New Jersey, Princeton University Press, 1963)

Oliver, Paul, contributing ed., *Shelter and Society*, (London, Barrie and Rockliff, 1969)

Oliver, Paul, contributing ed., *Shelter in Africa*, (London, Barrie and Jenkins, New York, Praeger, 1971)

Oliver, Paul, 'The Cones of Cappadocia', *Shelter*, ed., Kahn, Lloyd, (Bolinas, California, Shelter Publications, 1973)

Oliver, Paul, *A Navajo Hogan*, education wallsheet, (Oxford, Antipoverty, 1973)

Oliver, Paul, 'Primary Forms and Primary Considerations. The Future of Studies in Greek Vernacular Shelter' *Shelter in Greece*, eds., Doumanis, Orestis B. and Oliver, Paul, (Athens, Architecture in Greece Press, 1974)

Oliver, Paul, *English Cottages and Small Farmhouses*, exhibition and catalogue, (London, Arts Council of Great Britain, 1975)

Oliver, Paul, contributing ed., *Shelter, Sign and Symbol*, (London, Barrie and Jenkins, 1975; Woodstock, New York, The Overlook Press, 1977)

Oliver, Paul, 'The Anthropology of Shelter', *Market Profiles*, ed., Keniger, Michael, Architectural Education Conference, (Brisbane, August 1979)

Oliver, Paul, 'Organic Growth and Planned Development: The Example of Pre-Industrial Isfahan', paper to Conference on City Planning, (Development Planning Unit, University College, London, 1980)

Oliver, Paul, 'The Cultural Context of Shelter Provision', *Disasters and the Small Dwelling*, ed., Davis, Ian, (Oxford, New York, Pergamon Press, 1980)

Oliver, Paul, 'The Cultural Context of Earthen Housing in Seismic Areas', May, Gerald W., ed., *International Workshop Earthen Buildings in Seismic Areas*, Proceedings vol. 2 (Albuquerque, University of New Mexico for The National Science Foundation, 1981)

Oliver, Paul, 'Architectural Form and Symbolism: The Amer-Indian Example', paper for Institut für Geschichte und Theorie der Architektur, (Zurich, Nov. 1981)

Oliver, Paul, 'Binarism in an Islamic City—Isfahan as an Example of Geometry and Duality, *Islamic Architecture and Urbanism*, ed., Germen, Aydin, (Dammam, King Faisal University, 1983)

Oliver, Paul, 'Earth as a Building Material Today', *The Oxford Art Journal*, vol. 5, no. 2 (Oxford, Oxford Microform Publications, 1983)

Oliver, Paul, 'Cultural Factors in the Acceptability of Resettlement Housing', *Transactions of the Built Form and Cultural Research Conference, 1984*, (Lawrence, University of Kansas, 1986)

Oliver, Paul, 'Vernacular Know-How', *Material Culture*, vol. 18, no. 3 (Fall 1986)

Oliver Paul, 'Kaluderica: High-Grade Housing in an Illegal Settlement', eds., Carswell J. William and Saile, David G., *Purposes in Built Form and Culture Research*, Conference Proceedings, (Lawrence, University of Kansas, 1986)

Oliver, Paul, and Samuels, Ivor, eds., *Provins Action Pilote: A Report on the Ville Basse*, (Headington, Oxford, Department of Architecture and Joint Centre for Urban Design, Oxford Polytechnic for Le Patrimoine Historique et Artistique de La France, June 1980)

Oliver, Paul, Davis, Ian and Bentley, Ian, *Dunroamin: The Suburban Semi and its Enemies*, (London, Barrie and Jenkins, 1981)

Oliver, Paul, ed. and Shelter and Settlements Unit, *Kaluderica: Observations on the Wild Settlement*, (Oxford, Department of Architecture, Oxford Polytechnic, April 1985)

Oliver, Paul, (project leader), Aysan, Yasemin (co-ordinator) and Oxford Polytechnic Disasters and Settlements Unit Team, *Cultural Aspects of Housing in Seismic Areas (Turkey)*, report to the Overseas Development Administration, (Oxford, 1986)

Opher, Philip, Misson, M. A., and Samuels, O., *Provins Town Trail: La Ville Basse*, (Headington, Oxford, Urban Design, Oxford Polytechnic for Le Patrimoine Historique et Artistique de La France, 1981)

Orchardson, Ian Q., *The Kipsigis*, (Nairobi, East-African Literature Bureau, 1961)

Oswalt, Wendell H., *Alaskan Eskimos*, (Scranton, Pennsylvania, Chandler Publishing Company, 1967)

Ozkan, Suha, 'Roam Home to a Dome', *Architectural Design*, vol. 42, no. 5 (London, 1972)

Ozkan, Suha, and Onur, Selahattin, 'Another Thick Wall Pattern: Cappadocia', *Shelter, Sign and Symbol*, ed., Oliver, Paul, (London, Barrie and Jenkins, 1975; Woodstock, New York, The Overlook Press, 1977)

Pacey, Arnold, ed., *Sanitation in Developing Countries*, (Chichester, New York, John Wiley and Sons, 1978)

Parin, P., Morgenthaler, F. and Parin-Matthey, G., *Les Blancs Pensent Trop*, (Paris, Payot, 1966)

Parin, Paul, Morgenthalter, F., and van Eyck, A., 'Dogon', *Forum*, (Hilversum, July 1967)

Payne, Geoffrey K., *Urban housing in the Third World*, (London, Leonard Hill; Boston, Routledge and Kegan Paul, 1977)

Payne, Geoffrey K., 'The Gecekondus of Ankara', *Process Architecture*, no. 15 (Tokyo, May 1980)

Payne, Geoffrey K., 'Self-Help Housing: A Critique of the Gecekondus of Ankara', *Self-Help Housing: A Critique*, ed., Ward, Peter M., (London, Mansell Publishing Ltd., 1982)

Payne, Geoffrey K., ed., *Low-Income Housing in the Developing World*, (Chichester, New York, John Wiley and Sons, 1984)

Pearson, Kenneth, 'The Family that Came in from the Cold', *The Sunday Times Magazine*, (London, 1984)

Peristiany, J. G., *The Social Institutions of the Kipsigis*, (London, Routledge and Kegan Paul, 1939)

Pieper, Jan, 'Three Cities of Nepal, *Shelter, Sign and Symbol*, Oliver, Paul, ed., (London, Barrie and Jenkins, 1975)

Pinxten, Rik, van Dooren, I., and Harvey, F., *The Anthropology of Space*, (Philadelphia, University of Pennsylvania Press, 1983)

Prasad, Sunand, *The Haveli and the Hot Dry City*, (Mimeo), (Feb. 1985)

Prussin, Labelle, *Architecture in Northern Ghana*, (Berkeley, University of California Press, 1969)

Prussin, Labelle, 'Fulani-Hausa Architecture' *African Arts*, vol. X, no. 1 (Oct. 1976)

Prussin, Labelle, *Hatumere: Islamic Design in West Africa*, (Berkeley, University of California Press, 1986)

Queen, Stuart A., Habenstein, Robert W., and Adams, John B., eds., *The Family in Various Cultures*, (Philadelphia, J. B. Lippincott Co., 1961)

Raglan, Lord, *The Temple and the House*, (London, Routledge and Kegan Paul, 1964)

Raji, Abdul Shukoor, 'Traditional Domestic Heating Systems of Afghanistan', dissertation, degree M.Phil., (School of Architecture, University of Newcastle-upon-Tyne, June 1986)

Ramseyer, Urs, *The Art and Culture of Bali*, (Oxford, New York, Oxford University Press, 1977)

Rapoport, Amos, *House Form and Culture*, (Englewood Cliffs, New Jersey, Prentice-Hall, Inc., 1969)

Rapoport, Amos, 'Australian Aborigines and the Definition of Place', ed., Oliver, Paul, *Shelter, Sign and Symbol*, (London, Barrie and Jenkins, 1975)

Rapoport, Amos, 'Vernacular Architecture and the Cultural Determinants of Form', *Buildings and Society*, ed., King, Anthony D., (London, Boston, Routledge and Kegan Paul, 1980)

Ravuvu, Asesela, *Vaka i Taukei; The Fijian Way of Life*, (Fiji, Institute of Pacific Studies of the University of the South Pacific, 1983)

Read, Margaret, *Children of Their Fathers: Growing up among the Ngoni of Malawi*, (New York, London, Holt, Rinehart and Winston, 1968)

Redfield, Robert and Rojas, Alfonso Villa, *Chan Kom: A Maya Village*, (1934), (Chicago, London, The University of Chicago Press, 1962)

Reser, Joseph, 'Values in Bark', *Hemisphere*, vol. 22, no. 10 (Oct. 1978)

Reser, Joseph, 'A Matter of Control: Aboriginal Housing Circumstances in Remote Communities and Settlements', *A Black Reality*, ed., Heppell, M., (Canberra, Australian Institute of Aboriginal Studies, 1979)

Richards, J. M., 'Village Life—Nigerian Style', *Country Life*, no. 2 (London, 1978)

Riches, David, 'Three Life Styles for Ungava Eskimos, *Geographical Magazine*, vol. XLV, no. 7 (April 1973)

Rimsha, A. K., 'City Building in the Hot Climate Zones', *Desert Planning*, ed., Golany, Gideon, (London, Architectural Press, 1982)

Ritzenthaler, Robert and Ritzenthaler, Pat, *Cameroon Village*, (Milwaukee, Milwaukee Public Museum, 1962)

Roaf, Susan, 'Wind-Catchers', *Living with the Desert*, eds., Beazley, Elisabeth, and Harverson, Michael, (Warminster, Aris and Phillips, 1982)

Roberts, Bryan, *Cities of Peasants: Explorations in Urban Analysis*, (London, Edward Arnold, 1978)

Robson, David G. with Gormley, A., and Sonawane, D., *Aided Self-Help Housing in Sri Lanka 1977 to 1982*, report for Overseas Development Administration, (London, 1984)

Rodd, Francis Rennell, *People of the Veil*, (London, Macmillan, 1926)

Ron, Zvi Y. D., 'Climatological Aspects of Stone Huts in Traditional Agriculture in a Mediterranean Region', *Israel Journal of Earth Sciences*, vol. 31 (1982)

Rosser, Colin, 'Housing for the Lowest Income Groups: the Calcutta Experience', *Ekistics*, vol. 31, no. 183 (Feb. 1971)

Rowland, Benjamin, *The Art and Architecture of India*, (London, Baltimore, Penguin Books, 1953)

Russell, Trevor and Stowell, Roger, 'Ksar Tinezouline: A Vulnerable Community Located in the Draa Valley in Morocco', unpublished report (London, Architectural Association School of Architecture, 1969)

Ruud, Jorgen, *A Study of Malagasay Customs and Beliefs*, (Oslo, University Press, 1960)

Saini, Balwant, *Building Environment, Analysis of Problems in Hot Dry Lands*, (Sydney, London, Angus and Robertson, 1973)

Salim, S. M., *Marsh Dwellers of the Euphrates Delta*, (London, University of London, The Athlone Press, 1962)

Salmonu, S., 'Zanen Gida: Decorated Houses in Zaria', *Egghead*, Fine Art Department Students Magazine, (Zaria, Ahmadu Bello University, June 1963)

Sargeant, Geoffrey, 'House Form and Decoration in Sumatra', *AARP: Art and Archaeology Research Papers*, no. 12 (London, 1977)

Sargeant, Geoffrey, *Traditional Buildings of Indonesia: Batak Toba*, vol. 1 (Bandung-Indonesia, Building Research Institute and United Nations Regional Housing Centre, n.d.)

Sarma, Jvotirmoyee, 'A Village in West Bengal', ed., Srinivas, M. N., *India's Villages*, (London, J.J. Publishers, 1955)

Schapera, I., *Married Life in an African Tribe*, (London, Faber and Faber, 1940, 1956)

Schapera, I., *The Tswana*, Ethnographic Survey of Africa: Southern Africa, III (London, International African Institute, 1953)

Schoenauer, Norbert, *Introduction to Contemporary Indigenous Housing*, (Montreal, Reporter Books, 1973)

Schwerdtfeger, Friedrich, 'Housing in Zaria', *Shelter in Africa*, ed., Oliver, Paul, (London, Barrie and Jenkins, New York, Praeger, 1971)

Schwerdtfeger, Friedrich, *Traditional Housing in African Cities*, (Chichester, New York, John Wiley and Sons, 1982)

Scully, Vincent, *Pueblo: Mountain, Village, Dance*, (London, Thames and Hudson, 1975)

Seelig, Michael Y., *The Architecture of Self-Help Communities, The First International Competition for the Environment of Developing Countries*, (New York, Architectural Record Books, 1978)

Serjeant, R. B. and Lewcock, Ronald, *San'a'—an Arabian Islamic City*, (London, World of Islam Festival Trust, 1977)

Shah, Kirtee, 'People's Participation in Housing Action: Meaning, Scope and Strategy', ed., Payne G. K., *Low-Income Housing in the Developing World*, (Chichester, New York, John Wiley and Sons, 1984)

Shankland Cox Partnership, *Third World Urban Housing*, (Watford, Building Research Establishment, 1977)

Sharp, Thomas, *The Anatomy of the Village*, (Harmondsworth, Penguin, 1946)

Sherwin, Dean, 'From Batak to Minangkabau: an Architectural Trajectory', *Majallah Akitek*, vol. 1 (Kuala Lumpur, 1979)

Silas, Johan, 'The Kampung Improvement Programme of Indonesia: A Comparative Case Study of Jakarta and Surabaya, *Low-Income Housing in the Developing World*, ed., Payne, Geoffrey K., (Chichester, New York, John Wiley and Sons, 1984)

Simić, Andrei, *The Peasant Urbanites: A Study of Rural-Urban Mobility in Serbia*, (New York, London, Seminar Press, 1973)

Singh, Laxman B.,'Bhaktapur', *Masalah Bangunan*, vol. 23, nos. 3-4 (Bandung, Directorate of Building Research—UN, 1978)

Sinha, Bakshi D., *Housing Growth in India*, (New Delhi, Arnold-Heinemann, 1976)

Sjoberg, Gideon, *The Preindustrial City: Past and Present*, (New York, The Free Press; London, Collier-Macmillan Ltd, 1960)

Skinner, R. J. and Rodell, M. J., eds., *People, Poverty and Shelter*, (London, New York, Methuen, 1983)

Skinner, Stephen, *The Living Earth Manual of Feng-Shui*, (London, Boston, Routledge and Kegan Paul, 1982)

Snead, Rodman, E., *World Atlas of Geomorphic Features*, (New York, Robert E. Krieger Publishing Co. and Van Nostrand Reinhold Co., 1980)

Spence, Betty and Biermann, Barrie, 'M'Pogga', *The Architectural Review*, vol. CXVI, no. 691 (July 1954)

Spence, Robin, 'Laurie Baker: Architect for the Indian Poor', *Architectural Association Quarterly*, vol. 12, no. 1 (London, 1980)

Spence, R. J. S. and Cook, D. J., *Building Materials in Developing Countries*, (Chichester, New York, John Wiley and Sons, 1983)

Spencer, Paul, *Nomads in Alliance*, (Oxford, Oxford University Press, 1973)

Spini, Tito and Spini, Sandro, *Togu Na*, (Casa della parola, Struttura socializzazione della comunita', Dogan), (Milan, Electa Editrice, 1982)

Spink, John and Moodie, D. W., *Eskimo Maps from the Canadian Eastern Arctic*, Monograph 5 (Toronto, University of Toronto Press, 1972)

Srinivas, M. N. ed., *India's Villages*, (London, J. J. Publishers, 1955)

Steiner, Stan, *The New Indians*, (New York, Dell Publishing Co., 1968)

Stephens, William N., *The Family in Cross-Cultural Perspective*, (New York, Rinehart and Winston, 1963)

Stewart, Frances, *Technology and Underdevelopment*, (London, New York, the Macmillan Press, 1977)

Stewart, G. R. and Voon, S. M., 'Adaptation and Change in Housing, Temerloh, Malaysia', unpublished thesis, (Department of Architecture, Oxford Polytechnic, 1981)

Stirling, P., *Turkish Village*, (London, Weidenfeld, 1965)

Stoll, Gary, Ziersch, Rex and Schmaal, Joan, 'Principles Relating to Housing amongst Aboriginal Groups associated with Hermannsburg', ed., Heppell, M., *A Black Reality: Aboriginal Camps and Housing in Remote Australia*, (Canberra, Australian Institute of Aboriginal Studies, 1979)

Sumintardja, Djauhari, 'Poso-Toraja: Traditional Housing in Indonesia', *Masalah Bangunan*, vol. 23, nos. 3-4 (Bandung, Directorate of Building Research UN, 1978)

Sumintardja, Djauhari, 'Site Visits—Kampung Improvement Programme', *Housing Process and Physical Form*, ed., Safran, Linda, (Geneva, The Aga Khan Award for Architecture, 1980)

Suzuki, Makoto, ed., *Maisons de Bois en Europe*, (Fribourg, Switzerland, Editions du Moniteur, 1979)

Swan, Peter J., Wegelin, Emiel and Panchee, Komol, *Management of Sites and Services Housing Schemes*, (Chichester, New York, John Wiley and Sons, 1983)

Talib, Kaiser, *Shelter in Saudi Arabia*, (London, Academy Editions, New York, St. Martin's Press, 1984)

Terrell, John Upton, *Pueblos, Gods and Spaniards*, (New York, The Dial Press, 1973)

Thesiger, Wilfred, 'Marsh Dwellers of Southern Iraq', *National Geographic Magazine*, vol. CXIII, no. 2 (Washington DC, 1958)

Thesiger, Wilfred, *The Marsh Arabs*, (London, Longmans, Green and Co., 1964)

Tiemann, Harry Donald, *Wood Technology*, (New York, Pitman Publishing Co., 1942)

Tokman, K. Bulent, 'Ankara: Procedures for Upgrading and Urban Management', *Low-Income Housing in the Developing World*, ed., Payne, Geoffrey K., (Chichester, New York, John Wiley and Sons, 1984)

Trewartha, Glenn T., *The Earth's Problem Climates*, (Madison, The University of Wisconsin Press, 1961, London, Methuen and Co., 1962)

Trimingham, J. Spencer, *A History of Islam in West Africa*, (Oxford, New York, Oxford University Press, 1962)

Tserendulam, 'In Praise of Life in a Ger', collected by Jenkins, Jean and translated by Urgunge Onon, *Vocal Music from Mongolia*, (London, Tangent Records, TGS 126)

Tuan, Yi-Fu, *Topophilia*, (Englewood Cliffs, New Jersey, Prentice Hall, 1974)

Turner, John F. C., *Housing by People: Towards Autonomy in Building Environments*, (New York, Pantheon Books, 1976)

Turner, John F. C. and Fichter, Robert, eds., *Freedom to Build: Dweller Control of the Housing Process*, (New York, The Macmillan Co.; London, Collier-Macmillan Ltd., 1972)

Tussing, Arlon, R., Rogers, G. W. and Fischer, V., *Alaska Pipeline Report*, (Fairbanks, Institute of Social, Economic and Government Research, University of Alaska, 1971)

United Nations Centre for Human Settlements (Habitat), *The Residential Circumstances of the Urban Poor in Developing Countries*, (New York, Praeger, 1981)

United Nations Centre for Human Settlements (Habitat), *Development of the Indigenous Construction Sector*, report of the ad hoc Expert Group Meeting, Nairobi, Nov. 1981, (Nairobi, UNCHS—Habitat, 1982)

United Nations Centre for Human Settlements (Habitat), *Survey of Slum and Squatter Settlements*, (Dublin, Tycooly International Publishing, 1982)

United Nations Centre for Human Settlements (Habitat), *Small-scale Building Materials Production in the Context of the Informal Economy*, (Nairobi, UNCHS—Habitat, 1984)

United Nations Disaster Relief Co-ordinator (UNDRO), *Shelter After Disaster*, (New York, United Nations, 1982)

US Department of Agriculture, Foreign Agricultural Service, *Bamboo as a Building Material*, (Washington DC, n.d.)

Van Eyck, Aldo, 'Basket-House-Village-Universe', *Meaning in Architecture*, eds., Baird, George and Jencks, Charles, (London, Barrie and Jenkins, 1969)

Varanda, Fernando, *Art of Building in Yemen*, (Cambridge, Mass., London, MIT Press, London, 1982)

Van Stone, James, W., *Point Hope: An Eskimo Village in Transition*, (Seattle, University of Washington Press, 1962)

Walton, James, 'Nguni Folk Building, South African Peasant Architecture', *SA Architectural Record*, vol. 35, (South Africa, 1950)

Walton, James, *African Village*, (Pretoria, J. W. Van Schaik, 1956)

Walton, James, 'Megalithic Building Survivals', ed , Jenkins, Geraint, Studies in Folk Life, (London, Routledge and Kegan Paul, 1969)

Walton, James, 'Art and Magic in Southern Bantu Vernacular Architecture', ed., Oliver, Paul, *Shelter, Sign and Symbol,* (London, (Barrie and Jenkins, 1975)

Ward, Peter M., ed., *Self-Help Housing: A Critique*, (London, Mansell Publishing, 1982)

Warren, John and Fethi, Ihsan, *Traditional Houses in Baghdad*, (Horsham, Coach Publishing House, 1982)

Wheatley, Paul, *The Pivot of the Four Quarters*, (Edinburgh, Edinburgh University Press: Chicago, Aldine Publishing Co., 1971)

White, Leslie, A., *The A'coma Indians, People of the Sky City*, paper from the Bureau of American Ethnology, Annual Report 47, 1929-1930, (Glorieta, New Mexico, The Rio Grande Press, Inc., 1973)

Whittier, Herbert L. 'The Kenyah', *Essays on Borneo Societies*, ed., King, Victor T. (Hull, Oxford University Press, 1978)

Whorf, Benjamin Lee, 'Linguistic Factors in the Terminology of Hopi Architecture', *Language, Thought and Reality*, (Cambridge, Mass., Massachusetts Institute of Technology, 1956

Williams-Ellis, Clough, *Cottage Building in Cob, Pise, Chalk and Clay*, (London, George Newnes; New York, Charles Scribner's Sons, 1920)

Wilsher, Peter and Righter, Rosemary, *The Exploding Cities*, (London, André Deutsch, 1975)

Windass, Mark, 'ARTIC and the Construction of Houses in Andhra Pradesh', *Disasters and the Small Dwelling*, ed., Davis, Ian, (Oxford, New York, Pergamon Press, 1981)

Wirth, Louis, 'Urbanism as a Way of Life', *The American Journal of Sociology*, vol. 44 (Chicago, University of Chicago Press, July 1938)

World Employment Programme, *Poverty and Landlessness in Rural Asia*, (Geneva, International Labour Office, 1977)

Worth, R Hansford, *Worth's Dartmoor*, eds., Spooner and Russell, (Newton Abbot, David and Charles, 1967)

Wright, Leigh, Morrison, H. and Wong, K. F., *Vanishing World: The Ibans of Borneo*, (New York, Weatherhill, 1972)

Wyman, Leland C., *Blessingway: With Three Versions of the Myth Recorded and Translated from the Navaho by Father Berard Haile*, (Tucson, University of Arizona Press, 1970)

Yellen, John E., 'Settlement Patterns of the !Kung San', *Kalahari Hunter-Gatherers: Studies of the !Kung San and Their Neighbours*, eds., Lee, Richard B. and De Vore, Irven, (Cambridge, Mass., Harvard University Press, 1976)

Yousufi, Abdullah, 'Traditional Timber Dwelling Environments: Three Selected Case Studies in Afghanistan and South Korea', dissertation, degree M.Phil., (School of Architecture, University of Newcastle-upon-Tyne, May 1986)

INDEX